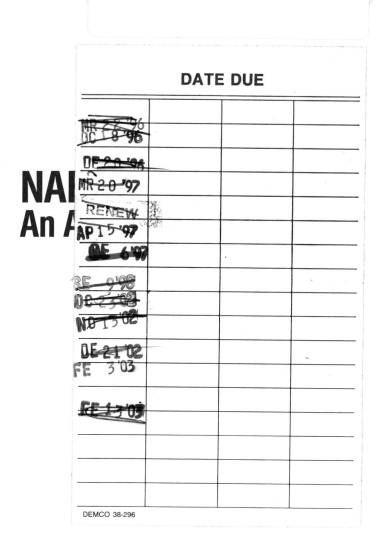

NA[
An A

GARY CLYDE HUFBAUER AND JEFFREY J. SCHOTT
assisted by
Robin Dunnigan and Diana Clark

NAFTA
An Assessment

Revised Edition

INSTITUTE FOR INTERNATIONAL ECONOMICS
Washington, DC
October 1993

(1979–81); Deputy Assistant Secretary for International Trade and Investment Policy of the US Treasury (1977–79); and Director of the International Tax Staff at the Treasury (1974–76). He has written extensively on international trade, investment, and tax issues, including *US Taxation of International Income* (1992), *North American Free Trade* (1992), *Economic Sanctions Reconsidered* (second edition 1990), *Trade Policy for Troubled Industries* (1986), and *Subsidies in International Trade* (1984).

Jeffrey J. Schott, *Senior Fellow*, was a Senior Associate at the Carnegie Endowment for International Peace (1982–83) and an International Economist at the US Treasury (1974–82). He is coauthor of *Completing the Uruguay Round* (1990); *Free Trade Areas and US Trade Policy* (1989); *North American Free Trade* (1992) *The Canada-United States Free Trade Agreement: The Global Impact* (1988), *Economic Sanctions Reconsidered* (Second edition 1990), *Auction Quotas and US Trade Policy* (1987), and *Trading for Growth: The Next Round of Trade Negotiations* (1985).

INSTITUTE FOR INTERNATIONAL
ECONOMICS
11 Dupont Circle, NW
Washington, DC 20036-1207
(202) 328-9000   FAX: (202) 328-5432

C. Fred Bergsten, *Director*
Christine F. Lowry, *Director of Publications*

Printed in the United States of America
96 95 94   8 7 6 5

Library of Congress Cataloging-in-Publication Data

Hufbauer, Gary Clyde.
    NAFTA : an assessment, revised edition, Gary Clyde Hufbauer and Jeffrey J. Schott.
    p.   cm.
    Includes bibliographical references and index.

    1. Free trade—North America.
    2. North America—Commerce.
    3. North America—Commercial policy.
    I. Schott, Jeffrey J., 1949–
    II. Hufbauer, Gary Clyde. North American free trade.
    III. Title.
    HF3211.H83   1993
    382'.71'097—dc20   92-38904
                                                     CIP

ISBN 0-88132-199-0

Marketed and Distributed outside the USA and Canada by Longman Group UK Limited, London

To Julius L. Katz,
for his lifelong achievements
in support of an open world trading system

Contents

Preface to the Revised Edition

In March 1992, the Institute released *North American Free Trade: Issues and Recommendations,* a comprehensive analysis of the negotiations then under way between the United States, Canada, and Mexico. The authors, Gary Clyde Hufbauer and Jeffrey J. Schott, assessed the likely economic impact of the prospective North American Free Trade Agreement (NAFTA) on the three countries and made specific recommendations as to how it should be crafted. The book quickly became the most frequently cited study of the NAFTA. It was circulated widely among policymakers in Washington, Ottawa, Mexico City, and elsewhere.

With the conclusion of the NAFTA negotiations in August 1992, Hufbauer and Schott prepared a sequel that examined the almost 2,000 pages of the NAFTA text. We published that volume, *NAFTA: An Assessment,* which summarized the key provisions of the agreement and analyzed their economic implications, in February 1993. In it, the authors made judgments on how well the negotiators met the high standards set by the original Hufbauer-Schott recommendations.

This update of *NAFTA: An Assessment* extends its original coverage to include appraisals of the three side agreements—on the environment, labor, and import surges—called for by President Clinton and concluded in August 1993. The revision also addresses some of the more recent views that have been expressed on the pact's economic effects, especially by its critics. This volume thus seeks to offer a comprehensive picture of the entire arrangement. We hope that it will be able to play a useful role in the ensuing public discussion of NAFTA and the ratification debate in the Congress, as did our *United States–Canada Free Trade: An Evaluation of the Agreement* (by Jeffrey J. Schott) in 1988.

The Institute for International Economics is a private nonprofit institution for the study and discussion of international economic policy. Its purpose is to analyze important issues in that area, and to develop and communicate practical new approaches for dealing with them. The Institute is completely nonpartisan.

The Institute is funded largely by philanthropic foundations. Major institutional grants are now being received from the German Marshall Fund of the United States, which created the Institute with a generous commitment of funds in 1981, and from the Ford Foundation, the William and Flora Hewlett Foundation, the William M. Keck, Jr. Foundation, the C. V. Starr Foundation, and the United States–Japan Foundation. A number of other foundations and private corporations also contribute to the highly diversified financial resources of the Institute. About 16 percent of the Institute's resources in our latest fiscal year were provided by contributors outside the United States, including about 7 percent from Japan. Partial support for this study was provided by grants from David Rockefeller and the Tinker Foundation.

The Board of Directors bears overall responsibility for the Institute and gives general guidance and approval to its research program—including identification of topics that are likely to become important to international economic policymakers over the medium run (generally, one to three years), and which should thus be addressed by the Institute. The Director, working closely with the staff and outside Advisory Committee, is responsible for the development of particular projects and makes the final decision to publish an individual study.

The Institute hopes that its studies and other activities will contribute to building a stronger foundation for international economic policy around the world. We invite readers of these publications to let us know how they think we can best accomplish this objective.

C. FRED BERGSTEN
Director
September 1993

Acknowledgments

The authors would like to thank C. Fred Bergsten, Richard N. Cooper, Tony Halliday, Murray Smith, and Rene Villarreal for their insightful comments on earlier drafts of the entire manuscript. Special thanks are also due to members of the Council on Foreign Relations' study group on NAFTA, chaired by James Jones and directed by C. Michael Aho, that held several meetings in New York to discuss our analysis of the agreement. We appreciate the work of Angela Barnes, who typed numerous drafts of the manuscript, Valerie Norville, who carefully edited the text, and Christine Flint Lowry, who ensured rapid publication.

Overview and Scorecard

On 17 December 1992, the United States, Canada, and Mexico signed a historic trade accord. The North American Free Trade Agreement (NAFTA) is the most comprehensive free trade pact (short of a common market) ever negotiated between regional trading partners, and the first reciprocal free trade pact between a developing country and industrial countries. The NAFTA is scheduled to enter into force 1 January 1994, after ratification by the three legislatures.

In the United States, the process of formulating implementing legislation will begin in the new Congress, which convened in January 1993. Because the NAFTA was signed before fast-track provisions of US trade law expired, there is no statutory deadline for submitting implementing legislation. However, as a practical matter, given the 90 session days allowed for congressional action and the political calendar in Canada and Mexico, US implementing legislation must be submitted to Congress by summer 1993 if the NAFTA is to enter into force, as envisaged, in January 1994.

Delay in US ratification of the NAFTA could complicate the timetable of parallel efforts in Canada and, to a lesser extent, Mexico. In Canada, the Mulroney government must stand for election by late November 1993, so it will likely seek to approve the NAFTA in advance of US action to preclude the pact from becoming the focal point of the election, as the Canada-US Free Trade Agreement (FTA) was in 1988. In Mexico, the Salinas government has a longer tenure but would like the NAFTA to enter into force before the ruling party (PRI) nominates its candidate in summer 1994 to succeed Salinas in December 1994.

In this book, we summarize the central provisions of the NAFTA text, evaluate the economic impact of the agreement, and score the results against the recommendations of our earlier book (Hufbauer and Schott 1992a). This assessment is not intended as a legal guide or a negotiator's memoir. We leave those books to other authors. Our purpose is to provide a road map so that legislators, businessmen, labor leaders, and environmentalists can get a quick handle on the agreement.

Much of our analysis focuses on issues related to Mexico's participation in the pact, and in particular, the labor and environmental concerns that have dominated the US debate on NAFTA during the 1992 election and that will be a central theme in the ratification debate. Since the NAFTA incorporates much of the existing Canada-US FTA, we have limited our analysis of US-Canada issues to those areas where the NAFTA modifies or augments FTA provisions.

NAFTA Highlights

In essence, the NAFTA is a new, improved, and expanded version of the Canada-US FTA. In large part, the agreement involves commitments by Mexico to implement the degree of trade and investment liberalization promised between its northern neighbors in 1988. However, the NAFTA goes further by addressing unfinished business from the FTA, including protection of intellectual property rights, rules against distortions to investment (local-content and export performance requirements), and coverage of transportation services.

The NAFTA provides for the phased elimination of tariff and most nontariff barriers on regional trade within 10 years, although a few import-sensitive products will have a 15-year transition period. US-Canada bilateral tariffs will continue to be phased out according to the FTA schedule, that is, by January 1998. In addition, the NAFTA extends the innovative dispute settlement procedures of the FTA to Mexico (in return for a substantial revamping of Mexican trade laws that injects more transparency into the administrative process and brings Mexican antidumping and other procedures closer to those of the United States and Canada); contains precedent-setting rights and obligations regarding services and investment; and takes an important first step in addressing cross-border environmental issues.

The agreement contains notable commitments with regard to liberalization of trade and investment. First, the NAFTA establishes within 15 years free trade in agricultural products between the United States and Mexico. The accord immediately converts key US and Mexican agricultural restrictions into tariff-rate quotas and sets a maximum 15-year period for the phase-out of the over-quota tariffs—an impressive achievement considering the dismal track record of other trade talks in reducing long-standing farm trade barriers.

Second, the investment obligations of the NAFTA (and related dispute settlement provisions) accord national treatment to NAFTA investors, remove most performance requirements on investment in the region, and open up new investment opportunities in key Mexican sectors such as petrochemicals and financial services. The investment provisions provide a useful model for future GATT trade accords, despite the notable exceptions for primary energy and Canadian cultural industries.

Third, the pact sets important precedents for future regional and multilateral negotiations by substantially opening the financial services market in Mexico to US and Canadian participants by the year 2000 and by removing significant obstacles to land transportation and telecommunications services.

Finally, the NAFTA offers a schizophrenic result in textiles and apparel. On the one hand, the pact calls for the elimination of all tariffs and quotas on regional trade in textiles and apparel (except for a special US quota for Canadian apparel producers that do not meet the strict regional rules of origin). This is the first time in this heavily protected sector that imports from an important developing-country supplier have been significantly liberalized by the United States and Canada. However, the rules of origin established to qualify for duty-free treatment are highly restrictive. If not coupled with prospective GATT reforms, the cumulative result could be strongly trade diverting.

The NAFTA is a noteworthy achievement, but its implications for Mexico, Canada, and the United States should not be exaggerated. By widening the scope of the market and enlarging the range of available labor skills, the NAFTA enables North American firms and workers to compete more effectively against foreign producers both at home and in world markets. But the ability of the NAFTA partners to gain maximum benefits from the pact with minimum adjustment costs depends importantly on maintaining domestic economic policies that ensure growth. Firms will still look first and foremost at the macroeconomic climate in each country in setting their investment priorities.

Implications for Mexico, the United States, and Canada

For Mexico, the NAFTA reinforces the extensive market-oriented policy reforms implemented since 1985. These reforms have promoted real annual growth of 3 to 4 percent in the 1990s and a falling rate of inflation. The NAFTA portends a continuation of the fast pace of change in the Mexican economy by extending the reform process to sectors such as autos, textiles and apparel, finance, telecommunications, and land transportation. Mexican exporters will also benefit in two distinct ways: the relatively unfettered access to the US market that they already enjoy under various unilateral US programs will be sustained, and the few remaining US trade barriers will be liberalized.

The prospect of NAFTA implementation has already generated strong expectational effects, with capital inflows to Mexico estimated at about $18 billion in 1992 (of which about $5 billion was probably foreign direct investment).[1] These large inflows are the financial counterpart to the growing Mexican current account deficit generated by imports of machinery, equipment, and other capital goods—all essential ingredients for the sustained development of the Mexican economy.

However, a major cloud must be noted over Mexican skies: the government of Mexico seems determined to bring inflation down from its current rate of 10 to 15 percent to the US rate of 3 to 4 percent through stringent monetary policy, without permitting a significant devaluation of the peso. This approach could put the Mexican economy in a straitjacket, akin to the experience of the United Kingdom prior to the breakdown of the exchange rate mechanism in September 1992, and possibly compel Mexican policymakers to institute policies entailing high interest rates, low growth, and a burgeoning trade deficit for several years. Recognizing these risks, Mexico altered its exchange rate policy on 20 October 1992 and doubled the pace of permitted depreciation of the peso against the dollar from 2 percent to 4 percent per year (*Wall Street Journal*, 21 October 1992, A13). Further steps in this direction may be needed.

For the United States, the NAFTA reforms should enhance an already-important export market. US exports to Mexico have grown sharply since 1986 and now run at an annual rate of about $42 billion. US suppliers of intermediates, capital goods, and high-technology products should continue to reap large benefits as prime suppliers of the growing Mexican market. Over time, the NAFTA should impel industrial reorganization along regional lines, with firms taking best advantage of each country's ability to produce components and assembled products and thus enhancing competitiveness in the global marketplace.

In addition, the NAFTA meets key US foreign policy objectives. The US debate often ignores the foreign policy dimension, blithely taking for granted that Mexican steps toward economic reform and political pluralism are irreversible. But Mexico's economic reforms are still vulnerable to political and financial shocks, and democratic reforms are still in their infancy. The NAFTA should anchor achievements already made in Mexico and reinforce efforts to promote economic growth and political pluralism in that country.

---

1. Investment has anticipated trade reforms in Mexico, just as it did in Europe after passage of the Single European Act in 1986, which presaged the internal market reforms of the EC 1992 process.

For Canada, the NAFTA reinforces, and in some cases strengthens, its FTA preferences in the US market. Canada achieved many of its specific objectives in the negotiations, such as clarifying the method used to calculate the regional content for autos and retaining the Canada-US FTA provision that exempts Canadian cultural industries from external competition. In addition, the NAFTA improves Canada's access to the Mexican market. Although Mexico is a relatively small export market for Canada (under $1 billion at present), the NAFTA will expand export opportunities for Canadian firms in several key sectors, such as financial services, automobiles, and government procurement.

NAFTA "Lowlights"

Despite its attractions, the NAFTA does contain warts and blemishes. For example, basic energy remains immune to free trade, progress on labor and environmental issues proceeds in half steps, and the accession clause is no more than a hortatory statement.

But the main area where the NAFTA is open to criticism is its enunciation of restrictive rules of origin. These arcane trade provisions have been aptly labeled "tools of discrimination": they are used to determine which goods qualify for preferential treatment under the NAFTA and to deny NAFTA benefits to those goods that contain significant foreign-sourced components.

Rules of origin are an integral part of all free trade pacts, but the NAFTA provisions pose two distinct dangers. First, to an undue extent, they penalize regional producers by forcing them to source from less efficient suppliers located in the region, thereby undercutting the global competitiveness of the buying firms. Second, the NAFTA rules could establish an unhappy precedent for other preferential trading pacts, which may choose to emulate the restrictive practices articulated in the NAFTA to the disadvantage of the original perpetrators.

The impact of rules of origin in limiting trade liberalization is suggested by comparing actual and hypothetical duty collections on US imports from Canada.[2] Based on 1991 data, duty collections from Canada will eventually drop to about 18 percent of the most-favored-nation (MFN) duty rates rather than the zero level that would occur without rules of origin. In other words, about 18 percent of US imports from Canada will not benefit from the FTA. Obviously, the stricter the rules of origin, the higher this residual percentage will be.

In general, the NAFTA adopts a standard rule that goods containing foreign components qualify for preferential treatment only if they un-

---

2. This exercise was carried out by Tom Dorsey (1992) of the Office of Management and Budget.

dergo a "substantial transformation" in the region that results in a change in tariff classification of the product. In addition, however, the NAFTA rules of origin for several key sectors have been encumbered by complex value-added tests and requirements that products not be contaminated by key components sourced abroad.

Our concerns about restrictive NAFTA rules of origin arise most prominently in two sectors: textiles and apparel, and autos. In textiles and apparel, the agreement establishes a triple transformation test that makes the already-protectionist rules of origin in the Canada-US FTA seem liberal by comparison. For most products, the NAFTA establishes a "yarn forward" rule, which requires an item to be produced from yarn made in a NAFTA country to qualify for regional preferences. The impact of this rule is somewhat softened, however, by the exemption of a small number of fabrics that only need pass a single transformation test to qualify for preferential treatment and by special quotas under which products that do not meet the origin requirements still qualify for preferential tariff treatment. The intense lobbying that prompted these restrictive NAFTA rules presages the industry's counterattack against the proposed global reform of the Multi-Fiber Arrangement in the Uruguay Round of GATT negotiations. The reform would phase out all quotas over 10 years.

For autos, the NAFTA adopts a "net cost" approach for origin calculations. By itself, this method is an administrative improvement.[3] However, the NAFTA value-added test (62.5 percent for autos, light trucks, engines, and transmissions; 60 percent for other vehicles and parts) is much higher than, and supersedes, the 50 percent requirement of the Canada-US FTA. Moreover, the NAFTA includes tracing requirements to ensure that the foreign component of engines, transmissions, and other specified parts is subtracted when determining whether a vehicle meets the new content requirements. Together these rules substantially raise the overall regional-content requirements for preferential trade in automotive products.

Foreign concern about the potentially adverse trade effects of these provisions will diminish if:

- The three NAFTA partners cut their MFN tariffs substantially in the Uruguay Round (thereby reducing the surviving margin of preference between the NAFTA zero rate tariffs and the MFN rate);

- The three countries move toward the adoption of a common external tariff, especially in autos, thereby mitigating the legitimate worries about potential transshipment of foreign components from one NAFTA partner to another.

---

3. The net-cost approach subtracts specified administrative expenses from the transaction price to determine the base for calculating the ratio of foreign to regional content.

In contrast to the textiles' and autos' rules of origin, a constructive precedent was set in the rule of origin for computers. The rule is relatively simple: computers qualify as a North American good if the circuit board is made in the region and is further transformed so as to change the tariff classification (e.g., from a circuit board to a partly assembled computer). In contrast to textiles and autos, the NAFTA establishes a common external tariff for computers and related products among the three countries: US and Canadian MFN tariffs (3.7 percent or 3.9 percent, depending on the product) will remain the same (subject to Uruguay Round cuts), but Mexico's external tariff will be reduced from rates of 10 and 20 percent, down to the US and Canadian levels over 10 years (annex 308.1).[4]

NAFTA Ratification: The Clinton Scenario

From the moment NAFTA negotiations were contemplated, US critics focused on environmental and labor provisions. These issues served as lightning rods for the congressional debate prior to the start of NAFTA talks in 1991. At that time, President Bush promised Congress to include environmental safeguards both in the agreement and in parallel bilateral initiatives with Mexico and to ensure that adequate programs address the adjustment needs of US workers dislocated by the NAFTA reforms.

While the NAFTA and the parallel US-Mexico side agreements arguably meet Bush's commitments, they clearly have not satisfied the critics. Even though the NAFTA is probably the "greenest" trade pact ever negotiated, the accord contains far less in terms of rules and enforcement than US environmental interests demanded. Similarly, the NAFTA drew sharp objections from US labor groups because it does not contain "hard" obligations in the area of workers' rights and related labor issues. In both cases, the critics complain that the consultative commissions are of the "meet and greet" variety, rather than forums for progressively upgrading standards and enforcement.

In October 1992 Governor Clinton delivered a major address in which he endorsed the NAFTA, rejected any renegotiation of the text, and enumerated important qualifications (Clinton 1992). With Clinton's election, these qualifications now provide a guide for the requirements for US ratification of the NAFTA.[5]

---

4. In addition, duty drawback benefits will be phased out over seven years for the maquiladoras, where most Mexican-made computers are produced (US Chamber of Commerce 1992, 32).

5. At a news conference held on 19 November 1992, President-elect Clinton affirmed that the NAFTA is a priority and that while "there are other things that have to be done before the treaty should be implemented by Congressional legislation," he looks forward to working with President Salinas to resolve the outstanding issues (*Washington Post*, 20 November 1992, p. A37).

In broad terms, Clinton sees NAFTA and other trade accords as part of a larger national economic strategy, including changes in the US tax system (i.e., investment tax credits), developing a "conversion plan" for the defense sector, and controlling health care costs. The NAFTA is accordingly regarded as a part of the overall US competitiveness strategy. Moreover, Clinton views the NAFTA as the first step toward developing stronger regional ties, as the United States "reaches down into the other market-oriented economies of Central and South America."

Clinton has enumerated five unilateral measures that the United States should enact in the context of NAFTA implementing legislation. The unilateral steps require worker adjustment assistance (training, health care benefits, income supports, and assistance to communities to create jobs); environmental funding (to ensure environmental cleanup and infrastructure investments in the United States); assistance to farmers (strict application of US pesticide requirements on food imports, plus help in shifting farmers to alternative crops); assurance that NAFTA "does not override the democratic process" (i.e., Clinton would give US citizens the right to challenge objectionable environmental practices in Mexico or Canada);[6] and assurance that foreign workers are not brought to the United States as strikebreakers.

In addition to these unilateral steps, Clinton stated his intention to negotiate three supplemental agreements that would be submitted to Congress in parallel with NAFTA implementing legislation. His proposal was ambiguous as to whether these pacts would be solely with Mexico or trilateral in nature. However, it clearly was motivated by political demands to strengthen US-Mexico provisions.

The first agreement would create an Environmental Protection Commission. The commission, which would be headed by Vice President Gore, would have "substantial powers and resources to prevent and clean up water pollution" and would "encourage the enforcement of the country's own environmental laws through education, training, and commitment of resources, and provide a forum to hear complaints" (Clinton 1992).

A second supplemental agreement would create a Labor Commission that would have powers similar to those of the environment commission to protect worker standards and safety. "It, too, should have extensive powers to educate, train, develop minimum standards, and have similar dispute resolution powers and remedies."

Finally, a supplemental safeguards agreement would be negotiated to deal with instances where "an unexpected and overwhelming surge" in imports from a partner country required temporary protection beyond that provided by the "snapback" clauses enumerated in the

---

6. This subject, of course, raises issues that could require negotiated commitments with US trading partners.

NAFTA text. The rationale for such a provision would be to provide an additional avenue for temporary import relief to deal with the aftershocks of regional integration. It does not encompass, however, the innovative safeguards mechanism that we advocated for sectors such as autos, textiles, and agriculture.

President Salinas has reacted positively, if not warmly, to these proposals. Indeed, he reportedly suggested that the agenda of these supplemental negotiations be expanded to include a special economic support fund for Mexican development (*Wall Street Journal*, 8 December 1992, A11).

In the relevant chapters that follow, we examine these proposed supplemental agreements in more detail. As with the completed NAFTA text, we offer recommendations regarding the scope and content of the prospective labor and environment pacts.

NAFTA Accomplishments: A Scorecard

In the remaining chapters of this assessment, we examine the accomplishments of NAFTA measured against the yardsticks set out in our 1992 book. When we drafted that book, we regarded our recommendations (which serve here as yardsticks) as the outer limits of what might be accomplished in a long process of integrating the economies of Canada, the United States, and Mexico. We have never viewed the NAFTA text as the final word on economic and social convergence within the huge North America market. Rather, we see the NAFTA as a very large first step, with the implication that further steps will be taken in later years.[7]

What follows are detailed assessments of the key provisions of the NAFTA text, both in terms of individual sectors and in terms of crosscutting rules. Readers who want a succinct appraisal should turn to the appendix, which summarizes our recommendations, the main elements of the NAFTA text, and the contrast between recommendations and results. For readers who want a very short scorecard, in table 1.1 we have assigned grades for achievements in each area. In this scorecard, a gentleman's B indicates that the outcome just met our recommendations (which demand a high standard of accomplishment), an A indicates an outcome that surprised us for the exceptional progress made toward a free regional market, and a C indicates that the outcome was disappointing.

---

7. In a sense, the NAFTA for North America is akin to the Treaty of Rome, signed by European Community members in 1957. The parallel is far from exact, however, in that the Treaty of Rome announced as its destination a common market with a major institutional superstructure. By contrast, the NAFTA has as its destination a free trade area with little institutional superstructure.

Table 1.1   Scorecard: How NAFTA rates against the recommendations

NAFTA results	Grade
Market access by sector	
Energy	C+
Automobiles	B
Textiles and apparel	B+
Agriculture	A
Financial services	B+
Transportation	A
Telecommunications	B+
Trade rules	
Rules of origin[a]	C+
Safeguards[b]	C
Subsidies and dumping[c]	B
Dispute settlement[c]	A
Government procurement[d]	B+
New issues	
Investment	A−
Intellectual property	B
Environment	B
Labor adjustment[e]	A
Maquiladoras[d]	B
Average grade	B+

a. Rules of origin are discussed in chapter 1 and in the automobiles and textiles and apparel sections of chapter 3.
b. Safeguards are discussed in chapter 2.
c. Subsidies and dumping are discussed in the dispute settlement section of chapter 4.
d. Government procurement and maquiladoras are not addressed separately in the assessment but are included in the appendix.
e. Labor adjustment is discussed in chapter 2. The grade of A assumes that President Bush's proposed labor adjustment program, or a better program, is adopted.

The overall grade we assign the NAFTA text is a B+. In most subjects, the agreement met our recommendations. In several areas—such as investment, agriculture, transportation, dispute settlement, and labor adjustment—the NAFTA text exceeded our recommendations and receives an A. However, in some areas—energy and rules of origin—the agreement falls short and earns only a C.

Trade and Employment

In the United States, opposition to the NAFTA has focused on potential job losses and downward pressure on American wages. The root fear is that low Mexican wages and poor enforcement of Mexican labor standards will attract investment, deprive US workers of their jobs, and drive down US wages. NAFTA opponents point to the fact that average hourly compensation in Mexican manufacturing is only about 14 percent of the US figure: $2.17 in Mexico in 1991 versus $15.45 for the United States (US Bureau of Labor Statistics, "International Comparisons of Hourly Compensation Costs for Production Workers in Manufacturing, 1991," Report 825, June 1992; Faux and Lee). In the third presidential debate, Ross Perot argued that equilibrium would not be reached between the United States and Mexico until Mexican wages rose to $7.50 an hour and US wages fell to $7.50 an hour (transcript of presidential debate, East Lansing, Michigan, 19 October 1992, excerpted in *New York Times*, 20 October 1992, A21).

Resurrection of the Pauper Labor Argument

The fears skillfully articulated in Perot's sound bites and by other NAFTA opponents basically amount to a restatement of the "pauper labor" argument: imports by a rich country from a poor country must inevitably reduce the standard of living in the rich country.[1] The best one-line

---

1. The "pauper labor" argument was reflected in the Tariff Act of 1922, which significantly

retort was offered by Ambassador Carla Hills: "If wages were the only factor, many developing countries would be economic superpowers" (remarks delivered at the Institute for International Economics, Washington, DC, 21 September 1992).

Ambassador Hills might well have noted that Puerto Rico has enjoyed free trade with the United States for decades. Yet a major gap still separates manufacturing wages in the United States and Puerto Rico. In 1987 the average payroll per production worker in Puerto Rican industry was only $11,170, compared with the US level of $20,540 *Statistical Abstract of the United States 1991*, tables 1305 and 1427). Nor has there been an outsize boom in Puerto Rican manufacturing jobs: between 1970 and 1990, employment in Puerto Rico only rose from 132,000 to 160,000 manufacturing workers, and these jobs actually fell as a share of the work force from over 17 percent to under 15 percent. If low wages were such a magnet for manufacturing activity, Puerto Rico should have gained more than 28,000 manufacturing jobs over two decades, and the proportion of the labor force engaged in manufacturing should have risen, not fallen *Statistical Abstract of the United States 1992*, table 1328).

More generally, while trade between developing and developed countries has mushroomed, differences in living standards are still very wide. Between 1975 and 1990, the dollar value of two-way trade between countries belonging to the Organization for Economic Cooperation and Development (OECD) and low-income countries tripled from $59 billion to $200 billion. Yet the per capita income gap between OECD countries and low-income countries actually increased over this period.[2] In 1975 the OECD-country average per capita GNP figure was $5,680 while the figure for low-income countries was $190 (OECD countries, 30 times higher); by 1990 the OECD country average reached $20,250 while the low-income country average was $350 (OECD countries, 58 times higher) (International Monetary Fund, *Direction of Trade Statistics, Yearbook 1981 and 1992*; The World Bank, *World Tables 1992*, 4–5).

Even in the highly successful instances of Hong Kong, Korea, and Singapore, a large gap still remains between wages paid to production workers and industrial-country wages. The total two-way trade of the three Asian "tigers" increased from $39 billion in 1975 to $475 billion by 1991 (International Monetary Fund, *Direction of Trade Statistics, Yearbook 1981 and 1992*). Yet in 1991 the average hourly compensation for production workers reached only $3.58 in Hong Kong, $4.32 in Korea, and

---

raised US tariffs after the First World War, and gave the president (acting on the advice of the Tariff Commission) the power to levy additional duties "to equalize costs of production" (the so-called "scientific tariff"). The pauper labor argument and the scientific tariff (which was seldom implemented) were attacked by, among others, Gottfried Haberler (1936, 251–53).

2. Low-income countries and OECD countries correspond to those listed in the World Bank's *World Tables 1992*, 684–85.

$4.38 in Singapore. These rates are still well below the hourly rates paid by their major trading partners: $15.45 in the United States, $14.41 in Japan, and $22.17 in Germany (US Bureau of Labor Statistics, "International Comparisons of Hourly Compensation Costs for Production Workers in Manufacturing, 1991," Report 825, June 1992, 6).[3]

To be sure, real hourly compensation in the United States has grown by only 0.7 percent annually since 1973—far less, for example, than the 2.1 percent figure achieved in Japan (*Economic Report of the President 1992*, 95–96). But the dismal wage performance for the average US worker has little to do with imports from developing countries. Instead, it reflects larger forces in the US economy, especially low rates of investment, both in human training and in physical capital. The right policy response to poor US wage gains will not be found in trade barriers. Rather, the response requires broad-gauged policies that, among other things, ensure a much higher rate of investment, and far better work force skills (Competitiveness Policy Council, "First Annual Report to the President and the Congress: Building a Competitive America," 1 March 1992, and forthcoming report, March 1993).

The reason why the pauper labor argument misstates the connection between trade and wages is simple. On average, high US labor productivity pays for high US wages. The US worker earns high wages because of his high output, which in turn reflects his work skills, his complement of sophisticated capital equipment, and the highly articulated infrastructure of the US economy. In the future as in the past, average US wages will increase primarily as a result of US success in raising productivity, a task that requires research outlays, capital investment, and worker training—not the erection of barriers to developing-country exports.

These statements about average wage levels do not mean that wage rates are irrelevant to international competition. In some industries and in some products, US wages are higher than US productivity can justify when compared with the juxtaposition of Mexican wages and productivity, for example. Those activities will tend to migrate from the United States to Mexico. Illustrative of this is the Smith Corona typewriter factory that plans to relocate from Cortland, New York, to Mexico in 1993.[4] But in other industries and products, the reverse is true. For example, US workers can make cheaper and better heavy

---

3. All figures are translated at commercial market exchange rates.

4. In July 1992 Smith Corona announced that about 870 workers would be laid off. The highly publicized closure is the last step in the technological replacement of typewriters by electronic word processors and the relocation abroad of the remaining segments of the typewriter industry. Smith Corona also has a plant in Singapore but had kept the bulk of its operations in Cortland (*US News and World Report*, April 1982, 71; telephone conversation with David Verostko, Smith Corona headquarters, Cortland, NY, October 1992).

trucks and photocopy machines than Mexican workers.[5] In such activities, the NAFTA will prompt investment and jobs to migrate from Mexico to the United States.

NAFTA opponents often charge that US multinationals use the threat (or the actuality) of moving to Mexico as a hammer to beat down the wages of US workers. We do not know how often such tactics are used. But we would not vilify private firms that balance wage rates against labor productivity when selecting plant sites. Such calculations affect the choice between Los Angeles and Salt Lake City, just as they affect the choice between Cleveland and Guadalajara. Cost-minimizing decisions are the bedrock of an efficient economy. The fact that some US plants close, just as some Mexican plants close, should be read as evidence that the market system is working, not that it is failing. From the standpoint of the US economy as a whole, what counts is how many net jobs are created by NAFTA.

US Jobs Created and Dislocated

According to our estimates, the NAFTA will exert a modest but positive effect on the US labor market. By our estimates, the agreement—in conjunction with Mexican domestic economic reforms—will create about 170,000 net new US jobs in the foreseeable future (that number should be reached by 1995, five years after the NAFTA talks were first proposed) by comparison with the 1990 position (table 2.1).[6] Indeed, with a surging US trade balance with Mexico (a $6.8 billion trade surplus in 1992, compared with a $2.4 billion trade deficit in 1990), many new US jobs have already been created. If the NAFTA is rejected, we would expect the United States to experience job losses relative to the situation in 1992. The reason is that a rejection of NAFTA would probably cause capital to leave Mexico, in turn forcing Mexico to contract its imports, thereby slashing the growth of US exports and drastically shrinking the US trade surplus with Mexico.

Our job projections reflect a judgment that, with NAFTA, US exports to Mexico will continue to outstrip Mexican exports to the United States, leading to a US trade surplus with Mexico of about $7 billion to $9 billion annually by 1995. How long can this scenario last? The answer fundamentally depends on investor confidence in Mexico, Mexican growth, and the ratio between Mexican external debt and Mexican GDP.

---

5. See, for example, *Washington Post*, 13 December 1992, H1, for an account of how Xerox and its union have boosted productivity at the Webster, New York, plant, thereby averting relocation of the plant to Mexico.

6. We start the clock from a 1990 base because the prospect of the NAFTA generated expectational effects that resulted in sharp increases in bilateral trade and investment.

In this regard, the experience of South Korea is instructive (table 2.2). For 25 years, between 1957 and 1981, Korea ran current account deficits which, for successive five-year periods, averaged between 5.0 and 8.5 percent of GNP.[7] At the start of the Korean growth spurt, in the late 1950s, gross external debt was only 4 percent of Korean GNP. Over the next 25 years, as Korean GNP grew rapidly, Korean corporations began acquiring foreign assets. In combination, these various forces gradually pushed the Korean gross external debt ratio up to about 50 percent of GNP by 1982.[8]

While similarities may exist between the prolonged Korean growth spurt that started in the late 1950s and the Mexican growth spurt that started in the late 1980s, important differences must also be noted. Mexico has a much higher initial external debt ratio than Korea: 47 percent of Mexican GDP in 1990 versus 4 percent of Korean GDP in 1957. Moreover, Mexico has already experienced a severe debt crisis, so lenders may be more cautious. On the other hand, even with its dramatic reforms, Mexico is unlikely to grow as fast as Korea. In our view, Mexico might achieve an annual real growth rate of 4 to 5 percent over the next 25 years, whereas Korea sustained an average real growth rate of 8 percent between 1957 and 1981. These factors suggest that even a very successful Mexico would not long incur the magnitude of current account deficits that Korea experienced. However, with a slower rate of growth, Mexico will have less need (relative to its GNP) than Korea for foreign capital.

All in all, Mexican annual current account deficits in the vicinity of 3 percent of GNP should be consistent with a manageable external debt position. The 3 percent figure would translate into current account deficits of $10 billion to $15 billion annually in the 1990s and $13 billion to $19 billion in the following decade. These magnitudes are consistent with our scenario of a US merchandise trade surplus with Mexico of $7 billion to $9 billion annually throughout the 1990s and perhaps $9 billion to $12 billion annually in the following decade. This surplus would ensure the net creation of about 170,000 jobs in the US economy.

Other investigators have reached very different conclusions on the job impact of NAFTA. Conspicuous among NAFTA critics are the Economic Strategy Institute (Prestowitz and Cohen 1991), the Economic Policy Institute (Faux and Spriggs 1991; Faux and Lee), former Secretary of Labor Ray Marshall (1992), the Cuomo Commission on Competitiveness (1992), and Timothy Koechlin and Mehrene Larudee (1992, 19–32).

---

7. Until 1966 these deficits were largely financed by official aid, but beginning in 1967 private foreign investment and credits basically funded Korean trade deficits.

8. In 1984 Korea experienced a minor external debt crisis, which was quickly resolved.

Table 2.1 US jobs supported by exports to Mexico and dislocated by imports from Mexico, 1990 and future scenario, resulting from the impact of NAFTA and related reforms[a]

	Median weekly wage (dollars)	Base level (1990)		Scenario for the foreseeable future				Very long-term scenario			
		Exports	Imports	Exports	Imports	Net job change vs. 1990	Percent of total US jobs	Exports	Imports	Net job change vs. 1990	Percent of total US jobs
Merchandise trade (billions of dollars)	n.a.	28.4	30.8	45.1	38.5	n.a.	n.a.	58.4	60.8	n.a.	n.a.
Average weekly wage (dollars)	n.a.	420	424	420	424	n.a.	n.a.	418	424	n.a.	n.a.
Total jobs supported/displaced (thousands of workers)	n.a.	538.0	579.9	854.4	724.9	171.4	n.a.	856.6	903.9	−5.4	n.a.
Jobs, by type (thousands of workers, except where noted)											
Executive, administrative, managerial	620	59.1	67.3	93.9	84.1	17.9	0.12	93.0	107.4	−6.2	−0.04
Professional specialty	634	29.6	33.8	47.0	42.2	9.0	0.06	53.7	60.4	−2.5	−0.02
Technicians and related support	508	12.8	15.5	20.3	19.4	3.7	0.10	22.9	28.3	−2.7	−0.07
Sales	418	75.6	80.4	120.1	100.5	24.4	0.17	85.3	88.0	2.1	0.02
Administrative support, including clerical	365	61.1	67.5	97.0	84.4	19.1	0.10	92.1	101.1	−2.6	−0.01
Service	280	34.6	37.0	54.9	46.3	11.1	0.07	39.4	41.5	0.3	0.00
Precision, production, craft, repair	483	83.5	94.1	132.6	117.6	25.6	0.19	133.1	151.3	−7.6	−0.06
Machine operators, assemblers, inspectors	336	85.7	76.9	136.1	96.1	31.2	0.41	166.1	131.1	26.2	0.34
Transportation and material moving	419	30.6	35.9	48.6	44.9	9.0	0.18	41.6	53.6	−6.7	−0.14
Handlers, equipment cleaners, helpers, laborers	305	31.3	32.0	49.7	40.0	10.4	0.23	45.2	43.7	2.2	0.05
Farming, forestry, fishing	263	34.1	39.3	54.2	49.1	10.2	0.30	86.8	97.4	−5.4	−0.16

n.a. = not applicable.

a. The assumptions behind the intermediate scenario for the foreseeable future are spelled out in the text. Basically, it was assumed that NAFTA and related Mexican reforms will boost US exports to Mexico by $16.7 billion over the levels otherwise obtained and boost US imports from Mexico by $7.7 billion. In this scenario, no allowance is made for normal trade growth in the absence of NAFTA and related reforms.

The long-term scenario depicts an expansion of exports and imports by $30 billion each. Again, these figures only reflect the effect of NAFTA and related Mexican reforms and not the normal growth in merchandise trade. To emphasize the influence of trade composition on occupational categories, the export expansion was confined to these sectors: agricultural products, chemicals, primary metals, nonelectric and electric machinery, and transport equipment. The $30 billion export expansion was distributed among the named industries in proportion to their relative amounts of 1990 exports. Likewise, to emphasize the influence of trade composition, the $30 billion import expansion was confined to these sectors: agricultural products; other nonmanufactured goods; textiles, apparel, and shoes; other nondurables; primary metals; and transport equipment. Again, the $30 billion import expansion was distributed in the same manner as the export expansion, in proportion to the relative amounts of 1990 imports.

To obtain figures for jobs by occupational category supported by exports to Mexico in 1990, the Department of Commerce figures for direct and indirect jobs supported by exports to Mexico in 1990, by industry, were multiplied by coefficients representing the ratio of specific occupations within an industry to total jobs within that industry for the United States at large. For example, the figure for sales jobs supported by agricultural exports to Mexico was obtained by multiplying the total number of jobs (direct and indirect) supported by agricultural exports to Mexico by the ratio of sales jobs to total jobs in US agriculture as a whole.

To obtain figures for jobs by occupational category displaced by imports from Mexico in 1990, a parallel method was used. Department of Commerce figures for direct and indirect jobs in each industry supported by exports were multiplied by the ratio between US imports from Mexico and US exports to Mexico for the products of that particular industry. To make the calculation manageable, only the top 100 imports and exports were used in calculating these ratios. The top 100 imports and exports account for 96.8 percent of total US imports and 96.7 percent of total US exports to Mexico in 1990.

Numbers for total jobs by occupation supported by exports, or displaced by imports, in 1990 were obtained by summing the figures for each industry.

The average weekly wage for jobs supported by exports to Mexico in 1990 was obtained by taking a weighted average of the median wage for each occupational category, where the weights are the proportion of each occupational category supported by exports to the total number of jobs supported by exports. The same procedure was used to obtain the average wage associated with jobs displaced by imports. In these calculations, 1991 median wage figures were used.

The figures for jobs by occupation supported by exports or displaced by imports in each of the two future scenarios was obtained by multiplying the respective 1990 figures by the ratio of scenario exports (or scenario imports) to base-year exports (or base-year imports). Average wages were calculated in the same way as those for 1990. This methodology does not allow for productivity growth either in terms of jobs or in terms of wages.

Sources: Data for total jobs, by industry, and supported by exports to Mexico in 1990 was obtained from the Office of the Chief Economist, Economics and Statistics Administration, US Department of Commerce, "U.S. Jobs Supported by U.S. Merchandise Exports to Mexico: Supplemental Report," May 1992. The coefficients representing the ratio of specific occupational categories within an industry to total jobs within that industry for the United States at large are derived from unpublished data for the year 1991, collected by the Bureau of Labor Statistics. The data for average weekly wages for the year 1991 for each occupation were obtained from Bureau of Labor Statistics, US Department of Labor.

Table 2.2   Korean GNP growth, current account deficit, and gross external debt, 1957–91

Year	Average real GNP growth (percent per year)	Average current account deficit (percent of GNP)[a]	Gross external debt (percent of GNP at beginning of period)[b]
1957–61	11.1	6.9	4.0
1962–66	7.9	6.7	3.8
1967–71	9.6	8.5	15.1
1972–76	9.2	5.7	33.9
1977–81	5.8	5.0	33.8
1982–86	9.8	0.8	52.0
1987–91	10.0	(2.8)	27.6

a. For these purposes, official aid is treated as a positive capital account item. Parentheses indicate a current account surplus.
b. Between 1957 and 1982, gross external debt increased as a percent of GNP, even though GNP was growing faster than the size of the current account deficit (as a percent of GNP), because Korean corporations and citizens were simultaneously acquiring foreign assets.

Sources: Il SaKong, *Korea in the World Economy*, Washington: Institute for International Economics, 1993; IMF, *International Financial Statistics*, various issues; OECD, *Financing and External Debt of Developing Countries*, 1990 Survey, Paris 1991.

The Cuomo Commission authored the most prominent criticism of NAFTA. Briefly, the commission was concerned that the NAFTA would have three adverse effects:

- it would shift new plant and equipment investment from the United States to Mexico;

- it would create "export platforms" by which multinational firms based in Japan and other countries would gain improved access to the US market;

- it would lead to more intense wage competition between US and Mexican workers.

The apprehension that, with NAFTA, Mexico will soon be sprinkled with export platforms was answered in a report issued by the Council of the Americas (US Council of the Mexico-US Business Committee 1992, chapter 3). Neither Japan nor other countries are clamoring to build export facilities in Mexico, and as our earlier calculations suggest, Mexico is likely to remain a large net importer from the United States for many years to come. Moreover, the tight rules of origin negotiated in some sectors, particularly autos and textiles and apparel, go a long way toward eliminating the attractions of Mexico as a place to assemble third-country components and to ship the finished goods to the United States and Canada.

We have already commented on wage competition between US and Mexican workers. The remaining issue raised by the Cuomo Commission is the potential shift of plant and equipment investment from the United States to Mexico. Among most NAFTA critics, including the Economic Strategy Institute and the Economic Policy Institute, this potential investment shift is the center point for scenarios of US job losses. A systematic exposition of the investment-shift and job-loss scenario was published by Koechlin and Larudee.

The key assumption they made is that increased investment flows from the United States will augment the capital stock in Mexico by an amount ranging from $31 billion to $53 billion between 1992 and 2000 and that these investment flows will cause an equivalent decrease in the US capital stock. From this key assumption, a very pessimistic scenario emerges. The United States loses 290,000 to 490,000 industrial jobs, while Mexico gains 400,000 to 680,000 industrial jobs.[9]

The assumption that larger investment in Mexico implies smaller investment in the United States (the substitution assumption) taps into a long debate on US foreign direct investment. In our view, the substitution assumption is based on an erroneous model of the international investment process. On balance, we think that investment by US firms in Mexico is a "good event" rather than a "bad event" for the United States. Foreign investment by US firms creates US jobs, both in the short run, by boosting US exports of capital goods, and in the long run, by establishing channels for the export of US intermediate components, replacement parts, and associated goods and services.[10] If US firms were to refrain from investing in Mexico, there is no reason to believe that the firms would invest in the United States instead (rather than, for example, Chile or Korea), nor is there any certainty that foreign multinational firms would not seize the investment opportunities in Mexico that were passed over by US firms. In any event, from a purely selfish US standpoint, the economic gains from additional investment and faster growth in Mexico are greater than the gains from corresponding activity in any other country (outside the US itself), since the Mexican propensity to import from the United States is among the highest in the world. On average, each Mexican imports $380 of US merchandise annually; by contrast, each Korean, with twice the per capita income, imports $360 of US merchandise annually.

There is another difficulty with the pessimistic scenario developed by Koechlin and Larudee: it ignores the dampening effect of a larger Mexican capital stock on illegal migration from Mexico to the United States. According to a computable general equilibrium model devised by Sher-

---

9. Koechlin and Larudee also forecast that between 0.8 million and 2.0 million Mexican rural jobs will be lost as a result of expanded US corn and bean exports to Mexico.

10. Early contributions to this debate were US International Trade Commission (1973, 645–72) and Bergsten, Horst, and Moran (1978). For a recent summary of the role of multinational firms in the international economy, see Hufbauer (1992, chapter 5).

man Robinson et al. (1992, 17), each 1 percent increase in the Mexican capital stock reduces the level of permanent migration from Mexico to the United States by about 44,000 workers. The Mexican capital stock in 1990 was probably about $500 billion,[11] so an increment of $31 billion to $53 billion owing to the NAFTA (the Koechlin and Larudee forecast) would augment the capital stock by between 6 and 10 percent. In turn, this would reduce permanent immigration by at least 260,000 workers from the levels that would otherwise be reached. Lower-skilled Americans who compete in the job market with immigrant Mexicans should welcome this by-product of Mexican prosperity.[12]

The Occupational Impact of NAFTA

Conflicting estimates of net jobs gained or lost in the intermediate term on account of NAFTA should be put in a broader perspective.[13] Over a period of 10 years or longer, total employment in the United States and the US merchandise trade balance with the world at large are essentially determined by macroeconomic conditions and policies: specifically, domestic and global business cycles, US fiscal and monetary policies, and the productivity of the US economy. Microeconomic events, such as defense conversion or NAFTA, will affect the distribution of employment throughout the economy, and perhaps the trade balance with individual countries, but they will not exert a perceptible long-run impact on overall employment levels or on the overall merchandise trade balance. In the long run, the impact of NAFTA will be offset by other changes in microeconomic policy or will be lost as noise in the background of macroeconomic events.

Nor will NAFTA make a significant addition to the large number of gross job displacements that occur annually in the dynamic US economy. For example, over the five years up to 1990, some 8.9 million workers reported that they had been displaced from their jobs, meaning that they had lost their jobs because of a plant closing, because the employer went out of business, or because they were laid off and not later recalled (Podgursky 1992, 19, table 1). By our calculations, a gross total of 316,000 US jobs will be created by NAFTA while a gross total of 145,000 US jobs

---

11. It is commonly assumed that the stock of reproducible capital is two to three times the level of GDP. In the United States in 1991, the estimate for the net stock of fixed reproducible private capital was $10.4 trillion while GDP was $5.7 trillion (*Survey of Current Business*, October 1992, 29).

12. One model suggests the return migration to Mexico could increase the wage rate for US rural and unskilled workers by between 1.8 and 5.7 percent (Hinojosa-Ojeda and Robinson 1991, 22–24 and table 8, scenarios 4B and 5B).

13. For a good summary of the broader economic perspective, see Alfred Reifman (1992).

will be dislocated.[14] Our estimate that 145,000 US jobs will be displaced works out to less than 2 percent of total displacements over five years. Even the far more pessimistic calculation of Koechlin and Larudee, namely that as many as 490,000 US workers will be displaced by NAFTA, works out to less than 6 percent of total displacements over five years.

Nevertheless, while the scale of NAFTA-related dislocations is small compared with economywide magnitudes, some US workers will inevitably lose their jobs. The volume of trade in both directions will rise dramatically, and increased two-way trade between the United States and Mexico will cause employment to shift within and between US industries. The challenge for the United States is to help such workers make the difficult transition to new jobs. In turn, this raises the question of whether the jobs created by NAFTA require very different skills from the jobs displaced by NAFTA. If this is the case, then on balance NAFTA would impose a heavier burden on some occupational categories than on others.

Because of the concern about the impact of NAFTA on US workers with different skill characteristics, it is worth taking a closer look at the likely impact by occupational category. Table 2.1 contains a breakdown, by occupational category, of US jobs "supported" in 1990 by exports to Mexico, and US jobs "dislocated" by imports from Mexico. These estimates rest on a number of assumptions that are summarized in the table notes.

Based on the 1990 composition of trade, the median weekly wage associated with US exports to Mexico and US imports from Mexico were practically the same: about $420 to $425 per week. This calculation is striking because it suggests that there is no overall tendency for US exports to Mexico to support high-skilled US jobs, nor for US imports from Mexico to displace low-skilled US jobs.

In our scenario for the foreseeable future, the impact of NAFTA and associated Mexican reforms is to increase US exports to Mexico by $16.7 billion and to increase US imports from Mexico by $7.7 billion.[15] For the purposes of this scenario, we ignore trade growth that would likely occur without NAFTA and Mexican domestic reforms. Based on this scenario,

---

14. We originally estimated that up to 112,000 workers would be dislocated by North American trade liberalization. In light of the latest Commerce Department coefficients of direct and indirect jobs per billion dollars of exports to Mexico (about 19,600 per billion dollars of exports) we have revised our earlier estimate upward to 145,000 jobs lost (US Department of Commerce 1992b).

15. A high-side estimate of trade diversion from all third countries as a result of NAFTA is about 35 percent of increased US imports from Mexico, or about $2.7 billion annually. The possibility of trade diversion is not factored into our job calculation, but it would increase the net number of US jobs created, since fewer US jobs would be dislocated owing to a smaller net increase in US imports (after making an allowance for diverted trade).

table 2.1 shows the number of US export jobs created, and the number of US import-competing jobs dislocated, by occupational category, assuming that the composition of trade by industry sector remains the same as in 1990. The important point to note is that the net job impact (by comparison with the 1990 position) is distributed fairly evenly across occupational categories. While all occupational categories show net job gains, relative to numbers employed in 1990 the net gains in the executive, professional, and administrative categories are actually smaller than for production workers and farmers.[16]

To depict the maximum plausible impact of NAFTA on the composition of the US job market, we have also calculated the very long-term scenario portrayed in table 2.1[17] This scenario does *not* reflect normal trade growth; instead, it only purports to calculate the incremental impact of *highly optimistic* two-way trade creation resulting from NAFTA. In this scenario, both merchandise imports and exports are projected to rise, as a consequence of NAFTA, by $30 billion over the levels that prevailed in 1990. As in 1990, Mexican merchandise trade is *assumed to be approximately balanced* and the United States *does not run a trade surplus* with Mexico.[18] These are assumptions for calculating the very long-term occupational impact; they are not trade forecasts for any point in the near future.

In order to develop plausible "worst case" estimates for this scenario ("worst case" from the vantage point of unskilled US workers), US merchandise import growth from Mexico is assumed to be concentrated in nondurables, while US merchandise export growth to Mexico is assumed to be concentrated in durables and capital goods. The results are noteworthy in two respects.

First, as the calculations in table 2.1 show, the distribution of the impact across occupational categories is *not* focused on lower-paid workers. Instead, even assuming a *major* change in the composition of trade, US factory workers benefit relative to US office workers, and less skilled workers do not incur disproportionate job losses compared with more skilled workers.

---

16. It is worth noting that the INFORUM-CIMAT study directed by Clopper Almon reached similar results. In their TAB scenario, in which the US trade balance improves by about $6.3 billion (1990 dollars) five years after the NAFTA enters into force, the calculated increase in US craft worker, operative, nonfarm labor, and farm employment is 31,500 jobs, while the calculated increase in professional and managerial employment is only 9,100 jobs (Shiells and Shelburne 1992, tables 1 and 7).

17. Because of its speculative character, this scenario was deleted from the first edition of our book. The *New York Times*, in its edition of 22 February 1993, called attention to the deletion and drew misleading conclusions about the underlying analysis. Contrary to the *New York Times* story, the scenario was designed to highlight the job impact *across* occupational categories, not the *net* job effects of the NAFTA accord.

18. The scenario assumes that, as in the recent past, Mexican payments for the import of services will approximately equal Mexican receipts for the exports of services plus remittances from immigrants working in the United States.

Second, these calculations do *not* represent estimates of net US job gains or losses over the long term. Rather they reflect the potential impact of NAFTA on the *composition* of US jobs.[19] The small net US job loss in our very long-term scenario is entirely due to the fact that we assumed balanced trade growth, starting from a base year in which Mexico ran a merchandise trade surplus with the United States of $2.4 billion. This trade surplus figure is an assumption, not a plausible forecast for events after the year 2000. Judging from Korean experience, Mexico is likely to run trade deficits, not trade surpluses, with the United States for many years.

To summarize: we estimate that NAFTA should generate small net positive US jobs gains over the next few years. Over time, the level of US employment will be determined by the broad array of US domestic economic policies rather than by its trade policies. However, in assessing the effect of NAFTA on the composition of US jobs, we found that there is little or no substance to the fear that NAFTA will worsen the job prospects for the lowest quartile of the US work force.

Long-Term Efficiency Benefits from NAFTA

Over the long term, the main impact of larger US-Mexican trade will be higher incomes made possible by greater efficiency and faster growth. Efficiency in both economies will be boosted by the tendency of each country to export those goods and services in which it has a comparative advantage. Faster growth will result from more intense competition among a larger number of firms in each segment of the market and from an expanded North American market that will enable each firm to realize economies of scale. In turn, this could result in an improved trade balance for North America with the rest of the world or better terms of trade for North America.[20]

Indirect evidence on the benefits of expanded trade is provided in a study by David Walters, Chief Economist in the Office of the US Trade Representative (1992a).[21] According to the Walters study, US direct and indirect private-sector jobs supported by nonagricultural exports to world markets pay wages that are about 16.7 percent higher than average nonagricultural jobs throughout the US economy. A parallel analysis by Walters for exports to Mexico (1992b) indicates that, on average, US jobs

---

19. Some commentators have deliberately misread and misrepresented our findings to suggest that NAFTA will ultimately lead to net US job losses. This error has been made most notably by Jeff Faux and his colleagues at the Economic Policy Institute, *Challenge*, July/August 1993, and by Jim Hightower, "NAFTA: WE DON'T HAFTA," *Utne Reader*, July/August 1993.

20. Whether a more competitive North America translates into an improved trade balance or an appreciated currency (and hence better terms of trade) will depend on macroeconomic conditions in North America and other regions of the global economy.

21. The data used in this study are for 1990.

supported by nonagricultural exports to Mexico pay 12.2 percent more than average US nonagricultural jobs.[22]

It should be noted that, in his calculations, Walters compared the average wage of export-supported employment to the average wage of all employment; Walters made no comparison to the average wage of import-dislocated employment. Our calculations in table 2.1 suggest that, in terms of bilateral US-Mexico trade, there is little difference in the average wage between export-supported and imported-dislocated jobs. These calculations accordingly suggest that US gains from NAFTA will result not from a shift in the occupational composition of the US work force but rather from greater efficiency within the traded goods sector and faster growth in the two economies.

One way to size up the efficiency benefits from trade liberalization is to examine the results of the hypothetical elimination of US trade barriers on a global basis for several highly protected industries. According to estimates made in the mid-1980s by the Institute for International Economics (Hufbauer, Berliner, and Elliott 1986, tables 1.2 and 1.4), if US import barriers on 31 highly protected industries had been eliminated, US imports would have increased by about $44.4 billion, and US efficiency gains would have been about $8.4 billion. These two numbers indicate that comparative-advantage gains from the elimination of trade barriers could be as large as 20 percent of trade expansion.[23] The industries in this sample were, however, subject to severe protection, a circumstance that overstates the size of possible efficiency gains relative to the volume of potential trade expansion in the North American context. Given the height of US and Mexican trade barriers prior to NAFTA, classic efficiency gains are likely to be in the range of 7.5 percent of two-way trade expansion.[24]

In addition to the classic efficiency benefits from harnessing comparative advantage, the larger number of firms in an expanded North American market should prompt all competitors to reduce their costs and to exploit economies of scale. This possibility has been widely discussed in the theoretical literature.[25]

---

22. The data are for 1990.

23. A recalculation based on our unpublished analysis for the year 1990 suggests that the 20 percent ratio still applies for highly protected industries.

24. This calculation assumes that additional Mexican imports account for two-thirds of the total two-way trade expansion and that the efficiency gain on these imports is 10 percent of the incremental trade (reflecting an assumption that the pre-NAFTA level of Mexican tariff and nontariff barriers is on average 20 percent). The other one-third of the trade expansion is additional US imports from Mexico, where the efficiency gain is assumed to be 2.5 percent of the incremental trade (reflecting an assumption that the pre-NAFTA level of US tariff and nontariff barriers is on average 5 percent).

25. For a survey of the literature, see J. David Richardson (1989) and Hufbauer (1992, chapter 5). Also see McKinsey & Company (1992) for an indirect assessment of the impact of competition on productivity in a number of service-sector industries.

In an unpublished study, the authors of this assessment have calculated the trade and growth gains for Latin American taken as a whole, based on a scenario of broad policy liberalization, including dramatic trade reform (Hufbauer and Schott 1992b, appendix B). The implication of our reform scenario is that, during 1990–2000, Latin American two-way trade would increase by $235 billion over the baseline level. The dynamic impact of trade gains, together with other reforms, would boost the region's GDP by $385 billion over the baseline level. The suggested ratio between induced GDP gains and trade expansion brought about by policy reform is an astonishing 1.65. This very high ratio is, of course, subject to estimation errors and assumes dramatic policy reforms. Even making liberal allowance for modeling errors and less-than-sweeping policy reforms, it seems plausible that trade liberalization could yield dynamic GDP gains of at least 50 percent of the resulting two-way trade expansion for the Mexican economy, which was highly protected in the late 1980s.

In round numbers, if two-way US-Mexico trade in the intermediate term expands by $25 billion on account of NAFTA, and if classic comparative-advantage benefits realized by both countries amount to just 7.5 percent of expanded trade, the annual efficiency gains would be about $1.9 billion. In addition, the growth gains from enhanced competition and larger markets might benefit the Mexican economy by as much as $12.5 billion annually. To an unknown extent, the larger and more competitive North American market would also confer dynamic gains on US producers.

Together, the efficiency benefits and growth stimulus of NAFTA could exceed $15 billion annually. Over the long term, this figure—not jobs gained or lost—is the true measure of the economic gain from the NAFTA agreement. Annual gains of $15 billion are equivalent to making an addition to the combined capital stock of the two nations of about $75 billion—not bad for government work.[26]

Migration

In keeping with our recommendations, the NAFTA text stayed well clear of the explosive issues raised by illegal immigration from Mexico to the United States. The NAFTA itself only addressed the entry of business and professional personnel.[27]

---

26. The $75 billion figure assumes that capital invested in the US and Mexican economies yields a real social return of 20 percent per year.

27. Intracompany transferees will be allowed to enter if they have been with the company for at least one year out of the previous three years. In addition, 5,500 Mexican professionals will be allowed to enter the United States annually in addition to those admitted under global immigration limits (see NAFTA appendix 1603.D.4).

While the NAFTA itself is silent on illegal immigration, this issue is very much on the minds of Americans. Over the long term, Mexican prosperity is the only practical answer to the problem of illegal immigration. As explained in our 1992 book, the NAFTA is likely to lead over the long term to strong growth in Mexican per capita income (Hufbauer and Schott 1992a, chapter 3). Over three or four decades, Mexican per capita income might reach half the US level, and this gain would substantially ease and perhaps even eliminate pressures within Mexico to emigrate.

Nevertheless, Mexican immigration is likely to increase in the short run for reasons having nothing to do with NAFTA. A study by the National Commission for Employment Policy (1992, 6–7) indicates that between 4 million and 5 million legal and illegal Mexican immigrants will enter the United States during the 1990s, not taking into account the effects of the NAFTA. Most of these migrants will return to Mexico, but a fraction (perhaps 10 percent) will settle permanently in the United States (Martin 1992, 5).

All in all, it would be prudent to expect more rather than less immigration during the next five years. The overriding pressures to emigrate will come from rural displacement in Mexico stemming from land reforms, increased demand for farm and service-sector workers in the United States, and rapid efficiency gains in the Mexican industrial sector. Compared with these pressures, the incremental impact of NAFTA in the next five years will be small—perhaps an additional gross 100,000 migrants annually (National Commission for Employment Policy 1992, 6–7).[28]

One way to reconcile these various estimates is to speculate that, in the short run, NAFTA may marginally increase the gross number of illegal immigrants. However, in the longer run, NAFTA should help create the level of Mexican prosperity that will substantially reduce the gross level of illegal immigration.

Over time, emigration pressures will be offset by faster economic growth in Mexico, assisted and reinforced by the long-run effect of NAFTA in boosting Mexican productivity. The consulting firm CIEMEX-WEFA, for example, calculates that, over the 10-year period ending in 2002, the gross number of illegal immigrants could decrease by 600,000 on account of economic growth stimulated by NAFTA (CIEMEX-WEFA 1992, 15).[29]

---

28. Of the additional migrants, perhaps 10 percent, or 10,000 annually, would settle permanently in the United States.

29. The National Commission also projects a decrease in Mexican immigrants in the first decade of the 21st century (National Commission for Employment Policy 1992, 7).

The US federal government already provides about $1 billion annually to state and local governments to cope with extra social costs associated with immigrants (Philip L. Martin, letter to authors, 28 October 1992).[30] About $600 million is spent annually on 13 programs for migrant and seasonal farm workers and their families. With the possibility of increased immigration in the short term, the federal government will probably have to augment these programs (Martin 1992, 17; National Commission for Employment Policy, letter to the president 13 October 1992).

We do not believe that the United States should put large amounts of money into building steel barricades, digging concrete ditches, or placing electronic sensors along its 2,000-mile border with Mexico.[31] Such measures would be rightly characterized as rebuilding the Berlin Wall, brick by brick, in North America. Unless border controls were comprehensive and draconian, they would not stem the aggregate flow. However, they would prompt a larger fraction of migrants to settle permanently, knowing that reentry to the United States had become more difficult. Whatever the effect on immigration flows, border fortification measures would be sure to sour US relations with Mexico for a very long time.

US Labor Adjustment Programs

In its May 1991 Action Plan, the Bush administration promised to address labor's concerns about NAFTA both in the agreement itself and through a new US-Mexico Labor Commission. In her September 1992 testimony to Congress, US Labor Secretary Lynn Martin argued that labor's concerns would be addressed through three mechanisms: explicit NAFTA provisions, a formal binational cooperation program with Mexico, and President Bush's new job training program (Secretary of Labor Lynn Martin, testimony before the Senate Finance Committee, 10 September 1992, 2). These responses did not satisfy organized labor. Not surprisingly, candidate Clinton promised a bigger and better approach to labor adjustment. But even President Clinton's approach will not satisfy those who are determined to take a negative view of the employment consequences of NAFTA.

---

30. A study by the Rand Corporation examined the impact on public services resulting from Mexican immigration, and noted *inter alia* that "California educators project they will need between $1.7 billion and $2.4 billion a year to give each immigrant adult an estimated 450 hours of schooling." To an unknown extent, additional taxes paid by immigrants offset some of these expenses (*The Washington Post*, 26 March 1991, A15).

31. The United States is helping Mexico police the Mexicans' southern border with Central America. This effort may retard the flow of Central Americans through Mexico to the United States.

Explicit NAFTA Provisions

According to Labor Secretary Martin, explicit NAFTA provisions that will smooth the transition for US workers include 15-year transition periods for the most sensitive sectors, such as glassware, some footwear, ceramic tile, broomcorn brooms, some watches, and certain fruits and vegetables; improved safeguard mechanisms to protect sensitive industries against a flood of imports; and strict rules of origin to "ensure that the free-trade benefits of a NAFTA accrue to North American products and their workers" (Secretary of Labor Lynn Martin, testimony before the Senate Finance Committee, 10 September 1992, 5). Interestingly, only the United States and Canada obtained 15-year transition periods for particularly sensitive manufactured goods. Mexican tariffs on all manufactured products will be eliminated within 10 years.

The NAFTA contains several bilateral safeguard provisions applicable during the transition. The main bilateral safeguard mechanisms are contained in Article 801. During the transition period, a tariff "snapback" to the pre-NAFTA level is allowed for up to three years for most products, and up to four years for the most sensitive products, in cases where imports from a NAFTA partner are a substantial cause of serious injury or threaten serious injury.[32] This mechanism augments the Canada-US FTA safeguard provisions by allowing a safeguard action even if increased imports only threaten injury and by allowing up to four years of relief rather than three. The NAFTA also establishes special safeguards in the form of tariff rate quotas for sensitive agricultural products and a different causation test ("serious damage") for textiles and apparel.

In addition to the bilateral provisions of Article 801, the NAFTA's global safeguard provision (Article 802) allows for the imposition of tariffs or quotas on imports from NAFTA partners as part of a multilateral safeguard action brought by any NAFTA country. Following the FTA precedent, however, imports from a NAFTA partner must be "substantial" before its trade can be included in a global safeguards action.[33]

In designing long transition periods and special safeguard mechanisms, the negotiators gave ample attention to the adjustment consequences of free trade within North America. Under the NAFTA approach, some products will continue to enjoy protection for long periods, even though the concerned firms might have been able to adjust on a faster

---

32. The current most-favored-nation (MFN) rates become the benchmark if, at the time of the snapback, the MFN rates are lower than the NAFTA rates (Article 801).

33. The NAFTA defines "substantial" differently from the US-Canada FTA. Imports from a NAFTA member is exempt from global safeguards unless that country "is among the top five suppliers of the good subject to the proceeding, measured in terms of import share during the most recent three-year period" (Article 802:2a). The FTA definition is 5 to 10 percent of total imports of the good.

timetable to competition from other NAFTA countries. However, this flaw can be redressed if the NAFTA follows the US-Canada FTA approach and accelerates tariff cuts through subsequent negotiations.

Binational Cooperation

The Bush administration's second mechanism to meet labor concerns—binational cooperation—has resulted in a series of bilateral agreements to promote closer cooperation and joint action on a variety of labor issues. The initial memorandum of understanding with Mexico (signed in May 1991) has produced an array of comparative studies of labor conditions and laws in each country that are designed to provide the substantive basis for new bilateral programs.[34]

In September 1992 the United States and Mexico further expanded their cooperative efforts in this area by concluding a bilateral agreement establishing a new Consultative Commission on Labor Matters. This permanent body will implement a bilateral work program and consult on the enforcement of national labor laws and regulations. However, the agreement itself does not contain a joint enforcement mechanism ("Agreement . . . Regarding the Establishing of a Consultative Commission on Labor Matters," 14 September 1992, Article 3:1). In addition to the consultative commission, the two countries have agreed to develop improved standards in the areas of industrial hygiene and work place safety.

Job Training Program

The third, and most critical, of the Bush administration's efforts to address labor adjustment issues came in August 1992, when President Bush proposed a new worker adjustment program: Advancing Skills through Education and Training (ASETS). ASETS was designed to replace two existing adjustment programs, under the Economic Dislocation and Worker Adjustment Assistance Act (EDWAA) and the Trade Adjustment Assistance Act (TAA), with a single new program. The new program called for $10 billion in new funding over five years for training and adjustment assistance for displaced workers, of which $1.67 billion, or $335 million annually for five years, was earmarked (if needed) for workers displaced by the NAFTA.[35]

---

34. See, for example, US Department of Labor and Mexican Secretariat of Labor and Social Welfare (1992a and b).

35. Up to an additional $335 million annually could be drawn from a discretionary fund, if required. The reserve-fund contingency implied an upper-level job-loss figure of about 300,000 workers over 10 years.

President Bush's plan easily beat our recommendation that the United States budget $1.2 billion over five years for NAFTA-related worker adjustment. Indeed, the Bush plan was much better and bolder than our proposals, since it subsumed NAFTA adjustment in the larger context of retraining workers, whatever the cause of dislocation. Further, as we had recommended, the bulk of the funding was scheduled for retraining rather than income maintenance, with vouchers issued for training at qualified private institutions in addition to federally run programs.

Clinton's Plan

Candidate Clinton said in his October 1992 speech that he would support the NAFTA as drafted but would negotiate a supplemental agreement to reinforce worker standards and safety (speech at North Carolina State University, 4 October 1992, 15). In addition, he promised a bigger and better approach to labor adjustment than that evinced in Bush administration programs.

To a large extent, Clinton's proposal for a supplemental pact on labor issues stems from concerns about the enforcement of national labor laws in Mexico. While specific objectives for such a pact have not yet been spelled out, we assume the supplemental negotiations would seek to establish commitments to the aggressive enforcement of national labor laws and regulations, monitoring of labor markets by a trinational commission, and dispute settlement provisions to encourage compliance. Such an agreement would subsume, but greatly expand upon, our recommendation that the NAFTA require trinational panels to issue biennial reports on labor market conditions (including immigration) in each country. In like fashion, it would sharply expand the responsibilities of the nascent US-Mexico Binational Commission, particularly with regard to enforcement mechanisms.

In essence, the commission should act as a roving spotlight. It should focus public attention both on inadequate enforcement and on labor standards that do not meet international norms. (It would thereby supplement the weak enforcement provisions of International Labor Organization conventions.[36]) To accomplish these tasks, the trinational commission would need to review the enforcement practices of national authorities, to send out field investigators, to hold public hearings, to publish reports, and to make recommendations to the NAFTA govern-

---

36. It should be recalled that Mexico has signed more ILO conventions that the United States or Canada, so in some respects Mexico could complain that its northern neighbors have not met international norms. In addition, Canadian unions would be happy to use the Trinational Commission as a forum to criticize state "right to work" laws in the United States.

ments. Labor unions and industry associations should be able to file reports on the labor practices in any member country. In some respects, the procedures would parallel the special dispute settlement process for unfair trade laws under NAFTA chapter 19, in which NAFTA panels rule on whether national authorities have faithfully pursued their own trade laws and administrative procedures. In this case, the issue would be whether the national authority has enforced its own labor laws and regulations.

However, we do not think the commission should have the power to levy fines or award money damages against particular firms or industries. Such remedies should remain the responsibility of national agencies and courts. In most cases, we believe the glare of publicity should be sufficient to promote compliance. If this spotlight and subsequent government measures prove inadequate, the commission, acting on a petition from a NAFTA country, should be empowered to authorize trade remedies against firms or industries that show a persistent pattern of labor abuse.[37]

In sum, the supplemental agreement could make an important contribution to the enforcement of labor standards by using the trinational commission to expose offenders and by ultimately authorizing trade countermeasures if governments do not succeed in halting the abuses. We believe the negotiation of such a pact would reinforce the NAFTA provisions in this area and would be desirable for all three countries.

Clinton also proposed a supplementary agreement that would allow a NAFTA member to take action if there is an "unexpected and overwhelming surge in imports into either country which would dislocate a whole sector of the economy" (speech at North Carolina State University, Raleigh, NC, 4 October 1992, 16). The US sugar and citrus industries have been strong proponents of a supplementary agreement on safeguards. Both industries are concerned about the potential rapid growth in Mexican exports to the United States, especially if the NAFTA reforms are supplemented by GATT trade liberalization. Accordingly, they would like to retain the possibility of reinstating high tariffs and/or quotas to protect against import surges from Mexico both during and after the transition period.

Basically, the Clinton supplementary agreement on safeguards seems designed to address cases that have three characteristics: trade injury is serious, Canada and Mexico would escape global trade remedies because

---

37. For trade remedies to be effective (and not give rise to spiraling countermeasures), the NAFTA parties would need to waive their GATT rights concerning the imposition of trade penalties for persistent labor abuse when the penalties are authorized by the Trinational Commission. In our view, the NAFTA commission, like a GATT dispute panel, should only authorize trade remedies in response to a petition from a member government. It should not become a court of original jurisdiction for labor unions, trade associations, or other petitioners.

their exports to the United States are not "substantial," and the snapback provisions in Article 801 are inadequate to stem the import surge from NAFTA partners.

A supplementary agreement, even if limited to these cases, would cause concern in Canada and Mexico. A major Canadian objective in the FTA was to contain the "sideswipe" risks of US actions under Section 201, and a supplementary agreement might threaten to undermine this objective. A possible solution is language that qualifies the circumstances in which Canadian and Mexican imports are excluded from global actions because they are not "substantial." In the case of an "unexpected and overwhelming surge" in a NAFTA country's imports (to use Clinton's language), the trajectory of import penetration as well as the level could be considered.

In addition to these supplementary agreements, Clinton promised to enact unilateral measures to facilitate labor adjustment within the United States. Clinton essentially pledged to reach more affected workers with better delivery systems than the Bush program. For example, farmers would be helped in the shift to alternative crops, and those farmers who do "lose out to competition should be just as eligible for transition assistance as workers in businesses" (speech at North Carolina State University, 4 October 1992, 13).

The dimensions of the Clinton labor training program remain to be spelled out, but a safe bet is that remedies for NAFTA-induced dislocation will eventually be part of a much larger program. As with the Bush proposals, the specific causes of worker dislocation may come to play a limited role in the availability of training, relocation, and income maintenance allowances. Instead, the program benefits will be geared to worker characteristics (e.g., the previous employment history of the worker, wage level, etc.) and features of the local labor market (e.g., the extent of unemployment in the area). Given mediocre US productivity performance over the past two decades, broad-gauged retraining programs make more sense than programs targeted on specific causes of worker dislocation. However, broad-based programs may not be in place by January 1994, when NAFTA implementation is supposed to start. Hence, as in the Bush program, Clinton should earmark money for NAFTA adjustment until a broader program has been adopted.

Finally, Clinton, Salinas, and Mulroney could make an important contribution to public acceptance of NAFTA by calling on their central banks and finance ministers to meet from time to time to review the macroeconomic situation in North America. In addition, when new fiscal, monetary, or exchange rate policies are adopted in one of the partner countries, the others should be consulted in advance. At a minimum, these meetings could help avert the tendency—so prominent in Canadian experience with the FTA—to blame the NAFTA for all plant closings, labor dislocation, and other bad economic tidings.

3

Market Access by Sector

1. Energy

The NAFTA negotiations offered an opportunity to integrate Mexico's abundant oil reserves with US and Canadian financial capital and technological expertise. But Mexico's historic commitment to oil as a symbol of national sovereignty prevented a sweeping liberalization of the energy sector. The agreement failed to break the monopoly held by Pemex (Mexico's national oil company) on oil exploration and development and on gasoline and fuel oil sales. Moreover, Mexican energy trade remains subject to a far wider range of contingent restrictions than US or Canadian energy trade. Despite these shortcomings, the NAFTA makes modest progress by increasing US and Canadian access to Mexican electricity, petrochemical, gas and energy services, and by opening up Mexico's substantial procurement of energy-related goods and services to NAFTA suppliers.

Public Procurement and Performance Contracts

One of NAFTA's most notable energy achievements is the opening of Pemex and CFE (the State Electricity Commission) contracts to foreign participation: 50 percent participation immediately, 70 percent by year 8, and 100 percent by year 10.[1] Moreover, Mexico will adopt procedures

---

1. Pemex contracts are currently worth about $5.5 billion a year, and CFE contracts are worth about $3.0 billion a year. According to an advisory committee report, "Despite a

comparable to those of the General Agreement on Tariffs and Trade (GATT) to ensure that US and Canadian firms have fair access to Pemex and CFE procurement.

In addition, Mexico will allow performance contracts, under which US and Canadian oil and gas field service companies operating in Mexico can be paid a bonus for exceeding contract targets. This creates a measure of flexibility so that agreements between Pemex and foreign companies can allow some sharing of the upside risk of oil and gas exploration.

Investment

Mexico will maintain most of its investment restrictions for the petroleum industry: the NAFTA does not ensure foreign investment in oil exploration, production, or refining; it does not provide for standard risk-sharing contracts; and it does not permit US and Canadian firms to enter the Mexican retail gasoline market.

By our standards, the NAFTA thus receives a low score for its failure to liberalize investment in the petroleum sector. The United States and Canada certainly would gain from the relaxation of Mexico's investment restrictions, but it is Mexico that would benefit most from opening its oil industry to North American firms. To avoid becoming a net oil importer, Mexico must dramatically overhaul its energy sector and invest heavily in new exploration and development just to meet domestic energy demand, which is increasing at 5 percent a year, and to maintain exports at 1.3 million barrels a day.[2] In particular, Mexico will need to augment its supply of petroleum products to compensate for refineries closed for environmental reasons and to provide more unleaded gasoline.[3]

Recognizing that the NAFTA would not fully liberalize energy trade with Mexico, we recommended that Mexico should restructure Pemex into three separate, semiprivate firms. In June 1992 Pemex did reorganize its operations into four distinct subsidiaries: an exploration and pro-

---

fairly long transition period for maximum access to energy sector procurement by Mexican Government agencies, the above provisions will eventually provide good access to Mexico's promising $20 billion oil service sector market" (Industry Sector Advisory Committee for Trade in Energy 1992, 11).

2. Mexico already runs a trade deficit in basic petrochemicals, and in 1991 Mexico quadrupled its imports of US natural gas (*Wall Street Journal*, 17 June 1992, A13). According to energy consultant Rafael Quijano, domestic demand alone could consume all of Mexico's petroleum output by the year 2004 unless there is a big boost in exploration and development.

3. In August 1992, just weeks after the NAFTA negotiations were concluded, Shell Oil announced a joint venture with Pemex under which it would sell Pemex 50 percent of Shell's Deer Park, Texas, refinery. The plant will be upgraded to refine heavy crude from Mexico.

duction unit, a refining unit, a natural gas and primary petrochemicals unit, and a secondary petrochemicals unit. This reorganization is a step in the right direction, but the restructuring of Pemex still has a long way to go. For example, while the new Pemex subsidiaries will use world market prices as reference points to price transactions with sister subsidiaries, they will not be allowed to buy or sell in the open market.

Although Mexico refused to open its petroleum industry to foreign investment, it did meet our recommendation to liberalize investment restrictions in two related areas: basic and secondary petrochemicals, and electricity. Mexico will immediately lift its investment embargo on 14 of the 19 previously restricted basic petrochemicals and controls on 66 secondary petrochemicals. Import and export licenses will be required only on the five remaining basic petrochemicals.

In electricity, Mexico will allow foreign investors to acquire, establish, and operate electric generating facilities for their own use, cogeneration, and independent power production, without any involvement from the state electricity monopoly, CFE. However, any surplus power generated by foreign facilities must be sold to CFE, and no cross-border sales will be allowed without the participation and agreement of CFE.

Trade

The NAFTA was partially successful in meeting our recommendation to liberalize cross-border trade in electricity and natural gas. The agreement permits US and Canadian suppliers of natural gas and electricity to negotiate contracts directly with Mexican firms. However, these suppliers still must pass all arrangements through Pemex or CFE, which gives the state monopolies blocking and delaying powers. We continue to recommend direct dealing between suppliers and end users so as to permit agreements to be made more quickly and to discourage anticompetitive practices by Pemex and CFE.

The Canada-US FTA confines energy trade restrictions to special circumstances: to protect national security, to conserve exhaustible natural resources, to deal with a short supply situation, or to implement a price stabilization plan. Under the FTA, the dislocation caused by energy trade restrictions (other than those imposed for national security reasons) is supposed to be shared between domestic and foreign users. Under the NAFTA, these norms are retained for Canada and the United States, but they are not extended to Mexico as we recommended.

Mexico did, however, agree to abide by GATT standards when intervening in international energy trade. In general terms, the GATT requires that quantitative restrictions take into account the historical market shares of importing and exporting countries. However, the GATT does not call on countries that limit their exports to share the dislocation burden between domestic and foreign users. In theory, therefore, Mexico could cut off petroleum exports to the United States and all other foreign countries without breaching NAFTA.

The NAFTA was successful in liberalizing investment and trade in the coal industry. Mexico will immediately permit US and Canadian firms to own 100 percent of new coal mines and facilities (up from the pre-NAFTA limit of 49 percent), but Mexico will continue for three years to limit US and Canadian ownership of existing mines and facilities to a ceiling of 49 percent. Mexico will eliminate its 10 percent tariff on coal immediately and will guarantee national treatment to coal imported from the United States or Canada. Mexico currently applies a 6 percent value-added tax on coal shipments to parastatal enterprises, and this tax will remain in force both for foreign and domestic coal sales.

Evaluation

Although the NAFTA falls short of achieving free market competition in energy for North America, it does achieve notable progress in opening up Pemex and CFE procurement to NAFTA suppliers and in liberalizing investment in secondary petrochemicals. But the governments of the three countries should consider the NAFTA as only a first step in liberalizing North American energy investment and trade. Because of Mexico's continuing investment needs, we believe the agreement should deter Mexico from returning to more restrictive policies and provide a precedent for further liberalization and privatization.

2. Automobiles

As with commerce between the United States and Canada, automotive products are the largest component of bilateral manufacturing trade between the United States and Mexico, and also between Canada and Mexico. Distinct and powerful constituencies with conflicting interests were thus involved in the NAFTA automotive negotiations: the US Big Three automakers (General Motors, Ford, and Chrysler), auto parts firms in all three countries, and ever more militant US and Canadian auto workers. On the sidelines, Nissan, Volkswagen, Toyota, Honda, and Hyundai were attentive watchers. Not surprisingly, with so much at stake, the automotive section of the NAFTA package was one of the last to fall in place. In the end, the auto section (annex 300-A) makes the significant accomplishment of pointing toward an integrated North American market, free of almost all trade barriers within 10 years.

A key US and Canadian objective in the negotiations was to open Mexico's highly protected automotive market. This goal was achieved. Mexico has the fastest-growing major auto market in the world, and improved US access to this market was critical to the Big Three's endorsement of the NAFTA.[4]

The Big Three are powerful in Mexico as well as in the United States; after Pemex, Ford, Chrysler, and GM are Mexico's three largest exporters. Not only did the Big Three want better access to the fast-growing Mexican market, they also wanted to ensure that their Japanese competitors would not use Mexico as a ready-made "export platform."[5] Meanwhile, as part of a defensive game to continue its assured access to the US auto market, Canada sought to prevent overly tight rules of origin that would handicap Canadian assembly operations. Canada also sought to clarify the method used by the US Customs Service to calculate North American content, with the express purpose of averting future "Honda cases."[6] Additionally, Canada sought to retain its own panoply

---

4. Automobile unit sales in Mexico are expected to reach 1 million by 1995, up from 740,000 in 1992 (*Financial Times*, 18 June 1992, 6). In our view, US-Mexico two-way trade in automotive goods could easily double or triple under NAFTA auspices, growing from $8.3 billion in 1990 to between $20 billion and $25 billion by 1995. Also see Berry, Grilli, and López-de-Silanes (1992), who foresee doubling of US auto exports to Mexico within five years under NAFTA auspices.

5. See, for example, the 23 October 1992 letter from Robert C. Stempel, then Chairman of General Motors, to Richard A. Gephardt (D-MO), House Majority Leader, for a summary of GM's negotiating objectives and an expression of satisfaction with the NAFTA outcome. In November 1992 the Motor Vehicles Manufacturing Association ejected Honda and limited its membership to GM, Ford, and Chrysler, partly because of different negotiating objectives between Honda and other MVMA members in the NAFTA talks (*New York Times*, 26 November 1992, D1).

6. The Canada-US FTA contains a "roll-up" method that enables a part to be counted as

of safeguards established under the 1965 US-Canada Auto Pact, even safeguards that were redundant (Hufbauer and Schott 1992a, chapter 11).[7]

For its part, Mexico wanted to continue liberalizing its own automotive sector, but at a pace that would protect its auto parts firms. Auto parts firms in the United States and Canada likewise sought to ensure that parts would be supplied by North American firms rather than by Japanese, European, or Korean firms.

Finally, US and Canadian auto workers were dead set against the agreement. They argued that Mexico's low wages and inadequate enforcement of labor standards would attract auto and parts firms to Mexico, causing a loss of production jobs and putting downward pressure on auto wages in the United States and Canada.

Mexican Liberalization

The NAFTA will eliminate all of Mexico's automotive tariffs and most of its nontariff barriers over a transition period lasting 5 to 10 years. Mexico's tariff on autos and light trucks (20 percent) will be cut in half immediately and then phased out either over 10 years (autos) or 5 years (light trucks).

Mexico's domestic-content requirement, as applied to the 1991–92 base level of production, will be phased out over 10 years, but at a slow rate: from 36 percent to 34 percent for the first five years, to 29 percent over the next five years, and to zero after 10 years. However, a special provision for established manufacturers liberalizes the phaseout schedule. During the first five years, established manufacturers are only held to the domestic-content percentage achieved in model year 1992. For nearly all firms, this level is less than 34 percent. In addition, lower domestic-content rules are applied to incremental growth in auto output: incremental growth in the first four years is multiplied by a factor of 0.65 before the content rule is applied, incremental growth in the next three years is multiplied by a factor of 0.60, and thereafter incremental growth

---

100 percent regional if its domestic value exceeds 50 percent. However, the FTA also contains a domestic value-added requirement: to qualify for zero tariffs, an assembled auto must be 50 percent North American. The ambiguous tension between "roll-up" for components and the value-added test for assembled autos led to the 1991 Honda case, in which the US Customs Service claimed that the regional content of Civics assembled in Honda's Ontario plant was only 15 percent, far below the 50 percent level required by the FTA for preferential treatment. In the Canadian view, the US challenge to Honda's duty-free treatment contained three objectionable elements: it dismissed the value of engines assembled in Ohio from the North American content calculation, it ignored the permitted "roll up" method, and it assaulted the security of investment in Canada.

7. The Auto Pact safeguards were discussed in detail in our 1992 book. The fact that these were untouched by NAFTA is a tribute to the negotiating skills, if not the economic wisdom, of the Canadian team.

is multiplied by a factor of 0.50. Taking these special features into account, the average domestic-content requirement quickly drops to 20 percent before going to zero.[8]

As a result of these factors, Mexican parts suppliers are guaranteed a declining percentage of any growth achieved in the Mexican auto parts market during the transition period (as a result of the factors mentioned above, the guaranteed percentage of growth starts at 65 percent and declines to 50 percent). Although the content rule has been liberalized, it survives for an extended period. Any guaranteed market share for Mexican parts suppliers, even if a declining share of the total market, necessarily discriminates against US, Canadian, and other non-Mexican parts suppliers.

In what the automotive industry calls "the single most significant accomplishment of the NAFTA automotive negotiations," Mexico will immediately reduce its trade balancing requirement from $2 of car exports for every dollar's worth of imported cars to 80 cents, then gradually down to 55 cents in 2003, and then eliminate the requirement in January 2004 (Industry Sector Advisory Committee for Trade in Transportation Equipment, Construction Equipment, and Agricultural Equipment 1992, 14). For parts, the trade balance ratio will immediately fall from a $1-to-$1 ratio to an 80 cents-to-$1 ratio and then decline on the same schedule as vehicles. Further, established manufacturers will be able to access trade balance "credits" earned on parts trade prior to model year 1991 (surpluses above the $1-for-$1 requirement). The credits may be used by each firm to import up to $150 million worth of automotive goods annually until the credits have been exhausted.

Mexico will immediately eliminate its quota on new-car imports (subject to the trade balancing requirement), but Mexico will retain for 10 years the requirement that manufacturers produce in Mexico in order to sell in Mexico. After the transition, any firm will be able to export new autos to Mexico without having to produce there. However, the ban on used car and truck imports will remain in place for 15 years and not be fully phased out for 25 years.

Mexico significantly liberalized its import regime on heavy trucks. Until January 1999, Mexican manufacturers will be able to import heavy vehicles equal to 50 percent of what they produced in Mexico that year; thereafter, import restraints on new trucks will be lifted.

Mexico abolished its restrictions on auto and truck financing subsidiaries of US firms, enabling them to do a much larger volume of business. The subsidiaries will now be able to act as nonbank banks in

---

8. We recommended a straight-line phaseout, lowering the domestic-content requirement by 3.6 percentage points a year. While the special features of the agreed phaseout schedule essentially meet our objectives, they do favor incumbent auto firms (the Big Three, Nissan, and Volkswagen) over newcomer firms.

Mexico, selling certificates of deposits denominated in pesos, thereby financing the purchase of vehicles and other equipment.

Level Playing Field

While the elimination of most of Mexico's nontariff barriers will open the Mexican market to US exports, the terms of the transition are designed to ensure that the overall package does not confer an advantage on new entrants in comparison with auto manufacturers already established in Mexico. This was a key negotiating objective for the Big Three, as well as for Nissan and Volkswagen, the two other foreign manufacturers established in Mexico. The slow phaseout of the domestic-content requirement, the long-term ban on used-car imports, and the remaining trade balancing requirements will ensure that new auto assembly firms that establish operations in Mexico face much the same hurdles as existing firms.[9]

One way these hurdles work is to force new assembly firms to source largely from Mexican suppliers, which is more difficult than importing parts and assembling them in Mexico. Another way the hurdles work is to force new assembly firms to build up their own exports from Mexico before selling into the Mexican market. A third way the hurdles work is to preclude Mexican imports of used cars, so that (for example) two-year old Hondas assembled in Ohio or Ontario cannot be resold in Mexico.

Auto Rules of Origin

At the end of the transition period, the NAFTA rules of origin for the automotive sector rises to 62.5 percent for autos, light trucks, engines, and transmissions, and to 60 percent for other vehicles and parts. Thus, when an assembled auto is shipped across one of the NAFTA borders, it must eventually contain 62.5 percent North American content in order

---

9. It can be argued that retention of some hurdles, and their application to new firms, is fair because in past years existing firms had to meet similar hurdles. That is akin to the argument that, because firm A had to spend $100 million to discover a new process, so should firms B, C, and D spend $100 million, even though the technology can now be created for $20 million. This example illustrates the tension between historical equity (in the sense of a level playing field throughout production history) and efficiency. In the Mexican auto market, we advocate efficiency; established producers advocate historical equity.

An additional argument for historical equity is that it fulfills implicit Mexican promises made to automotive investors in years past and thereby demonstrates to future investors that they, too, can rely on a stable Mexican policy regime. However, we are skeptical of maintaining trade barriers as a way of ratifying past investment decisions. In our view, when firms make investments, they should anticipate the possibility of trade liberalization.

to receive duty-free treatment. This rule supersedes, and is probably stricter than, the existing Canada-US FTA rule of 50 percent (we recommended keeping the rule of origin at 50 percent).[10] For established auto manufacturers, the rule of origin starts at 50 percent, rises to 56 percent after four years, and to 62.5 percent after eight years. New firms that open in North America will have a five-year grace period (during which they will be subject to a 50 percent content requirement) before they have to meet the 62.5 percent rule. In this respect, the rules of origin are relatively generous to new firms.

In a side agreement, the Honda dispute has apparently been settled to Canada's satisfaction. However, the long-term outcome will depend on whether the Honda cars produced in Canada can meet the new NAFTA origin requirements. The new rules will apply to all Honda imports not yet "liquidated" (i.e., a final determination made on US customs duties).[11]

Under the NAFTA, regional content will be calculated using a net-cost method in which key foreign components will be "traced" to measure their own North American content (with a 60 percent minimum content requirement). The new tracing test was designed as an administratively easy way to prevent the sort of "roll-up" anomaly that characterized the FTA: counting a foreign part as 100 percent regional if the domestic share of value added in one of the partner countries exceeds 50 percent, combining that part (which could be 49 percent foreign) in a larger assembly that is also 49 percent foreign, and then counting the whole assembly as 100 percent regional, even though it might be 70 percent or more foreign in terms of value added.

Under the new tracing rule, the value of the foreign content of 69 specified parts will be subtracted in calculating the net cost of the vehicle. Some of these parts can be regarded as the "heart and lungs" of an automobile (e.g., engines and transmissions); others are less vital (e.g., bumpers, mirrors). The tracing requirement introduces an administrative bias in favor of 100 percent North American content of the traced parts, simply to avoid the paperwork of a customs service audit. However, without a tracing requirement or some similar test, the auto section

---

10. Because the method of calculating North American content differs between NAFTA and the FTA, the 62.5 percent figure cannot be directly compared with the 50 percent figure. In fact, under some production circumstances, the new rule could be less strict than the old rule. Moreover, as Ronald Wonnacott points out, since the FTA has now been effectively enlarged to include Mexico, a higher percentage rule (with the same method of calculation) is not necessarily more protective, since it may be satisfied by parts that would have been shipped from Mexico without the rule.

11. The existing Honda case remains to be resolved by a binational panel. However, US Trade Representative Carla Hills has recommended that the NAFTA's implementing legislation state that the new NAFTA rules of origin apply to outstanding disputes, which could include the Honda case (*New York Times*, 9 October 1992, D1).

would have met enormous political opposition. Not surprisingly, US parts and vehicle manufacturers applaud the tracing rule as an answer to their demand that a higher percentage of regional content be required in assembled autos (e.g., 75 percent).[12] Combined, the stricter rules of origin and supplemental tracing requirements should eliminate the roll-up problem, but at a price of reduced efficiency.

The stricter rules of origin will not significantly affect foreign producers who export assembled autos to the United States because the US tariff on automobiles is currently only 2.5 percent and averages only 3.1 percent on auto parts; moreover, these rates will be reduced even further in the Uruguay Round. On the other hand, tariffs are somewhat higher in Canada (9.6 percent) and much higher in Mexico (20 percent on autos; 13.2 percent on parts). The stricter rules will thus primarily affect foreign transplant firms operating in North America by forcing them to source more parts regionally if they want unfettered access to the Canadian and Mexican markets.

US Liberalization

The NAFTA meets our recommendation to remove the few US barriers to automotive trade. The United States will eliminate its auto tariff immediately, will reduce its tariff on light trucks from 25 percent to 10 percent immediately (matching Mexico's reduction of light truck tariffs to 10 percent), and will phase out the remaining tariff over five years.

The overall benefit to US consumers of cutting the US truck tariff will be significantly offset if Congress passes a bill reclassifying more vehicles as trucks.[13] Moreover, it should be noted that the promise extracted from Japanese auto firms in January 1992 by President Bush that they will source a larger volume of auto parts from the United States was not generalized to sourcing from Canada and Mexico as well.

Three years after the NAFTA is implemented, automotive production in Mexico or Canada may be designated as "domestic" or "foreign" for

12. According to the automotive industry report on the NAFTA: "With the adoption of North American content tracing requirements to improve the accuracy of value-content determinations in the NAFTA, most ISAC 16 members agreed that a 65 percent minimum level would accomplish their original goals in this area" (Industry Sector Advisory Committee for Trade in Transportation, Construction, and Agricultural Equipment 1992, 9).

13. Senator Riegle (D-MI) is pushing a bill that would reclassify imported minivans and sport-utility vehicles as trucks rather than cars, which in turn would raise their tariff from 2.5 percent to 25 percent (25 percent being the so-called "chicken war" tariff introduced in 1963 to retaliate against the common European Community tariff on US chicken exports, which was much higher than the previous German tariff). Under the NAFTA, the 25 percent tariff would be lowered to 10 percent for vehicles from Mexico when NAFTA is implemented; nevertheless, 10 percent is far higher than 2.5 percent. It has been estimated that the bill would raise consumer prices on affected vehicles by between $1,300 and $3,700 (*New York Times*, 22 September 1992, A26).

US Corporate Average Fuel Efficiency (CAFE) purposes at the option of the producer (this follows our recommendation of leaving the choice to the producer).[14] However, new manufacturers will be required to designate all Mexican production as domestic, and after 10 years all Mexican production will be counted as domestic. All in all, this provision somewhat alleviates the protective effect of CAFE rules, and gives US auto firms greater flexibility in rationalizing production as between the United States, Mexico, and Canada.[15]

Evaluation

As a consequence of NAFTA, within 10 years an integrated auto market will exist in North America. By world standards, the regional industry should be highly competitive. In fact, drawing on economies of scale and a variety of labor skills, North America could become the world's low-cost producer of autos and trucks, and a major net exporter of these products. Nonetheless, in our view, the interim transition rules are unnecessarily slow. As the NAFTA evolves, we recommend an accelerated pace of internal liberalization of domestic-content and trade balancing requirements by Mexico and deep cuts in Canadian and Mexican tariffs on autos and parts in the Uruguay Round, in conjunction with auto trade reforms by Europe, Japan, and others.

---

14. Car makers currently must maintain separate average fuel efficiencies of 27.5 miles per gallon for both their domestic and imported fleets. One purpose of the NAFTA rule allowing Mexican producers to choose how to classify their vehicles is to allow Volkswagen to continue producing the fuel-efficient Golf in Mexico and classify it as foreign in order to balance less fuel-efficient models like the Audi, which it exports from Germany to the United States (*Inside U.S. Trade*, 7 August 1992, 4).

15. From the standpoint of the United Auto Workers (UAW), a major purpose of the "two-fleet" CAFE rules was to ensure that US auto firms maintained a certain volume of small-car production in the United States or Canada. Now the auto firms can meet the CAFE standard for their domestic fleets by producing small cars in Mexico as well—not an outcome wished by the UAW.

3. Textiles and Apparel

The textile and apparel negotiations were watched anxiously by various participants in the industry: US producers, who are divided in their support of the NAFTA; Canadian producers, who depend heavily on the US market and offshore inputs; Caribbean producers, who fear trade diversion in favor of Mexico; and Mexican textile and apparel producers, who anticipate big export increases as a result of the NAFTA.

The final agreement is notable (and beats our recommendation) for its speedy elimination of virtually all quotas on North American trade in textiles and apparel, and its fast phaseout of tariffs. However, the benefits of liberalization will be limited by the NAFTA's ultrastrict rules of origin that determine which textiles and apparel will be eligible for tariff and quota elimination.

Rules of Origin

A major shortcoming of the NAFTA is the strict rules of origin it establishes for textiles and apparel (paralleled by the similarly strict rules of origin for autos). To qualify for preferential treatment, textile and apparel goods must normally pass a "triple transformation test," which essentially requires that finished products be cut and sewn from fabric spun from North American fibers in order to qualify for NAFTA preferences.[16]

This rule is significantly stricter than the US-Canada FTA rule, which calls for a "double transformation" in order for a traded item that contains foreign yarn or fabric to qualify for FTA preferential treatment (e.g., foreign fabric must be both cut and sewn into garment parts either in Canada or in the United States).[17] We recommended that the NAFTA rule of origin not be stricter than that of the US-Canada FTA; while some tightening might have been expected, the triple transformation test sets a high-water mark for protective rules of origin. A limited amount of flexibility survived this onslaught. Yarns, fabrics, and apparel that are made in North America but do not meet the rule of origin can still qualify for preferential treatment up to specified import levels (so-called tariff preference levels, or TPLs).[18]

---

16. However, 13 fabrics are eligible for single transformation, in which imported fabrics can be used to manufacture apparel products (Industry Sector Advisory Committee for Trade in Textiles 1992, 2).

17. The Textile and Apparel Advisory Committee applauded the strict rules of origin and recommended that they be "incorporated into the implementing legislation" of the agreement (Industry Sector Advisory Committee for Trade in Textiles 1992, 3). The committee hopes to freeze the rule in the implementing legislation, thereby deterring future liberalization. Canada, together with US retailers and importers, resisted the strict rules of origin. The NAFTA itself calls for a review of the rules of origin before January 1998.

18. See NAFTA appendix 6.0-B. The Textile Advisory Committee strongly opposes the

North American Liberalization

Despite the strict rules of origin, the NAFTA represents the first attempt by the United States or Canada to subject its heavily protected textile and apparel sector to significant trade liberalization with a large developing country.[19] The agreement meets our recommendation to eliminate all tariffs on textile and apparel trade within 10 years.[20] In addition, the United States will immediately lift its import quotas on Mexican textile and apparel products that meet the new rules of origin and will gradually phase out quotas on Mexican goods that do not qualify for preferential treatment. For all but 14 categories of goods (listed in schedule 3.1.2), the NAFTA establishes tariff-rate quotas for those products that do not meet the strict NAFTA origin rules. Imports up to the quota level are subject to NAFTA's preferential duty; over-quota shipments will pay the most-favored nation (MFN) rate.

Soon after the negotiations were completed, Canada announced it would unilaterally cut many of its textile yarn and fabric tariffs on an MFN basis. The reason for this proposal, which had long been planned, is to ensure that Canadian apparel producers will have access to cheap early-stage materials.[21] The US textile advisory committee recommends that, if Canada implements these tariff cuts, the United States should renegotiate the NAFTA textile provisions with Canada because Canada will have "shifted the balance of concessions in the textile sector decidedly against US textile producers" (Industry Sector Advisory Committee for Trade in Textiles 1992, 14). This call for renegotiation should be rebuffed. The NAFTA only governs trade among the three partners and does not contemplate that any one of them will concede control over its commercial policy vis-à-vis fourth countries.

Threatened Trade Diversion

A side effect of eliminating quotas on Mexican products is the potential for discrimination against fourth countries, particularly the Caribbean

---

TPLs, claiming that they will "provide a major loophole from the rules of origin" and will provide an "incentive for fraud, transshipment, and other kinds of abuse." The committee recommends that the TPL levels be capped and phased out during the NAFTA transition period (Industry Sector Advisory Committee for Trade in Textiles 1992, 4).

19. Textile and apparel trade between the industrial countries has long been free of quota restrictions, but even among industrial countries the trade is hampered by high tariffs.

20. Most US and Mexican tariffs will disappear after six years; the rest will be phased out in 10 years. Tariffs between the US and Canada will be phased out by 1999 according to the US-Canada FTA schedule.

21. The Canadian apparel industry sees early tariff cuts as a way to offset the NAFTA's stricter rules of origin. By contrast, the Canadian textile industry wants the cuts to be offered only as concessions in the Uruguay Round.

Basin Initiative (CBI) nations.[22] While we recommended that NAFTA benefits not be extended to the CBI countries until they join the agreement, we also recognized that the CBI countries (among others) will suffer if the NAFTA reforms are not matched by a multilateral commitment to phase out quotas imposed under the Multi-Fiber Arrangement (MFA) and to lower textile and apparel tariffs. Whereas Mexican exports to the United States will soon be free of tariffs and quotas, CBI exports will remain subject to a flexible quota system and to normal US tariffs.

In our view, this problem cannot be addressed by rapid accession of CBI nations to the provisions of the NAFTA. However, the CBI nations could seek a more limited agreement with the United States that provides access to the US market for textiles and apparel (and sugar)—equivalent to that granted to Mexico under the NAFTA—in return for CBI acceptance of investment and intellectual property accords and a relatively low external tariff. In this regard, the CBI nations are busy preparing a new initiative, CBI 3, which would address their problems in the textile and apparel sector well before any sweeping decision is made to join the NAFTA (*Journal of Commerce*, 9 October 1992, 1C).

A bigger problem is looming just over the horizon. Now that North American producers have acceded to regional free trade, they may insist even more loudly that the United States and Canada adopt a go-slow approach to proposed Uruguay Round reforms of the MFA quotas and high textile and apparel tariffs. In our view, it would be a great mistake for the United States to abandon its long-standing position in favor of gradual, multilateral liberalization.

Evaluation

The NAFTA textile and apparel provisions could signal a historic break with the protectionist traditions of this sector. Conceivably, as the US industry adjusts to Mexican competition and enjoys far larger sales in the Mexican market, it will come to accept an even wider geographic scope of liberalization. This is the optimistic interpretation. A pessimistic interpretation is that NAFTA, with its strict rule of origin, will lead to the creation of a textile and apparel fortress in North America. Whether events point toward the optimistic or pessimistic interpretation will soon be indicated by the outcome of GATT talks, and later by discussions between the United States and the CBI nations.

---

22. The apparel industry provides 200,000 jobs in the Caribbean and Central America, and accounts for $2.4 billion, or 24 percent, of the region's total exports.

4. Agriculture

Agriculture is the only area where the NAFTA does not involve a tri-lateral agreement between the three countries. Instead, two separate bilateral agreements were negotiated: one between the United States and Mexico, and another between Mexico and Canada. For US-Canada agricultural trade, the provisions of the US-Canada FTA continue in force. However, the NAFTA does establish trilateral obligations regarding rules of origin, safeguards, and sanitary and phytosanitary standards.

Bilateral Mexico-US Agreement

To a large extent, the NAFTA incorporates the grand bargain on agriculture that we recommended: linking Mexican liberalization of field crops to US horticultural reforms. The bargain achieved provides for the elimination of US trade barriers on a large variety of horticultural products, cotton, and sugar, in exchange for the phaseout of Mexican import restrictions on some field crops, dry beans, pork, potatoes, apples, and nonfat dry milk.[23]

In most cases, tariffs on US-Mexico farm trade will be phased out within 10 years. In addition, nontariff barriers (quotas, import licensing requirements) will be transformed into tariff-rate quotas (TRQs) and phased out over 10 to 15 years. Tariffs will be immediately eliminated on $3.1 billion, or 57 percent, of the value of bilateral US-Mexico farm trade. The figure will rise slightly to 63 percent after 5 years, to 94 percent after 10 years, and the remaining 6 percent will be eliminated after 15 years (table 3.1).[24] Because of the seasonal nature of farm trade, the liberalization schedule for some products will vary depending on the month of shipment (table 3.2).

To accommodate this broad liberalization, the accord establishes special safeguards to protect against import surges during the first 10 years of the agreement; it also establishes longer transition periods for the most import-sensitive products. While these provisions limit the scope of trade expansion during the next 10 to 15 years, they smooth the path to eventual trade liberalization.

Products for immediate tariff elimination (schedule A). The NAFTA will immediately eliminate tariffs on goods accounting for 57 percent of

---

23. In 1991 Mexico's exports of horticultural products to the US amounted to $1.3 billion; US field crops exports to Mexico totaled $740 million, of which sorghum represented $371 million and corn $147 million. However, the potential for increased corn exports was demonstrated in 1990 when US shipments rose to $400 million due to a Mexican drought (Agricultural Policy Advisory Committee for Trade 1992, 14 and 17).

24. These totals include goods subject to TRQs.

Table 3.1 Liberalization of US-Mexico agricultural trade (in millions of dollars)[a]

Transition period	US imports from Mexico	US exports to Mexico	Bilateral trade
Already duty-free or immediate elimination (category A)	1,600	1,500	3,100
Five-year transition (category B)	177	131	308
Ten-year transition (category C)	375	875	1,250
Fifteen-year transition (category C+)	75	0	75
Ten-year transition with a TRQ	330	155	485
Fifteen-year transition with a TRQ	45	208	253
Total	2,602	2,869	5,471

TRQ = tariff-rate quota
a. Based on 1991 trade.

Source: Data from Agricultural Policy Advisory Committee for Trade on the North American Free Trade Agreement, 1992 (September). Washington: Office of the US Trade Representative.

Table 3.2 Liberalization schedule of US tariffs on selected horticultural products

Commodity[a]	Jan	Feb	Mar	Apr	May	June	July	Aug	Sep	Oct	Nov	Dec
Fresh strawberries	A	A	A	A	A	A	A	A	A	A	A	A
Mangoes	A	A	A	A	A	B	B	B	A	A	A	A
Cut flowers	B	B	B	B	B	B	B	B	B	B	B	B
Limes and oranges	C	C	C	C	C	A	A	A	A	C	C	C
Bell peppers	C	C	C	C	C	B	B	B	B	B	C	C
Tomato paste	C	C	C	C	C	C	C	C	C	C	C	C
Frozen asparagus, broccoli, cauliflower	C	C	C	C	C	C	C	C	C	C	C	C
Avocados	C	C	C	C	C	C	C	C	C	C	C	C
Frozen strawberries	C	C	C	C	C	C	C	C	C	C	C	C
Prepared olives	C	C	C	C	C	C	C	C	C	C	C	C
Cantaloupes	A	A	A	A	A/C+	C+	C+	A	C/C+	C+	C+	A
Cucumbers	A	A	C+	C+	C+	B	A	A	B	C+	C+	A
Asparagus	C+	C+	C+	C+	C+	C+	B	B	B	B	B	B
Eggplant	A	A	A	C TRQ	C TRQ	C TRQ	A	B	A	B	B	C
Watermelons	A	A	A	A	C TRQ	C TRQ	C TRQ	C TRQ	C TRQ	A	A	A
Onions	C TRQ	C TRQ	C TRQ	C TRQ	C	C	C	C	C	C	C	C
Chili and other peppers	C TRQ	C TRQ	C TRQ	C TRQ	C TRQ	C TRQ	C TRQ	A	A	C TRQ	C TRQ	C TRQ
Tomatoes	C TRQ	C TRQ	C TRQ	C TRQ	C TRQ	C TRQ	C TRQ/B	B	B	B	B/C TRQ	C TRQ
Squash	C TRQ	C TRQ	C TRQ	C TRQ	C TRQ	C TRQ	B	B	B	C TRQ	C TRQ	C TRQ
Orange juice	C+TRQ	C+TRQ	C+TRQ	C+TRQ	C+TRQ	C+TRQ	C+TRQ	C+TRQ	C+TRQ	C+TRQ	C+TRQ	C+TRQ

TRQ = tariff-rate quota

a. These commodities accounted for $1.2 billion of the $1.3 billion in Mexican horticultural exports to the US in 1991.

Source: Data from Agricultural Policy Advisory Committee for Trade on the North American Free Trade Agreement, 1992 (September). Washington: Office of the US Trade Representative.

the value of Mexico-US farm trade. This category includes products already receiving duty-free treatment under the Generalized System of Preferences (GSP) as well as other commodities that currently face very low tariffs.

Mexican tariffs on US exports of cattle, beef, and selected hides and skins will be eliminated immediately (affecting about $450 million in US exports), as will those on most fresh fruits and vegetables, hops, nuts, and nursery products (affecting about $90 million in US exports).[25] Mexico will also extend duty-free status for US exports of soybeans shipped between January and September, affecting about $289 million of US exports.

US tariffs will be immediately eliminated on Mexican exports of most livestock, poultry, and eggs. Mexico will also be exempt from quotas established pursuant to the Meat Import Law.[26] In addition, US tariffs will be eliminated on a broad range of out-of-season fruits and vegetables, such as July-to-September strawberries and June-to-September oranges.

Products subject to five-year tariff elimination (schedule B). The products placed under this schedule amount to 6 percent of Mexico-US farm trade. This transition period will apply to Mexican tariffs on US exports of offal worth $70 million and selected horticultural products worth $25 million. It will also apply to US tariffs on Mexican exports of selected fresh fruits and vegetables and cut roses.

Products subject to 10-year tariff elimination (schedule C). A relatively large percentage—23 percent—of Mexico-US farm trade will be subject to the 10-year transition period.[27] This category mainly comprises Mexican tariffs on US exports of October-to-December soybeans, which face a 10 percent tariff and represent $57 million in US exports to Mexico; wheat, which faces a 15 percent tariff and represents $39 million of US exports to Mexico; rice, which faces a 20 percent tariff and represents $25 million in trade; and selected horticultural products, which represent $35 million in trade (including fresh grapes, fresh onions, fresh peaches, preserved cherries, dried mushrooms, canned corn, and prepared peanuts).

US tariffs on Mexican exports that are subject to the 10-year liberalization schedule include avocados, frozen strawberries, limes, tomato

---

25. All dollar figures for US-Mexico trade are based on 1991 data (Agricultural Policy Advisory Committee for Trade 1992, 10–13).

26. In 1991 Mexico exported $391 million in livestock and products and $16 million in sausage casings to the United States (Agricultural Policy Advisory Committee for Trade 1992, 11).

27. This category does not include products phased out over 10 years but also subject to TRQs.

paste, sauces and purees, frozen asparagus, broccoli, cauliflower, August-to-September cantaloupes, and November-to-May bell peppers. In 1991 Mexico exported $375 million of these goods to the United States.

Products subject to 15-year tariff elimination (schedule C+). Only 1 percent of the Mexico-US bilateral trade will be liberalized over 15 years, not including products subject to TRQs. This schedule covers only a small number of Mexican exports of fruits and vegetables to the United States and no Mexican tariffs on US goods. However, Mexico will maintain TRQs for corn and beans for 15 years (see below).

Products covered by tariff-rate quotas. For the most import-sensitive products that account for about 13.5 percent of bilateral farm trade, nontariff barriers will be converted into TRQs and phased out over 10 to 15 years. The treatment of goods subject to TRQs is summarized in tables 3.3 and 3.4.[28] The most important products for which the United States will establish TRQs are sugar, orange juice, and peanuts. Mexico will impose TRQs primarily on corn and dry beans.

Sugar. For the 1992–93 crop year, the United States has established a sugar import quota of 1.234 million metric tons (MT) spread among 40 countries. Although it has recently been a net importer of sugar, Mexico has a token US import quota of 7,258 MT, which it generally fills.

The NAFTA allows shipments of sugar under the Mexican quota to enter the United States duty-free and shipments in excess of the quota to enter subject to a tariff of 16 cents per pound (which will be reduced over 15 years). Over the first six years, the over-quota tariff will be reduced by 15 percent of its base level; starting in year 7, the remaining tariff surcharge will be phased out linearly through year 15. By contrast, the transition period for refined sugar will be 10 years. By year 6, Mexico will align its MFN tariff on sugar and kindred sweeteners to the level set by the United States (annex 703.2, section A (17)).

If Mexico becomes a net sugar exporter on a global basis, the quota will increase by the amount by which Mexico is a net exporter, up to 25,000 MT during the first six years and 150,000 MT starting in year 7 (increased annually by 10 percent through year 15). If Mexico continues to be a net exporter for two consecutive years, after year 6 the quota will be waived, and Mexico will be able to export all its surplus production to the United States.[29]

---

28. Mexico's over-quota tariffs will be reduced in most cases by 24 percent of the base tariff over the first six years, and then in equal annual installments. US over-quota tariffs will be eliminated linearly except for orange juice, where the tariffs will be cut by 15 percent of the base tariff during the first six years, left unchanged from years 7 to 10, and then phased out in equal annual installments.

29. In 1991 Mexican sugar production was 3.5 million tons and consumption was 4.5 million tons (*Journal of Commerce*, 22 June 1992, 5A).

Table 3.3 Tariff-rate quota system for US-Mexico agricultural trade liberalization: Mexican treatment

Mexico's treatment of US and Canadian products	Treatment of quota amounts			Treatment of over-quota amounts		Rate of quota increases (compound percentages)
	Amount	Tariff	Transition (years)	Tariff	Transition[a] (years)	
Products in Annex 703.3						
Slaughter pork and hogs and pork cuts	68,600 MT (US) 6,000 tons (Can)	20%	10	20%	c	3
Apples	55,000 MT (US) 1,000 tons (Can)	20%	10	20%	c	3
Frozen potatoes	2,000 MT (US) 2,000 tons (Can)	free	n.a.p.	n.a.	10	3
Potatoes prepared or preserved	3,100 (US)	n.a.	n.a.	20%	n.a.	3
Potato chips	5,400 (US)	n.a.	n.a.	20%	n.a.	3
Extracts; essences, or concentrates	200 (US)	n.a.	n.a.	20%	n.a.	n.a.

Products with license system

Fresh potatoes	15,000 MT (US) 4,000 MT (Can)	free	n.a p.	272% or $354/MT	10	3
Barley, malt	120,000 MT (US) 30,000 MT (Can)	free	n.a.p.	128% or $155/MT (barley) 175% or $212/MT (malt)	10 n.a.	5
Poultry meat	95,000 MT (US)[d]	free	n.a.p.	260% or $1,680/MT (chicken) 133% or $1,880/MT (turkey)	10 n.a.	3 3
Fresh and fertilized eggs	6,500 mill. MT (US)[d]	free	n.a.p.	50%	10	3
Animal fats and oils	35,000 MT (US)	n.a.	n.a.p.	282% or $930/MT	10	3
Nonfat dry milk	40,000 MT (US)[d]	free	n.a.p.	139% or $1,160/MT	15	3
Corn	2.5 mill. MT (US) 1,000 MT (Can)	free	n.a.p.	215% or $206/MT	15	3
Dry edible beans	50,000 MT (US) 1,500 MT (Can)	free	n.a.p.	139% or $480/MT	15	3

n.a. = not available
n.a p. = not applicable
MT = metric tons

a. Unless otherwise indicated, over the first six years, the over-quota tariff will be reduced by 24 percent of its base level, and the remaining tariff will then be phased out in equal annual installments.

b. Phased out in equal annual installments.

c. The over-quota tariff will not be phased out. It will become zero after 10 years.

d. Excluded from the agreement with Canada.

Source: Data from Agricultural Policy Advisory Committee for Trade on the North American Free Trade Agreement, 1992 (September). Washington: Office of the US Trade Representative.

Table 3.4. Tariff-rate quota system for US-Mexico agricultural trade liberalization: US treatment

US treatment of selected Mexican products[a]	Treatment of quota amounts			Treatment of over-quota amounts		Rate of quota increases (compound percentages)
	Amount	Tariff	Transition (years)	Tariff	Transition (years)	
Section 22 products						
Peanuts	3,377 MT	free	n.a.	123.1% or 80.3 cent/kg (shelled) 186.1% or 53 cent/kg (in-shell)	15[b]	3
Cotton	10,000 MT		n.a.	26%	10[b]	3
Frozen and concentrated orange juice	40 million gallons	4.625 cent/liter	No change until equal to over-quota rate.	9.25 cent/liter or UR	15[c]	no change
Fresh orange juice	4 million gallons	2.65 cent/liter		5.3 cent/liter	15[b]	no change

Products in
Annex 703.3

Product		Quota	Rate				
April to June	Eggplant	3,700 MT	3.3 cent/kg	10	MFN[d]	e	3
May to Sept	Watermelons	54,400 MT	20%	10	MFN[d]	e	3
Jan to July	Onions	130,700 MT	3.9 cent/kg	10	MFN[d]	e	3
Oct to July	Chili peppers	29,900 MT	5.5 cent/kg	10	MFN[d]	e	3
15 Nov to Feb	Tomatoes	172,300 MT	3.3 cent/kg	10	MFN[d]	e	3
Mar to 14 July	Tomatoes	165,500 MT	4.6 cent/kg	10	MFN[d]	e	3
Oct to June	Squash	120,800 MT	2.4 cent/kg	10	MFN[d]	e	3

n.a. = not applicable
MT = metric tons
MFN = most-favored nation
UR = Uruguay Round

a. Sugar is not included in this table. It has a special tariff rate quota described in the text.
b. Phase out in equal annual installments.
c. Over the first six years, the over-quota tariff will be reduced by 15 percent of its base level, and the remaining tariff will be held constant from years 7 to 10, and then it will be phased out in equal annual installments.
d. The lower of MFN or the prevailing tariff at the time the agreement is signed will be applied.
e. The over-quota tariff will not be phased out; it will become zero after 10 years.

Source: Data from Agricultural Policy Advisory Committee for Trade on the North American Free Trade Agreement, 1992 (September). Washington: Office of the US Trade Representative.

The US sugar industry is concerned about several aspects of the NAFTA provisions: the method of calculating Mexico's net sugar exporter status, the large quota expansion starting in year 7 (and potentially reaching about 325,000 MT), the "fast" phaseout of protection on refined sugar and sugar-containing products (which the US industry argues should be extended from 10 to 15 years to parallel the liberalization of cane sugar), and the delay in reaching a common external sugar tariff until year 7 (letter to the members of Congress from US sugar associations, 14 September 1992, reprinted in *Inside US Trade*, 2 October 1992, 15; and NAFTA annex 704.2, section I, appendix B).

Specifically, US sugar producers argue that corn sweeteners as well as cane sugar should be counted in the calculation of surplus production to avoid the substitution of corn sweeteners for cane in domestic consumption (as has occurred to some extent in the US market), thus freeing up cane sugar for export.[30] In addition, they contend that surplus producer status should be based on actual production over two consecutive years, not one year of actual production and one year of projected production, as set out in the NAFTA.

With the incentive of increased access to the US market, Mexican cane producers could well shift to higher sugar-bearing cane, increase their yields, and generate an "exportable surplus." In this scenario, other countries exporting sugar to the United States would suffer, assuming the United States retains its present stiff protection against third-country suppliers. Indeed, Mexican exports could displace more than 25 percent of total US imports, even without a shift in Mexican consumption from cane to corn sweeteners, if the stringent US quotas on other suppliers remain intact.

On the other hand, the NAFTA might accelerate reform of the US sugar import program, especially if coupled with implementation of the Uruguay Round proposals to convert sugar quotas into their tariff equivalents. Indeed, the US-Mexico farm pact seems to have been drafted with the GATT talks in mind. The big sugar quota expansion for Mexico only begins in year 7, giving ample time for the Uruguay Round reforms to be substantially implemented. In that scenario, any increase in Mexican exports would not significantly reduce US sugar imports from other countries.

Orange juice. The NAFTA sets two different quotas for orange juice: 40 million gallons for frozen and concentrated orange juice (FCOJ) and 4 million gallons for fresh orange juice. At the start of the NAFTA (January 1994), the in-quota amounts will be subject to half of the current

---

30. In the extreme case, they argue that high-fructose corn syrup could supplant 1.5 million MT of sugar currently used in Mexico's beverage industry (*Inside US Trade*, 3 July 1992, 16; and 21 August 1992, 18).

tariff.[31] US imports from Mexico that exceed the quotas will be subject to the current MFN tariffs. The quotas will not increase over time but will be effectively phased out as in-quota and over-quota tariffs are equalized. Over the first six years, the over-quota tariff will be reduced by 15 percent of the tariff base. The remaining tariff will be held constant for years 7 to 10, and then reduced to zero in equal annual installments from years 10 to 15. The over-quota tariffs for fresh orange juice will be phased out in equal annual installments over 15 years (table 3.4).

Imports account for one-third of US consumption of orange juice. Brazil is the main supplier, while Mexican exports presently represent only 3 percent of the US market (*Journal of Commerce*, 20 May 1992, 1A). Concerns that Brazilian juice would be transshipped through Mexico have been answered by NAFTA provisions that establish a 100 percent rule of origin for all fruit juices (frozen, concentrated, fresh, reconstituted, or fortified; see Article 405.4).

Peanuts. Under NAFTA, Mexico will be allowed to export up to 3,377 MT of peanuts to the United States duty-free. Over-quota shipments will pay either a tariff of 186 percent or 53 cents per kilo for in-shell peanuts, and 123 percent or 80 cents per kilo for shelled peanuts (see table 3.4).[32]

Here again, US producers voiced concern about transshipments from third countries, especially Argentina and China.[33] However, the rule of origin provides that only NAFTA-grown peanuts may be used to make peanut products shipped within the NAFTA region. Unlike orange juice, the *de minimis* test of NAFTA Article 405 will be applied. This test allows goods to meet North American content requirements, even if up to 7 percent of the transaction value of the product is of foreign origin.

Corn. The agreement converts Mexican import licenses for corn into TRQs, which will be phased out over 15 years. At the start, Mexico will create a duty-free US quota of 2.5 million MT (and a Canadian quota of 1,000 MT). The over-quota tariff is set initially at 215 percent, or $206 per MT. Over the first six years, the over-quota tariff will be reduced by 24 percent of the base tariff. The remaining tariff will then be phased out linearly through year 15. The quotas will expand by 3 percent per year (table 3.3).

---

31. The tariffs will be immediately reduced from 9.25 cents per liter for FCOJ and 5.3 cents for fresh juice to 4.6 cents and 2.7 cents, respectively.

32. Currently, peanuts in the US market are sold for $700 a ton while the world market price is $300. (*Window on Washington: A Monthly Report from Consumers for World Trade* 1992).

33. In 1991 the United States imported 1.7 million pounds of raw peanuts and 67 million pounds of processed peanuts. Two-thirds of the raw peanuts and most processed peanuts came from Argentina (*Journal of Commerce*, 12 August 1992, 4A).

US-Canadian Agricultural Trade

The NAFTA does not change the provisions of the Canada-US FTA. Accordingly, the ongoing US-Canadian dispute over Canadian wheat export subsidies remains unresolved. The issue is particularly sensitive in the NAFTA context because of increased competition faced by US exporters from subsidized Canadian exports to the Mexican market.[34] In most instances, the United States can match subsidized competition in its export markets by drawing on countervailing subsidies under the US Export Enhancement Program (EEP). However, Mexico is not on the list of markets eligible for EEP subsidies.[35]

Bilateral Mexico-Canada Agreement

The bilateral Mexico-Canada farm deal is small potatoes. Between 1989 and 1991, Canadian exports to Mexico averaged $112 million, and Mexican exports to Canada averaged $150 million. Over 85 percent of Canada's agricultural imports from Mexico already enters duty-free (*Inside US Trade*, 21 August 1992, p. 20). Following the FTA precedent, most nontariff barriers on sensitive farm products remain intact: Canada will maintain its import quotas, and Mexico its import licenses, on bilateral trade in dairy, poultry, and eggs (Agricultural Policy Advisory Committee for Trade 1992, 3).[36] All tariffs will be phased out over 10 years. However, Mexico will continue to apply its MFN tariffs on sugar imports from Canada (annex 703.2, section B (11,12)). In most other cases, Mexican tariffs on bilateral trade with Canada will be the same as those applied to trade with the United States. The Canadian schedule ensures that tariffs on Mexican imports will not be phased out more rapidly than those subject to liberalization under the Canada-US FTA.

Safeguards

NAFTA Article 703.3 allows a country to impose special safeguard measures in the form of tariff quotas during the 10-year transition period for listed products.[37] The US safeguards list includes seasonal vegetables

---

34. According to Senator Max Baucus (D-MT), Canada has used export subsidies to capture 76 percent of the Mexican market (*Inside US Trade*, 28 August 1992, 15; and 2 October 1992, 4).

35. The EEP applies to shipments of up to 29 million MT of wheat, representing about $3 billion in US export sales (*Journal of Commerce*, 3 September 1992, 5A).

36. Milk and poultry imports currently represent 27 percent of Mexican farm imports from Canada (*Inside US Trade*, 28 August 1992, 17).

37. These tariff quotas are different from the TRQs created as substitutes for existing nontariff barriers (e.g., US Section 22 and Mexico's license system). For a more detailed description of TRQs, see tables 3.3 and 3.4.

and fresh watermelons; the Mexican list includes swine, certain potatoes, and fresh apples; and the Canadian list includes certain vegetables, fresh cut flowers, and frozen strawberries (tables 3.3 and 3.4).

The NAFTA also establishes a bilateral safeguard mechanism (Article 801) that can be applied during the transition period only. It allows a tariff "snapback" to the pre-NAFTA level for up to three years for most products, and up to four years for the most sensitive products, in cases where imports from a NAFTA partner are a substantial cause of—or threaten—serious injury. The current MFN rates become the benchmark if at the time of the snapback the MFN rates are lower than the NAFTA rates. However, Article 801 safeguards cannot be applied to those agricultural products covered at the same time by tariff quotas under Article 703.3.

Sanitary and Phytosanitary Procedures

The NAFTA provisions for food safety standards improve upon similar obligations included in the Draft Final Act of the Uruguay Round negotiations. Several obligations that were unclear in the GATT text have been clarified by the NAFTA. For example, the NAFTA establishes that a party is free to choose its own level of protection and thus can maintain standards higher than international standards such as the Codex Alimentarius (see NAFTA Articles 712.1 and 713.2). The GATT provisions have been criticized for giving priority to the use of harmonized international standards rather than national standards. Even in the NAFTA, however, a few issues remain vague, particularly those relating to the use of harmful pesticides and food additives.

Rules of Origin

The NAFTA rules of origin for agricultural products apply on a trilateral basis and strengthen the rules adopted under the Canada-US FTA in some key areas. For a processed farm product to qualify as being of North American origin, generally 7 percent or less of its transaction value may originate in non-NAFTA countries (Article 405). The main exceptions are tobacco (9 percent) and fruit juices (100 percent North American fresh fruit) (annex 401-10 and annex 703.2, section A (10,11)).

Evaluation

The US-Mexico bilateral farm trade agreement makes laudable progress in the liberalization of farm trade barriers. As we recommended, the negotiators dealt with the most sensitive barriers to imports of field grains and fruits and vegetables. While the liberalization of the most sensitive farm products will be gradual and phased in over a longer period than most products covered by the NAFTA, trade barriers will be eliminated on bilateral US-Mexico farm trade within 15 years—a notable achievement compared with the snail's pace of GATT negotiations.

The biggest disappointment is the failure to build on the limited results of the FTA with regard to US-Canadian bilateral farm trade. As a result, US-Canada farm trade will continue to face important constraints. Moreover, both countries failed to resolve long-standing disputes, particularly with regard to transport subsidies for wheat exports. Like their FTA predecessors, the NAFTA negotiators dodged the nettlesome subject of farm export subsidies by establishing a trilateral Working Group on Agricultural Subsidies and by awaiting results in the GATT talks.

5. Financial Services

In time, the NAFTA will dramatically improve investment access for US and Canadian financial firms doing business in the Mexican market.[38] However, the right to establish a business presence in Mexico is phased at a measured pace, with interim caps placed on the share of market that can be controlled by foreign financial firms.[39] Nonetheless, these caps will allow a significant number of firms to enter the Mexican market when the agreement goes into effect. By 1 January 2000 all Mexican restrictions on entry into the financial services market and individual firm size will be eliminated. After that, temporary safeguard measures may be applied in the banking and securities sectors, but not beyond January 2007, and only if foreign market shares reach high levels.

Rules of origin were a modest problem in the financial sector. In this context, the rule-of-origin issue is the "true nationality" of a financial firm seeking to do business in one of the partner countries. The United States and Mexico will use a "residency" test, which has generally become the international standard, while Canada will use the more restrictive "control" test. Using a residency test, a firm's nationality is determined by the place in which it is incorporated, provided the firm has a substantial presence in that place. In the Canadian control test, the financial institution must be more than 50 percent owned by shareholders that are residents of the NAFTA countries (annex VII(B)–Canada).

Banking and Securities

US and Canadian commercial banks will have practically unlimited access to the Mexican market after a long transition period; in the meantime, caps will be placed on the permitted market shares. Foreign banks will be allowed a gradual expansion in their aggregate share of the Mexican banking market, from 8 percent in 1993 to 15 percent by 1999.[40] Throughout this period, individual foreign banks will be limited to 1.5 percent of the capitalization of the Mexican market (Intergovernmental Policy Advisory Committee for Trade 1992, 31). All restrictions will be eliminated by January 2000.

However, the NAFTA provides a special safeguard for a limited period after the market share caps are removed. Between 2000 and 2004, if US

---

38. The agreement covers both traditional financial service providers (banking, securities, and insurance firms) and nontraditional providers such as nonbank banks and financial affiliates of commercial entities (e.g., General Electric or AT&T).

39. The interim caps apply to the number and size of foreign firms permitted access to the Mexican market but do not constrain the scope of their operations.

40. The initial market share of 8 percent affords room for substantial entry by US and Canadian banks.

and Canadian banks obtain more than 25 percent of the market, Mexico will be able to impose a one-time, three-year moratorium. After 2007, no caps will be permitted on aggregate market share. However, a limit will still be applied to US and Canadian banks operating in Mexico whose acquisitions (as contrasted to internal growth) result in the bank achieving more than a 4 percent market share (Advisory Committee for Trade Policy and Negotiations 1992, 61; Intergovernmental Policy Advisory Committee for Trade 1992, 31). The 4 percent ceiling effectively protects the largest Mexican banks from foreign takeovers.[41]

Parallel restrictions are placed on foreign entry into the Mexican securities market. Foreign securities firms initially will be limited to 10 percent of the Mexican market; their share will rise in equal increments to 20 percent by 1999, and then to 30 percent over the next four years. Like banks, brokerage firms will face individual caps on market share until 1 January 2000, and one-time safeguards can be imposed from 2000 to 2004 if foreign firms obtain 30 percent or more of the Mexican market. However, unlike the largest banks, Mexican securities firms will not be protected against takeovers because the individual market share caps for foreign firms expire on 1 January 2000 and cannot be reimposed.

For the time being, US and Canadian banking and securities industries seem more concerned about minimum capital requirements than size limitations. They welcome increased access to the Mexican financial sector, especially after a long history of a closed Mexican financial market (Advisory Committee for Trade Policy and Negotiations 1992, 61).

The NAFTA does not require a country to allow establishment of both subsidiaries and branches. In light of US restrictions on branch banking, Mexico and Canada will not allow US banks or securities firms to establish branches in Mexico or Canada, only subsidiaries.[42] This restriction will result in somewhat higher operating costs since legally distinct subsidiaries (unlike branches) must meet capital requirements and reserve ratios of the host country standing on their own. However, Mexico and Canada have stated that they will consider modifying the "subsidiary-only" restriction when the United States repeals the McFadden Act and allows interstate branch banking (*Journal of Commerce*, 3 September 1992, 5A).[43]

---

41. Given the very high premiums over book value paid for these banks when privatized in 1991 and 1992, such protection seems to have been a modest concession to the new Mexican bank owners. Privatization of the Mexican banks was prompted by the 1990 reforms and ended with the sale of Banco del Centro in July 1992. Some analysts wonder if the newly privatized banks will have enough money to make needed improvements (*New York Times*, 7 July 1992, D2).

42. Moreover, the subsidiaries of US banks will not be allowed to establish branches in Mexico and Canada.

43. If the United States repeals the McFadden Act, Mexico and Canada will likely allow

Furthermore, under Mexican law, US and Canadian bank subsidiaries operating in Mexico can establish financial groups that include securities and insurance firms. However, Mexican and Canadian banks operating within the United States, like US banks, will continue to be subject to Glass-Steagall restrictions that separate investment and commercial banking.[44] These restrictions have been interpreted to deter ties between banks and securities firms (although both US and foreign banks can have "section 20" subsidiaries that engage in underwriting to a limited extent). In Canada and Mexico, no such barriers exist. Both countries (as well as most US banks) would like to see further liberalization of Glass-Steagall rules. Canada is particularly interested in easing a US restriction on transactions that may be performed by securities firms that are in turn owned by banks.[45]

In the United States, banks and securities houses are regulated by the states as well as the federal government; regulation of insurance firms is at the state level only. This raises the possibility that NAFTA could preempt state laws that affect foreign financial institutions. The advisory committee report cautions against the invocation of preemption powers: "NAFTA should not be used to preempt state law with respect to those laws that apply with equal force for both domestic and foreign institutions. The developments of implementing legislation must take place in close consultation with state governments, particularly with respect to any state laws deemed to be discriminatory" (Intergovernmental Policy Advisory Committee for Trade 1992, 32).

A country can obtain reservations from NAFTA obligations for nonconforming state laws. Nonconforming measures of major banking states must be reported by 1 January 1994 (other states have an additional year) to qualify for the NAFTA reservation. Accordingly, states will be bound only with regard to future changes in nonconforming measures, provided the existing law has been reserved under the NAFTA.

Insurance

Insurance industry experts estimate that Mexico could become one of the world's top 10 insurance markets by the next century. By the time NAFTA reforms are fully implemented, the Mexican market could gen-

---

branching of a subsidiary. However, the requirement that the initial banking establishment take the form of a subsidiary will not change.

44. However, the United States will allow securities firms that become affiliated with Mexican banks a five-year exemption from the Glass-Steagall divestiture requirements.

45. Revenues from nonallowed activities (for example, the underwriting of corporate securities) cannot exceed 10 percent of total revenues earned by "section 20" subsidiaries. Canada sought to increase that limit to 25 percent (*Inside U.S. Trade*, 26 June 1992, 3; and 3 July 1992, 12).

erate $50 billion in life and casualty insurance premiums annually.[46] US and Canadian insurers will have improved access to the booming Mexican market, subject to three different transition periods. Generally speaking, the phasing periods for foreign entry into the Mexican insurance market are far more liberal than for foreign entry into the Mexican banking and securities markets. In January 2000 all limits on foreign insurance firms will disappear.

One transition period applies to US and Canadian firms that currently have partial ownership interests in Mexican firms. These US and Canadian firms may increase their equity participation to 100 percent by 1 January 1996 (Intergovernmental Policy Advisory Committee for Trade 1992, 32). No market share cap is applied.

A second transition period applies to US and Canadian firms that form joint ventures with Mexican firms. These firms may take an equity stake of up to 30 percent by 1994; this cap increases to 51 percent by 1998 and to 100 percent by 2000 (Intergovernmental Policy Advisory Committee for Trade 1992, 32). Again, no market share restriction applies.

A third transition period applies to new insurance subsidiaries wholly owned by foreign firms. These will be subject to an aggregate market share limit of 6 percent, beginning in 1996; beginning in 1999 this limit will be raised to 12 percent. Individual market share caps will be 1.5 percent (Intergovernmental Policy Advisory Committee for Trade 1992, 32). Here again, all limits will be removed by 2000.

Cross-Border Services

NAFTA accomplishments with respect to cross-border financial services are very limited. Present restrictions are grandfathered. However, the NAFTA ensures that existing restrictions on marketing of financial services across borders will not be made more burdensome. Moreover, the agreement precludes restrictions on the purchase of financial services across borders, when the purchase is initiated by the buyer. Finally, the NAFTA countries agreed to consult on further liberalization no later than January 2000 (Advisory Committee for Trade Policy and Negotiations 1992, 57 and 58).

Evaluation

While the pace of liberalization of the Mexican financial services market is slower than we recommended, the NAFTA reforms do establish sig-

---

46. The three NAFTA countries combined represent 45 percent of the world's non–life insurance premiums and 31 percent of life premiums (*Journal of Commerce*, 24 September 1992, 11A). On a smaller scale, US marine insurers are also pleased with the possibility of insuring cargo moving between the US and Mexico. They estimate that Mexico's restrictions have prevented them from competing for as much as $100 million in premiums each year (*Journal of Commerce*, 4 September 1992, 2C).

nificant new opportunities for US and Canadian firms right from the start. By the year 2000, most controls on the entry of US and Canadian firms will be removed, subject to the imposition of one-time safeguards up until 2004, if the foreign share of the Mexican market exceeds certain thresholds. After a 10-year period, the only significant barrier will be the implicit takeover protection for the largest Mexican banks afforded by the individual market share caps on foreign firms.

6. Transportation

Rail and truck transportation together carry about 85 to 90 percent of bilateral trade between the United States and Mexico, while air transportation currently accounts for less than 5 percent (*Journal of Commerce*, 30 September 1991, 7).[47] The value of two-way truck shipments in 1990 has been estimated at approximately $50 billion of merchandise, and Department of Transportation officials believe it may exceed $100 billion by the year 2000 (*Traffic World*, 2 December 1991, 22; Whalen 1992, 2).

Efficient US-Mexican truck transportation requires several improvements by both governments: expedited inspection at border crossings, through access for trucks without changing rigs, harmonized safety and regulatory standards for drivers and rigs, and improved infrastructure of all kinds (roads, bridges, inspection facilities).[48] In addition, the fast-growing transportation sector in Mexico will need a great deal of private investment in trucks, buses, air, rail, and terminal facilities.

The NAFTA improves cross-border access for bus and trucking services, frees up investment both in bus and trucking services and in landside aspects of maritime transportation, and calls for the harmonization of technical and safety standards.

Truck Transportation

Prior to the NAFTA talks, Mexican carriers were limited to operations to and from the United States only within the border commercial zones defined by the Interstate Commerce Commission (ICC).[49] Two of these zones extend more than 25 miles into the United States: the San Diego zone (75 miles) and the Rio Grande Valley Zone, encompassing four Texas counties (US Department of Transportation 1992).[50] By contrast,

---

47. *Journal of Commerce*, 30 September 1991, Air Commerce, p. 7. Some estimates indicate that 85 percent of the trade is transported by truck (*Journal of Commerce*, 18 June 1992, 1A). The USTR says that over 90 percent of US trade with Mexico is shipped by land (USTR 1992a).

48. It is worth noting that Mexico has already taken important steps to improve its infrastructure. According to a world comparison done by the OECD, Mexican roads, with an index of 57, are equivalent to those of Greece (48), Spain (54), Australia (57), Ireland (49), or Portugal (61) (OECD 1992, 96).

49. Mexican motor carriers were confined to these zones by the Bus Regulation Reform Act of 1982 and the Motor Carrier Safety Act of 1984 (US Department of Transportation 1992).

50. In March 1992 the ICC proposed to expand the zone around El Paso, Texas, to 60 miles beyond the current El Paso commercial zone (*Journal of Commerce*, 11 March 1992, 3B).

US drivers were allowed only limited access into Mexican territory.[51] The asymmetrical scope of cross-border access has been a sore point for US truckers, in addition to equipment damage and late returns when trailers entering Mexican territory are handed over to Mexican truckers (*Journal of Commerce*, 12 August 1992, 1A).

The NAFTA establishes a much larger zone of trucking access on both sides of the border. US and Mexican charter and tour buses will be ensured immediate access to each other's market; regularly scheduled route buses will gain full cross-border access three years after the NAFTA enters into force.[52] US and Canadian trucking companies will be permitted to carry cargo both to and from the Mexican states contiguous to the United States by the end of 1995 and will have unfettered access to all of Mexico by 2000.[53] Likewise, Mexican trucking companies will get reciprocal access to the contiguous United States and then to the whole United States on the same timetable.[54]

Safety Regulations

Under a memorandum of understanding (MOU) signed in November 1991 between the United States and Mexico, each country committed to accept the other's commercial driving licenses beginning April 1992. Accordingly, US states now treat Mexican truck-driver licenses as out-of-state US truck driver licenses. In both countries, drivers must pass a written knowledge exam and a driving skills exam; these tests were harmonized in the MOU.

Nevertheless, California truckers and Teamsters union officials complain that Mexican drivers are not subject to the same safety rules—especially random drug testing—as US drivers. The difficulty with this objection is that Canadian carriers, which operate freely in the United States, are also not subject to random drug testing (*Journal of Commerce*,

---

51. Only charter and tour buses are allowed to cross the border. In October 1990 Mexico said it would allow US truckers to drive their rigs 26 kilometers beyond the Mexican border. However, this liberalization was never implemented (*Transport Topics*, 22 October 1990, p. 1).

52. Mexico will also extend these rights to Canada.

53. See annex I–Mexico, transportation sector. After pressing for reciprocity for almost a decade, US truckers would have preferred quicker access to Mexican territory but consider the three-year transition period some consolation (Jay Van Rein, spokesman for the California Trucking Association, as quoted in *Journal of Commerce*, 13 August 1992, 3A).

54. See annex I–US, transportation sector. During the first three years after the signature of the NAFTA, US and Canadian truckers will continue to pick up Mexican goods at the US border cities.

24 August 1992, 1A). Behind the drug-testing issue is the much bigger question of the difference in wages: Mexican drivers are said to make a fraction of the earnings of a US driver, who earns about $140 daily (*Journal of Commerce*, 10 August 1992, 1A).

The NAFTA establishes a Land Transportation Standards Subcommittee that will implement a work program to harmonize nonmedical standards for drivers (including age and language) within 1.5 years after entry into force of the NAFTA, and medical standards within 2.5 years. The subcommittee will also work to achieve more compatible vehicle standards in the three countries—including standards on weights, dimensions, inspections, and emissions—to the extent these standards are not already covered by the North American Standards Council work program.[55]

Each country has a thick book of vehicle standards: 250 safety and technical standards in Mexico and more than 1,370 in the United States, not including emission standards or sizes and weights (*Refrigerated Transporter*, December 1991, 80). While many of the differences can be sorted out at a technical level, difficult issues are sure to remain for a long time (for example, NAFTA dispute resolution in issues concerning state technical and safety standards). However, the most difficult issue to be addressed will probably be the question of differing vehicle size and weight standards of the US, Canadian, and Mexican truck fleets.[56] Mexico wants the United States to allow heavier vehicles (60,000 – pound triaxle trailers) to cross the border (Whalen 1992), Canada wants the United States to permit double and triple trailers to cross, and US truckers are pressing Mexico and Canada to allow 53-foot trailers. Until these fundamental differences are resolved, a truly integrated continental transportation system will not be achieved.[57]

Investment Reforms

As a result of NAFTA, US and Canadian bus and truck companies may acquire up to 49 percent ownership in Mexican companies that provide international cargo services by the end of 1995, 51 percent owner-

---

55. Between 1994–96, the subcommittee will work toward compatibility of road signs and the supervision of motor carrier safety compliance (see annex 913.5.a-1). The Automotive Standards Council will be responsible for the compatibility of measures that apply to automobiles, including fuel emissions (see annex 913.5.a-3).

56. It is worth noting that truck size and weight limits have also been a highly contentious issue in the European Community.

57. While the NAFTA establishes a working party to study these issues, harmonization is not required; instead, each country is allowed to maintain its own trucking standards as long as its overt purpose is not to block trade.

ship by 2001, and 100 percent by 2004. But Mexican carriers that only carry domestic cargo will continue to be insulated from foreign ownership.[58]

In addition to the NAFTA provisions, Mexico has independently taken steps to modernize its trucking industry. Tax incentives for truck acquisition are being sweetened. More important, Mexico will lower its import barriers on heavy vehicles. NAFTA establishes that, until January 1999, each Mexican manufacturer of heavy vehicles will be able to import 50 percent of the annual number of vehicles that it produced in Mexico. By 1 January 1999 there will be no restrictions on the importation of new vehicles.[59]

Overall, US carriers welcome the eventual enlargement of investment and leasing rights in Mexico, while Mexican carriers welcome the delayed phase-in of cross-border access, which gives them an opportunity to modernize their fleet.[60] The widespread support for the NAFTA on both sides of the border reflects the prospects for very rapid growth in the Mexican trucking sector.

The NAFTA made no major changes in the investment regime applied to rail services. Any NAFTA investor—not just US and Canadian railroads—will be able to market their services, construct and own terminals in Mexico, and build spur lines (*El Nacional*, 1 September 1992, p. 23). The operation and administration of Ferrocarriles Nacionales de Mexico (FNM) will continue under government control, as required by the Mexican Constitution. US railroads will continue agreements with FNM that allow them to use their own locomotives and railcars on Mexican track; however, crews will still have to be changed at the border. To reduce day-to-day operating frictions, rail companies in the three countries signed a letter of intent in August 1992 to integrate their rail systems.[61]

---

58. See annex I–Mexico, transportation sector.

59. In addition, firms that do not assemble trucks will be able to import an additional 15 percent of Mexico's total production in 1994 and 1995, 20 percent in 1996, and 30 percent in 1997 and 1998. Again, by 1 January 1999 there will be no restrictions on the importation of new vehicles. Also, by 2019, there will be no restrictions on imports of used vehicles regardless of age (appendix 300-A.2 (21-23)).

60. The Mexican fleet, with 230,000 vehicles, has an average age of 15 years, while the US fleet, with 2.7 million medium and heavy trucks, has an average age of 4.5 years (*Journal of Commerce*, 11 May 1992, p. 1A; 13 August 1992, p. 3A).

61. The letter was signed by Ferrocarriles Nacionales de Mexico, Canadian National Railway Co., Protexa Burlington, and Burlington Northern Railroad (*El Nacional*, 24 August 1992, p. 3). This joint-venture agreement will allow the companies to move goods from land to sea and vice versa by means of the "multimodal system"—that is, cargo containers can be transported directly from a railroad car to a ship (*Wall Street Journal*, 22 September 1992, B13).

Air and Maritime Transportation

The NAFTA text liberalizes the land-based aspects of port activities. Mexico will immediately afford US and Canadian firms the right to maintain wholly owned investments in port facilities to handle their own cargo. But approval by the Mexican Foreign Investment Commission will still be needed for up to 100 percent investment in companies handling the cargo of other companies.

While the United States and Canada permit Mexican firms to invest in similar port facilities, highly restrictive national cabotage laws, such as the US Jones Act, remain in place. These laws limit the ability of foreign ships to carry cargo from port to port within a partner country.[62] Under the NAFTA, the Jones Act will continue in force, and Mexican law will continue to restrict US-owned barges from operating between Mexican ports (*Journal of Commerce*, 13 April 1992, 1A).[63]

Bilateral agreements already govern US air transport with Canada and Mexico. The NAFTA makes few changes in the managed regime that has long characterized civilian air transport—allocation of landing rights, flight schedules, and terminal facilities. Foreign investment in commercial air services (both domestic and international) will be limited to 25 percent in all three countries—resulting in a modest liberalization of Mexico's current investment ban. However, the provision of specialty air services will be liberalized in all three countries by 1 January 2000.[64]

As business links increase between the three countries, and as tourist facilities in Mexico are upgraded, passenger traffic should rapidly increase. Air cargo will play a more limited role in North American trade because truck transportation should become far more efficient as the NAFTA provisions are implemented.

---

62. The potential gains from reforming the US Jones Act were highlighted in a recent ITC study. But maritime reform was quickly put on the back burner in the NAFTA talks in light of the experience of the US-Canada FTA, which nearly foundered because of its liberalizing provisions for maritime services (US International Trade Commission 1991, I-2-7).

63. "Maritime cabotage services, including off-shore maritime services, are reserved to Mexican-flagged vessels" unless Mexican-flagged vessels are not able to provide such services (annex I–Mexico, freight and passenger water transportation).

64. For the United States and Canada, the provision of services such as aerial construction and heli-logging will be open to citizens of another NAFTA country two years after entry into force of the agreement (by 1996); aerial sightseeing, flight training, and aerial inspection and surveillance services by 1997; and aerial spraying services by 2001. For Mexico, the provision of services such as aerial advertising, aerial sightseeing, aerial construction, and aerial spraying services will be open to US and Canadian citizens by 1997 and inspection, mapping, photography, surveying, and aerial spraying services by 2001 (see annex I).

Border Inspection Facilities

According to a GAO report, the main obstacle to efficient border inspection operation is the inadequate number of customs and immigration inspectors. The GAO report estimated that a doubling of trade would require an additional 1,740 US Customs Service inspectors and 1,463 Immigration and Naturalization Service (INS) inspectors.[65] Calculated at $75,000 per inspector (including backup and existing staff), the annual budget outlay would be $375 million.

On the Mexican side, dramatic progress has been made. Since December 1991 a brand-new corps of 1,200 customs officers has taken charge of the country's 47 customs points and another 243 "points of vigilance" (i.e., smuggling zones). In an anticorruption and proefficiency measure of draconian proportions, all 3,600 members of the previous customs police were retired overnight (*Journal of Commerce*, 26 August 1992, 4A).

NAFTA chapter 5 (customs procedures) emphasizes cooperation to enforce customs-related laws, to exchange information, and to standardize data elements in order to facilitate the flow of trade within North America. Noteworthy among its provisions are the advance-ruling procedures that provide importers and exporters greater certainty as to the customs status of traded goods (see Article 509). The NAFTA also creates a Working Group on Rules of Origin and a Customs Subgroup to ensure, among other things, "the effective administration of the customs-related aspects" of the NAFTA; agreement on "tariff classification and valuation matters relating to determination of origin"; and consideration of changes in customs procedures that could affect regional trade (see Article 513). These provisions establish an early-warning system that should help forestall technical differences from escalating into full-blown bilateral trade disputes (as in the Honda case).

Infrastructure

Border infrastructure projects have been on the drawing board well before the NAFTA text was drafted. The highway departments of the US border states have identified projects needed to meet current and increased levels of border traffic. Their estimates range from $2 billion for Texas to a California assessment that the present infrastructure is adequate for current traffic levels (US General Accounting Office 1991, 4).

---

65. In 1990, 1,188 Customs Service inspectors and 640 INS inspectors were authorized. A doubling of trade would require a total of 2,928 Customs inspectors and 2,103 INS inspectors (US General Accounting Office 1991, 3).

However, some projects are plagued by inadequate coordination between US and Mexican authorities.[66] The cities of Laredo and Nuevo Laredo provide an example: "While I-35 provides good access to the downtown bridge from the US side, on the Mexican side there are only narrow, congested city streets. However, at the Columbia Bridge, Mexico is building a four-lane highway from Monterrey to the bridge crossing, while on the US side there is only a two-lane farm road, which the local business community considers to be inadequate and unsafe for commercial traffic" (US General Accounting Office 1991, 50).

Additional problems arise with regard to the review, authorization, and implementation of infrastructure projects. For example, at least 30 US agencies are involved in evaluating a given proposal, but funding for bridge or land border crossing projects must be raised at the state or local level (Interview with Irwin Rubinstein, US Department of State, in Whalen 1992, 25). On top of that, each country is responsible for building its half of the bridge.

Mexico's infrastructure has significantly improved in the past few years. According to an OECD study, the present state of Mexican infrastructure is comparable to that of some Mediterranean countries. Mexico has been particularly bold in involving the private sector. By allowing the private sector to build and operate toll roads, the Mexican government will spur the construction of 6,000 kilometers of toll roads and bridges at a cost of $10 billion between 1989 and 1994.[67] Typically, the private sector constructs the road, bridge, or terminal and collects revenue as an operating concession for a fixed number of years, at which point the project reverts to the government. Whether similar imagination can be applied to US and cross-border infrastructure remains to be seen.

Changes are also expected in the railway and port infrastructure systems. Rates have been rationalized and the railway-car manufacturing company, CONCARRIL, was sold to Canadian investors (Organization for Economic Cooperation and Development 1992, 97). Regulations that gave exclusive rights to companies and unions in the ports have been revoked, and private-sector companies are planning to invest over $150 million in port facilities under build-operate-transfer arrangements.[68]

---

66. Although the interagency Committee on Bridges and Border Crossings meets regularly with its Mexican counterparts, this group has not addressed borderwide issues (US General Accounting Office 1991, 51).

67. The overall expansion of the highway system between 1989 and 1994, including public roads as well as toll roads, will be about 12,000 kilometers, or by about 80 percent (Organization for Economic Cooperation and Development 1992, 96).

68. In 1991 three corrupt union leaders were incarcerated, and three stevedoring firms were privatized (*Journal of Commerce*, 3 December 1992, 7C).

Evaluation

In the transportation sector, the NAFTA negotiators accomplished far more than we had expected. Within a few years, the United States and Mexico will be connected by a common network of trucking, rail, and other transportation services. The remaining major barriers, including differences in truck weights and sizes and the highly restrictive cabotage laws, might be liberalized in later talks under NAFTA auspices. The major task ahead is to build large amounts of road and bridge infra-structure. This will either require huge amounts of public money or an imaginative extension of the Mexican approach to the use of toll roads and toll bridges.

7. Telecommunications

The NAFTA provisions on telecommunications build on the model established by the telecommunications annex of the draft General Agreement on Services negotiated in the Uruguay Round. Like the GATT text, the NAFTA sets out a framework of rights and obligations regarding access to, and use of, public telecommunications networks. By assuring access to the public network on a nondiscriminatory basis, these provisions should greatly expand both cross-border trade and investment in enhanced or value-added services.[69] They do not apply, however, to basic telecommunications services.[70] Increased trade in enhanced telecommunications services should boost regional trade in telecommunications equipment.

Access to and Use of Public Networks

The NAFTA provides that North American firms have access to use of public networks and services on a reasonable, nondiscriminatory, cost-oriented basis for the conduct of their business. The NAFTA commits the three countries to ensure that the pricing of public telecommunications transport services reflects underlying economic costs and that private leased circuits are available to users for a flat-rate fee.[71] As generally accorded to cross-border trade in services, North American firms that provide telecommunications services across borders will receive most-favored-nation or national treatment, whichever is better (Articles 1202-1204).

Open and nondiscriminatory access to the public network means that North American firms will be allowed to lease private lines; attach terminal or other equipment to public networks; interconnect private circuits to public networks; perform switching, signaling, and processing functions; and use operating protocols of the user's choice. The NAFTA also affords US and Canadian firms the right to operate private intracorporate communications systems in Mexico and between Mexico and their home country. Increased access to and use of the public network in turn should expand opportunities for cross-border trade in banking, data, and other enhanced services.

---

69. Enhanced or value-added services refer to those telecom services employing computer processing applications such as electronic mail, on-line information and data base retrieval, electronic data interchange, store and forward facsimile services, and alarm services.

70. Nonetheless, the three countries agreed to consult on "the feasibility of further liberalizing trade in all telecommunications services, including public telecommunications transport networks and services" (Article 1309:2).

71. Currently, leased circuits have a flat rate based on the average usage of a switched circuit, and not on the cost of providing the service (*Inside US Trade*, 4 October 1991, 15; Industry Sector Advisory Committee on Services 1992, 12).

The NAFTA attempts to reconcile differences in standards and testing procedures (Article 1304). Qualifying standards are established for the attachment of private telecommunications equipment to public networks. The general thrust of these standards is to limit only private equipment that threatens technical damage, network interference, or user safety. Within one year of the implementation of the NAFTA, equipment test results conducted in each NAFTA country will be accepted by the other countries (Article 1304:6).[72]

In addition, the NAFTA contains quasi-regulatory provisions to ensure that, if a national monopoly is maintained, it must compete fairly with foreign firms in the provision of enhanced or value-added services, or other telecommunications-related goods and services. These provisions prevent a company such as Teléfonos de México (Telmex) from abusing its monopoly position through cross-subsidization or restricted access to public networks (Article 1305).

Trade and Investment Reforms

The NAFTA calls for the quick phaseout of most trade and investment barriers affecting telecommunications goods and services. From the outset, tariffs will be eliminated on the majority of telecommunications products, including private branch exchanges, cellular systems, satellite transmission and earth station equipment, and fiber-optic systems. Remaining tariffs will be phased out within five years.[73]

Regarding investment, the main NAFTA accomplishment is the opening up of the Mexican market for enhanced or value-added services. Mexico currently limits foreign investment in Mexican firms that provide enhanced telecommunications services to a maximum equity stake of 49 percent. The NAFTA eliminates at the outset foreign investment restrictions and local presence requirements for enhanced or value-added service providers in Mexico, except restrictions for videotext and enhanced packet switched data services, which will be removed by July 1995 (annex I–Mexico, telecommunications sector). However, existing ownership restrictions in all three countries for radio and television stations may be maintained.[74] In addition, Mexico will not lift its restrictions on invest-

---

72. In addition, a Telecommunications Standards Subcommittee (established in Article 913) will develop, within six months after the agreement is in force, a work plan for making compatible the standards-related measures for authorized equipment. See annex 913.5.a-2.

73. For example, the Mexican 20 percent tariff on office switches will be phased out at 4 percent per year over five years (*Telecommunications Reports*, 17 August 1992, 2).

74. The NAFTA thereby sanctions the restrictions established under the US Communications Act of 1934, as amended. Under these restrictions, the United States will apply

ment in companies that provide telecommunications transport networks (e.g., local basic and long-distance telephone services) and telecommunications transport services (annex II–Mexico, telecommunications sector).

Trade in Telecommunications Equipment

NAFTA reforms will provide further opportunities for US and Canadian firms to supply the already rapidly growing market for telecommunications equipment in Mexico. The Mexican market for those goods totaled $790 million in 1991 and may exceed $1 billion in 1992. Much of the projected increase involves equipment purchases by Mexico's public telephone company, Teléfonos de México (Telmex).[75]

While Telmex has been privatized, it remains a regulated monopoly.[76] The Mexican government has required Telmex to invest heavily ($2 billion to $3 billion annually) to improve service in exchange for less obtrusive regulation of prices and generous tax treatment. Since privatization, Telmex has been on an extensive buying spree of telecommunications equipment from foreign (mostly US and Canadian) suppliers. Current spending plans are well above target, and some estimates indicate that Telmex will spend $13 billion for equipment in 1992 and 1993 (*Telecommunications Reports*, 17 August 1992, 2).[77] The NAFTA provides a further stimulus to Telmex's investment plans, since the company has only five years before it faces strong competition for the provision of most value-added services.

---

reciprocal limitations on investment on cable television and reserves the right to adopt or maintain any measure relating to investment in, or the provision of, radio communications including broadcasting (annex II–US, communications sector). Canadian restrictions include the right to adopt or maintain any measure relating to radio communications including ownership restrictions (annex II–Canada, communications sector). Finally, Mexico prohibits foreign governments and foreign state enterprises from investing in a Mexican enterprise providing services related to the general means of communication, radio, and television; US and Canadian investors are limited to minority ownership in Mexico's cable television systems; and a majority of personnel involved in the production and performance of a live broadcast programming activity must be Mexican nationals (annex I–Mexico, communications sector).

75. For example, AT&T is scheduled to provide 60 percent of Mexico's new fiber-optics network (*Journal of Commerce*, 25 September 1992, 4A).

76. In December 1990 a controlling interest (20.4 percent) of Telmex was sold to a consortium formed by Grupo Carso (a Mexican diversified company), Southwestern Bell, and France Telecom.

77. For 1993 investment plans call for increasing the number of lines to 7.5 million, installing 13,500 km of fiber-optic cables, and digitizing 60 percent of local exchanges (*Financial Times*, 22 July 1992, 7).

Evaluation

The NAFTA makes substantial and rapid progress in opening up access for North American firms to Mexico's telecommunications market for enhanced or value-added services, and it should accelerate both cross-border trade and investment in telecommunications goods and enhanced services. US and Canadian exporters should benefit both from the immediate elimination of most Mexican tariffs and nontariff barriers on telecommunications equipment and from the rapidly growing Mexican demand for telecommunications services and equipment. Mexico will benefit by the rapid conversion of its third-world telecommunications system to first-world performance levels. As a result, North American producers of all kinds of goods and services should find it easier to do business in Mexico.

4

Trade Rules and New Issues

1. Investment

The three countries of North America are already linked by an extensive network of cross-border investment: bilateral US-Canada investments are predominant, but US direct investment in Mexico has grown significantly. The stock of US direct investment in Mexico on a historic cost basis was $11.6 billion at the end of 1991 compared with $4.9 billion at year end 1987. Additional capital inflows are critical for Mexico to boost production, improve productivity, and help finance the burgeoning Mexican current account deficit. The stock of US direct investment in Mexico represents only 2.6 percent of overall direct investments by US firms ($450.2 billion). However, new equity capital flows from the United States to Mexico over the past three years represent 6.7 percent of the overall total.[1]

The NAFTA liberalizes restrictions on the flow of investment within the North American region. This section is a major achievement for two reasons: it allows firms to rationalize production on a regional basis, underpinning their efforts to become more competitive in a global market, and it strongly reinforces Mexican economic reforms designed to improve the investment climate in that country.

---

1. In addition, a large amount of portfolio capital circulates among the three partners. The policy issues surrounding portfolio capital are less contentious, especially following the resolution of Mexico's external debt problems.

Extending and Augmenting FTA Rules

We recommended that the NAFTA require Mexico to accept obligations comparable to those in the Canada-US Free Trade Agreement regarding national treatment and limitations on the use of performance requirements and to go beyond the FTA commitments by allowing foreign participation in the energy sector.[2] In addition, we suggested that the United States and Mexico conclude a new tax treaty to deal *inter alia* with problems relating to Mexico's high withholding tax rates on interest and royalties (see below). Except for exemptions for the primary energy and basic petrochemical sectors, the NAFTA meets or exceeds our recommendations.

First, the NAFTA commits all three countries to provide national treatment to investors from NAFTA partners. In other words, US, Canadian, or Mexican investors must be treated at least as well as domestic-based investors; this obligation also holds for practices applied by states or provinces. In addition, the NAFTA contains a most-favored-nation (MFN) obligation that ensures that NAFTA investors are treated as well as any other foreign investor in the country.

NAFTA provisions on performance requirements are detailed and more demanding than either the Canada-US FTA or the draft General Agreement on Tariffs and Trade accord on trade-related investment measures (TRIMS). The FTA bans all new export performance, import substitution, and domestic-content requirements affecting US or Canadian investments. It also phases out existing export and production-based requirements, but it allows all three countries to impose non–trade-related performance requirements (e.g., employment targets). The list of proscribed practices in the NAFTA includes export performance, domestic content, domestic sourcing, trade balancing, product mandating, and technology transfer requirements. Most existing requirements of this type are to be phased out over periods up to 10 years. Like the FTA, the NAFTA allows some non–trade-related performance requirements, involving, for example, commitments to undertake worker training, construction or expansion of facilities, and local research and development.

By comparison, the coverage of the TRIMS accord in the draft Uruguay Round text is much more limited, covering primarily domestic-content and trade balancing requirements. Interestingly, the NAFTA provisions on performance requirements parallel the initial US proposals for the TRIMS negotiations, which were subsequently watered down because of the unwillingness of developing countries to accept constraints on their ability to control multinational firms resident in their territory. Since the GATT round began, however, many developing countries (including

---

2. For a discussion of the investment provisions of the Canada-US FTA, see Schott and Smith (1988, chapter 6).

Mexico) have unilaterally liberalized their investment regime, recognizing that their past policies had discouraged investment. For that reason, we believe the NAFTA text will become a useful model for future GATT accords and US bilateral free trade agreements.

Other provisions deserve mention. The NAFTA forbids restrictions on capital movements, including profit remittances and other payments and fees, except for prudential or balance of payments reasons (Article 1109:1). It outlaws expropriation—a historic problem in US-Mexico economic relations—except for a public purpose, on a nondiscriminatory basis, after due process, and upon prompt payment of fair compensation (Article 1110). In addition, the NAFTA forbids governments from dictating the nationality of corporate senior managers, but it may require that a majority of the board of directors be of a particular nationality or be residents (Article 1107).

The investment provisions of the NAFTA deal to some extent with environmental concerns. The NAFTA permits each country to require that investors adopt pollution abatement and other environmental technologies and satisfy specified environmental prerequisites such as submission of an environmental impact analysis. Furthermore, it recognizes that governments "should not" lower national standards to lure footloose firms attracted by lax pollution controls. However, it provides no concrete remedies (only consultation rights) if such actions are taken (Article 1114:2).

Dispute Settlement

Section B of the NAFTA chapter on investment contains extensive provisions regarding the settlement of disputes. These rules are so well drafted that NAFTA critics have argued that comparable enforcement procedures should be applied to the labor and environmental areas.

The NAFTA provides new rights for private investors to obtain relief directly against governments for NAFTA violations. Instead of seeking relief in courts or administrative tribunals of the host country, or trying to get his home government to pursue a claim against the host government, an investor may seek binding arbitral rulings directly against the host government in an international forum, following rules established by the World Bank's International Center for the Settlement of Investment Disputes (ICSID) or the UN Commission on International Trade Law (UNCITRAL). Remedies for violations of NAFTA obligations include monetary damages and return of property. However, the arbitration panels themselves cannot enforce money damages or compel the return of property. Instead, the investor can take the arbitral awards to a court in any of the three NAFTA countries and seek enforcement under treaties to which all three countries are parties.

These new provisions amount to a repudiation of the Calvo Doctrine, long espoused in Latin America, that all disputes involving foreign investors should be settled solely in local courts.

Coverage

The NAFTA provisions on investment apply to all investors in the North American region, including companies controlled by non–North American owners. There are, however, notable exceptions in the coverage of the investment chapter. In particular, the obligations do not apply to:

- measures related to investments in financial services "to the extent that they are covered by Chapter Fourteen (Financial Services)";

- existing federal measures listed in annex I of the NAFTA (which notably exempts Mexico's primary energy sector and railroads, US airlines and radio communications, and Canada's cultural industries);

- state or provincial measures notified within two years of entry into force of the pact, as well as their renewal or amendment (as long as such changes do not increase the burden of requirements that would otherwise be proscribed by the pact);

- public procurement by governments or parastatal enterprises;

- investment incentives (including government-supported loans, guarantees, and insurance);

- export promotion and foreign aid programs, which are exempt from some obligations not to set performance requirements;

- restrictions on investments for national security reasons (thus the NAFTA does not constrain application of the US Exon-Florio law).

Following precedent set in the Canada-US FTA, the NAFTA accords Mexico the right to continue to screen foreign acquisitions above an initial threshold of $25 million. The threshold figure will be progressively increased to $150 million (plus inflation adjustments) over 10 years. The FTA gave Canada similar rights to screen acquisitions above C$150 million (plus inflation and growth adjustments), and that provision remains in force. In Canada, the threshold effectively preempted screening of foreign acquisitions in all but the largest Canadian companies. In Mexico, while the initial threshold is lower, most Mexican companies are smaller, so the impact of screening is also likely to be limited.

US-Mexico Tax Treaty

Bilateral tax treaties are an important thread in the fabric of institutions that facilitate international investment. Treaties set maximum rates on taxes imposed on the repatriation of investment income (e.g., dividends or royalties), they ensure that foreign investors are not subject to discriminatory taxation, they divide overlapping parts of the income tax base between the two countries, and they promote cooperation between the tax authorities to avert double taxation and thwart tax evasion.

Just as the United States and Mexico have parallel agreements on labor and environmental issues that complement the NAFTA, both countries concluded a bilateral tax treaty in September 1992 that reduces the high statutory withholding rates charged on interest, dividends, and royalties flowing in both directions. In addition, the treaty breaks new ground with respect to charitable organizations, threatened congressional overrides of treaty terms, anti–treaty shopping provisions, and arbitration provisions (*Tax Notes International*, 19 October 1992, 825–35).[3]

Interest paid on Mexican government bills or bonds, interest paid to an official lender (such as the US Export-Import Bank), interest on certain loans guaranteed or insured by an official lender, and interest paid to a tax-exempt pension fund will be free of Mexican withholding taxes. Similar exemptions apply to US interest payments to Mexican holders, either by virtue of the treaty or by virtue of US statutory exemptions.

Interest paid to US banks will initially be subject to a 10 percent withholding rate; after five years, the rate will drop to 4.9 percent. This peculiar figure was chosen so that interest from Mexico would be placed in the same "basket of income," for US foreign tax credit purposes, as other "low-tax" foreign interest income, rather than "high-tax" foreign interest income.[4]

Interest paid to foreign lenders to finance the purchase of inventory, machinery, or equipment will be withheld at 15 percent for five years and 10 percent thereafter. The same rates apply to interest paid by Mexican banks to finance similar investments. Other interest payments (e.g., on a certificate of deposit issued by a Mexican bank and held by a US citizen) will be withheld at 15 percent.

The withholding tax on portfolio dividends starts at 15 percent and drops to 10 percent after five years. The tax on direct investment dividends (10 percent or more stock ownership) is 5 percent. However, the rate will go to zero if the United States negotiates another tax treaty with a zero rate.[5] The treaty provides a 10 percent tax on royalties, a fairly standard rate.

---

3. The innovations in the US-Mexican tax treaty generally accord with the recommendations offered in Hufbauer (1992, chapters 4 and 7).

4. When foreign interest income is assigned to the "high-tax" basket, the foreign tax credits associated with that income are likely to expire unused, with no benefit to the bank.

5. Mexico wanted a zero rate on direct investment dividends. The United States was unwilling to take that step in this treaty.

Evaluation

The NAFTA negotiators produced a landmark agreement on investment that meets or exceeds our recommendations, with the notable exception of obligations relating to the primary energy sector (see the section on energy, p. 33). Under the NAFTA, the three countries agreed to obligations more comprehensive than those contained in the Canada-US FTA (or any other US agreement, for that matter), and to new procedures that provide binding arbitration of investment disputes. In parallel, they negotiated a tax treaty that breaks new ground in a constructive direction.

The NAFTA provisions will require substantial revisions of Mexico's Law on Foreign Investment but little change in current US law and regulations. In particular, the United States will be able to continue to implement the Exon-Florio law to screen acquisitions of US firms by foreign investors that raise national security concerns.

The NAFTA marks the first time that a developing country both has accorded to foreign investors from developed countries the more favorable of either national treatment or MFN treatment, has adopted rigorous dispute settlement procedures, and has accepted comprehensive constraints on its use of performance requirements.[6] We regard the NAFTA agreement on investment as far superior to that produced in the Uruguay Round on TRIMS. Ideally, the GATT negotiators should replace the TRIMS accord with an investment code based on the NAFTA text—if not in the Uruguay Round then in subsequent talks. In addition, the United States should use the US-Mexico tax treaty as a model not only for other Latin American countries, but also on a wider scale.

---

6. In its network of bilateral investment treaties, the United States has secured the more favorable of national treatment or MFN treatment for US investors but has made only modest strides in limiting performance requirements.

2. Intellectual Property Rights

Following the enactment of comprehensive patent and copyright laws in Mexico in June-July 1991, the NAFTA negotiations on intellectual property rights focused on "locking in" the Mexican reforms, expanding the coverage of existing national laws to new areas, and resolving long-standing bilateral disputes.[7] The big question ahead is how the new Mexican laws will be enforced.[8]

The NAFTA also settled the US-Canada dispute over compulsory licensing of pharmaceutical patents. However, as in the FTA, Canada maintained its right to exempt cultural industries from NAFTA obligations, thus leaving the sector open to potential bilateral disputes.

Copyrights

As a result of NAFTA, literary, artistic, and industrial works to be covered by Mexican copyright laws include two new areas: computer programs and compilations of individually unprotected material (for example, a data base of economic statistics drawn from public sources).[9]

In addition, the intellectual property rights chapter includes provisions for the protection of satellite transmissions. Encrypted program-carrying satellite signals are vulnerable to decoding with the use of commercially available decryption equipment. The NAFTA agreement requires parties to make this practice a criminal offense (Industry Functional Advisory Committee for Trade in Intellectual Property Rights 1992, 14).

Mexico will also extend its copyright law to cover sound recordings, giving them a 50-year term of protection, the same as for motion pictures (Industry Functional Advisory Committee for Trade in Intellectual Property Rights 1992, 8). In principle, program owners and producers of sound recordings will now be able to prohibit knock-off copies or the rental of their products (Industry Functional Advisory Committee for Trade in Intellectual Property Rights 1992, 2). However, Mexico will not protect sound recordings published before the NAFTA goes into effect,

---

7. Intellectual property rights embrace patents, copyrights, trademarks, industrial design, trade secrets, and similar rights.

8. An example of poor enforcement in Mexico is the large number of unauthorized music tapes sold in the market. It is estimated that half of the music tapes sold annually are pirated, representing an annual loss to US producers of $75 million (*The Financial Post*, 18 September 1992, 9).

9. In 1990 US industries concerned with copyrights accounted for about $332 billion in value added. Of that total, the primary ones (motion pictures, publishers, and computer software) accounted for $190 billion (Industry Sector Advisory Committee on Services 1992, 31).

nor will it cover "parallel imports."[10] Clearly, after making dramatic changes in its laws, Mexico does not want to enlarge further the scope of intellectual property rights without US and Canadian concessions in return.[11]

Generally, each country accords national treatment in its intellectual property laws to corporations and citizens of the other NAFTA countries. One major exception in the copyright area involves Mexican broadcasting rights. Mexico takes the view that the original performer holds the right to the secondary use of a sound recording in a public performance or a broadcasting context. US law does not protect a performer's rights *per se* to the broadcasting of his recording. Instead, these rights are held by the copyright owner, who may or not may be the performer. Because of this fundamental difference between US and Mexican law, Mexico was unwilling to extend its law, under the national treatment principle, to foreign performers. Instead, the rights of US and Canadian performers in Mexico will be subject to a rule of reciprocity, which for the foreseeable future means no protection.[12]

Another major exception to the national-treatment standard, carried over from the US-Canada FTA, is the Canadian "cultural industries" exemption.[13] In the NAFTA, by comparison with the FTA, the cultural exemption applied to Canada has been expanded to include copyrights (*Journal of Commerce*, 3 August 1992, p. 10A).[14] As a result of the sweeping exemption of cultural industries from the FTA and from NAFTA rules that govern services, investment, and copyright protection, Canada in

---

10. A "parallel import" is the import of a protected work legitimately produced under license but not authorized for distribution in the importing country (Industry Functional Advisory Committee for Trade in Intellectual Property Rights 1992, 37).

11. Illustrative of outstanding issues is a Mexican proposal to establish a statutory scheme for distributing revenues generated at movie theaters. In the view of the US movie and record producers, this scheme would infringe upon their freedom to negotiate contract terms (Intergovernmental Policy Advisory Committee for Trade 1992, 40).

12. Another example of the result of applying the principle of reciprocity, rather than national treatment, involves Canada. Under a reciprocity rule, Canada would be allowed to "levy royalty fees on blank tapes and recording machines in order to compensate all copyright holders harmed by home recording, but not distribute the collected fees to US copyright holders" (Intergovernmental Policy Advisory Committee for Trade 1992, 40).

13. The industries potentially affected by this exemption include the motion picture, TV, and video production industries; the music and recording industries; the book, journal, magazine, and newspaper publishing industries; and the US radio, television cable, and satellite transmission industries. Industries not affected include computer programs and those protected by Canadian adherence to other international agreements, such as the Berne Convention (Industry Functional Advisory Committee for Trade in Intellectual Property Rights 1992, 14).

14. Under Article 2006 of the US-Canada FTA, Canada provided copyright protection for the retransmission of satellite programming.

principle "would be able to discriminate against these industries through the denial of national treatment or through the failure to provide the NAFTA minimum level of protection."[15]

In response to the Canadian exemption, the United States has reserved its right to withdraw comparable benefits if Canada exercises the cultural industries exemption (Intergovernmental Policy Advisory Committee for Trade 1992, 40). In practice, it seems unlikely that Canada will exercise the exemption to any greater extent than it has in the past.[16] However, film and sound-recording producers argue that the Canadian exemption sets a very bad precedent, which the European Community may attempt to emulate in the GATT accord.[17] If the reciprocity standard, rather than the national treatment standard, becomes the norm for film and sound recordings, it is conceivable that the US industry will try to build a reciprocity rule into US law.

Trademarks, Industrial Designs, and Geographical Indicators

US, Mexican, and Canadian laws differ little on the protection of trademarks (including service marks) and industrial designs. To reinforce established practice, the NAFTA protects trademarks, and it prohibits compulsory licensing or mandatory linking of trademarks. Initial registration of a trademark is for 10 years, and the trademark is renewable for successive terms of not less than 10 years. The use of the trademark is required to maintain its registration. US and Canadian firms are generally pleased with this outcome. However, they would like Mexico to amend its trademark laws to allow interested parties (e.g., an opposing trademark owner) to petition for cancellation of a trademark (Industry Policy Advisory Committee for Trade 1992, 38).

---

15. For example, the exemption allows Canada to maintain quotas on foreign-produced films (Intergovernmental Policy Advisory Committee for Trade 1992, 39).

16. To a small extent, Canada subsidizes the production of Canadian film and sound artists, gives preference to Canadian distributors, and allows tax benefits for advertising in Canadian-owned publications. An editorial in *The Financial Post*, a Canadian business journal, points out that, while it is very unlikely that the Canadian cultural exemption will be invoked, it gets a great deal of adverse attention, even though nobody worries about "an [actual] exception granted to Mexico in NAFTA that guarantees a minimum of 30 percent of that nation's movie screens be reserved for homegrown productions" (*The Financial Post*, 18 September 1992).

17. Around 55 percent of international revenues for the US film, TV, and home video industries come from Western Europe. Several European countries are considering the adoption, or already have adopted, "levy, rental, and even public performance regimes which discriminate against US rights holders." If the Canadian cultural exemption is emulated in Europe, the industry spokesman claims that "it would shrink, by tens of millions of dollars, legitimate revenues to American companies" (Jack Valenti, Motion Picture Association of America, Inc., memorandum, 10 September 1992).

NAFTA provides protection for independently created industrial designs that are new or original. However, "NAFTA does not dictate the form that industrial design protection must take in each country." Specifically, it does not incorporate the US standards of "ornamentability" and "unobviousness," which are prominent features of US design patent law. Instead, the NAFTA text uses the less archaic term "significantly differ" instead of "unobviousness," and the term "technically/functionally driven" design instead of "ornamentability" (Industry Functional Advisory Committee for Trade in Intellectual Property Rights 1992, 21). Conceivably, these differences could alter the outcome in particular disputes.

US firms find the provisions on geographical appellations (e.g., Bordeaux wine) potentially troubling for their activities in Mexico and Canada. Under the NAFTA, third countries (for example, the European Community) can establish separate bilateral agreements with Mexico and Canada in which geographical appellations preclude or supersede the use of conflicting trademarks (Industry Functional Advisory Committee for Trade in Intellectual Property Rights 1992, 21).

Patents, Mask Designs, and Trade Secrets

Better patent protection in Mexico and Canada is a significant NAFTA accomplishment, as is the protection given to trade secrets in Mexico. In the course of the NAFTA negotiations, Canada introduced legislation (C.91) to eliminate its compulsory licensing system for pharmaceutical patents, a contentious issue left over from the FTA. Moreover, the parties are required to recognize importation as meeting the local working requirement for compulsory licensing purposes.[18]

The NAFTA also requires that each country provide a minimum patent term of 20 years. While the NAFTA regime does not fully apply to patent rights obtained before the NAFTA enters into force, the NAFTA does provide "pipeline" protection for pharmaceutical and agrichemical products already patented elsewhere.[19] The industry advisory report regards the extent of pipeline protection in the NAFTA as a major improvement over the draft Uruguay Round text, which only provides pipeline pro-

18. The NAFTA text established that "patents shall be available and patent rights enjoyable without discrimination as to . . . whether products are imported or locally produced" (North American Free Trade Agreement, text prepared 6 September 1992).

19. "Pipeline" protection broadly refers to protection for products whose patent applications are being evaluated by the national patent office (which can take several years), products that are in the development stage, and products that are not yet sold in countries that are updating their intellectual property laws (*Journal of Commerce*, 20 August 1992; Industry Functional Advisory Committee for Trade in Intellectual Property Rights 1992, 17).

tection for patents filed after the entry into force of the GATT agreement.[20]

Products and process inventions will be patentable in all fields of technology unless the invention endangers public order or morality; the environment; or human, animal, or plant life or health (Industry Functional Advisory Committee for Trade in Intellectual Property Rights 1992, 16). The latter exception allows the continued exclusion from patentability of biotechnology inventions and diagnostic, therapeutic, and surgical methods (Advisory Committee for Trade Policy and Negotiations 1992, 65). This exclusion is a major concern to US firms. It mirrors the refusal of most developing countries to cover biotechnology inventions in the Uruguay Round draft text on intellectual property rights. Other exceptions to patent rights are permitted under a vague "exceptions provision," which is loosely governed by a rule of reason.[21] Parallel imports of patented products are not addressed under the NAFTA.

NAFTA provisions protect mask designs for semiconductors. The term of protection is equivalent to US law (at least 10 years), although Mexico is not required to meet these obligations until four years after the agreement is in effect (Industry Functional Advisory Committee for Trade in Intellectual Property Rights 1992, 38).

NAFTA is the first international regime to guarantee the protection of trade secrets and proprietary information. It also protects proprietary test data submitted by firms to government agencies for approval (regarding the safety and efficiency of new pharmaceutical and agrichemical products) for at least a five-year period of exclusive use.

The provisions on trade secrets do not meet all US demands. NAFTA adopts a "gross negligence" rather than a "negligence" standard for the proscribed disclosure of trade secrets to third parties (Advisory Committee for Trade Policy and Negotiations 1992, 66). The NAFTA text is ambiguous as to whether protection is provided not only against improper "acquisition" but also against "continued use" of an improperly acquired trade secret. Specifically, the definition of a "manner contrary to honest commercial practices" does not expressly preclude continued use or further dissemination of a trade secret by an innocent third party, even though improper practices were involved in the acquisition of the

---

20. However, Canada has declared that pipeline protection under the GATT (assuming the Uruguay Round package is concluded and ratified) should commence 20 December 1991 (the date the Dunkel draft was released) and has challenged other GATT parties to accept the same date.

21. The exceptions provision permits exceptions to patent rights so long as the exceptions do not unreasonably conflict with a normal exploitation of the patent right, do not unreasonably prejudice the legitimate interest of the patent owner, and do take into account the legitimate interest of other persons.

trade secret by the second party (Industry Functional Advisory Committee for Trade in Intellectual Property Rights 1992, 20).

Evaluation

In the intellectual property area, NAFTA stands as a model both for resolving outstanding disputes and for locking in reforms previously enacted. The two major shortcomings are the cultural exemption and the exclusion from patentability for biotechnology inventions. However, the accomplishments in NAFTA are so striking that it has quickly become the preferred benchmark for evaluating the accomplishments of GATT and other trade agreements.

The value of NAFTA provisions on intellectual property rights will clearly depend on the effectiveness of enforcement, and this is largely a matter of practice in each partner country. The US industry is concerned with the Mexican record of administrative inefficiency in controlling the abuse of intellectual property rights. As might be expected, US firms recommend close monitoring of the implementation of the NAFTA enforcement provisions. Our expectation is that, within five years, Mexico will protect intellectual property as well as the United States or Canada.

3. Environment

With the election of President Clinton, environmental issues stand at the center of questions to be resolved before the United States ratifies the NAFTA. Environmental issues were certainly not forgotten in the NAFTA negotiations, and many points raised in our 1992 book were addressed.[22] Indeed, the NAFTA stands as a landmark accord for handling environmental issues in a trade agreement. But the Bush administration's solutions fell behind the rising curve of environmental concerns. In contrast with goals advocated by environmental groups, the NAFTA provisions appear "mild in terms of obligations on Mexico, and vague in terms of substance" (Uimonen and Whalley 1992, 113). In recent years Mexico has unilaterally raised its standards and will probably continue to do so. The NAFTA attempts to ensure that existing standards are maintained, but the NAFTA does not contain provisions to upgrade the enforcement of existing standards or to adopt enhanced standards.

Mexican Unilateral Actions

Under President Salinas, Mexico has constructed a solid legal framework for protecting the environment.[23] All new investments must be accompanied by filing of an environmental impact assessment and meet from the outset Mexico's recently strengthened environmental standards. But Mexico's strong legislation has not yet been complemented by equally strong enforcement, directed both at individual industrial plants and at common municipal services.

Much has been done to correct the pollution created by individual plants. The number of Mexican environmental inspectors was increased from 109 in 1991 to more than 300 in 1992, including 200 inspectors operating in Mexico's border areas. As of August 1992, over 200 plants in the US-Mexico border region had been shut by Mexican officials for noncompliance with Mexican environmental laws. These efforts will be

---

22. For a good legal summary of the NAFTA accomplishments on the environment, see McKenna & Cuneo (1992).

23. US environmental groups acknowledge that Mexico has strong environmental laws. Justin Ward of the Natural Resources Defense Council recently testified that, "Mexico has made important strides in development of strong environmental laws and regulations . . . we are impressed by their rapid progress in crafting a legal and institutional framework for pollution control and natural resource protection." However, Ward emphasized the enforcement lapses that have plagued Mexico's environmental laws, including weak environmental impact assessment requirements for private and public developments. He also cited key areas, such as the lack of community "right-to-know" provisions for toxic releases, in which the scope of Mexican environmental law is more limited than requirements in the United States (Justin Ward, testimony before the Subcommittee on International Trade, Committee on Finance, US Senate, 16 September 1992).

strengthened by a recently approved $50 million World Bank loan to modernize and decentralize SEDESOL, the Mexican environmental authority.[24]

More difficult to solve are environmental problems associated with inadequate municipal services: contaminated drinking water, unauthorized hazardous waste dumps, poor sewage treatment, polluted rivers, and bad air quality. Over the last four years, President Salinas has increased the country's environmental budget sevenfold; in 1992 Mexico will spend 1 percent of its GDP on the environment, an unusually high figure for a developing country (*Journal of Commerce*, 24 August 1992, 8A).[25] But after decades of neglect, Mexico's environmental problems are deep-rooted and will require sustained long-term attention.

Bush Administration Actions

In its May 1991 Action Plan, the Bush administration promised to address environmental issues both in the NAFTA text and through bilateral and trilateral cooperative efforts.[26] When the NAFTA text was released, the administration argued that it had met its commitment to address environmental concerns through three mechanisms: explicit NAFTA provisions, the Integrated Environmental Plan for the Mexican-US Border Area (the "Border Plan"), and additional bilateral and trilateral arrangements, including a newly established North American Environmental Commission.

Explicit NAFTA Provisions

The NAFTA explicitly addresses environmental issues in four chapters: sanitary and phytosanitary measures (S&P, chapter 7b), standards-related measures (chapter 9), investment (chapter 11), and dispute settlement (chapter 20).[27] Much of the language in these chapters relating to the environment is either new to trade agreements or clarifies ambiguous

---

24. SEDESOL is the Secretariat of Social Development, which includes the former environmental agency SEDUE. SEDESOL has an enforcement budget of roughly $68 million for 1992, up from $4 million in 1989.

25. An increasing percentage of Mexico's environmental budget is being designated for enforcement purposes.

26. Soon after the administration released its Action Plan, the House of Representatives passed the Gephardt-Rostenkowski resolution (H.Res. 146), which bound the administration to meet its outlined commitments regarding labor, environmental, and health concerns in the NAFTA talks.

27. In addition, the preamble commits the three countries to "promote sustainable development" and to "strengthen the development and enforcement of environmental laws and regulations."

provisions in GATT articles and codes (and in the Uruguay Round draft text). The new and stronger language underpins the claim, often voiced by Ambassador Carla Hills, that the NAFTA is the "greenest" trade agreement ever negotiated.

In the S&P and standards chapters, the NAFTA meets our recommendation to maintain existing federal and subfederal health, safety, and environmental standards. These chapters permit a country to ban all nonconforming imports, so long as the country's standards are nondiscriminatory, are "based on data or information derived using scientific methods,"[28] and respect both the national treatment and MFN principles. The NAFTA states that the parties may enact standards stricter than those at the international level (Article 905.3).[29] While the text does not explicitly ensure that subfederal governments can also enact standards stricter than the international norm, Article 902 states: "Each Party shall seek . . . to ensure observance of Articles 904 through 908 by provincial or state governments . . ." This language would seem to permit subfederal governments to enact standards that are stricter than international ones if stricter measures are otherwise permitted by national law.

Some critics view parts of the NAFTA text as hostile to environmental measures. David Wirth, for example, points to Article 712.1, which establishes the right of NAFTA parties to take measures "for the protection of human, animal, or plant life," provided that the measures are applied "only to the extent necessary to achieve the appropriate level of protection, taking into account technical and economic feasibility" (David Wirth, Assistant Professor of Law at Washington and Lee University, statement before the House Committee on Science, Space, and Technology, 30 September 1992).[30] Wirth is troubled by the phrase "to the extent necessary" because this phrase has been interpreted in similar

---

28. The reference to scientific methods (Article 724) hardly provides a touchstone for quick and easy resolution of disputes. Scientists often disagree on the harm associated with a given chemical or environmental change. And it is a value judgment, not a scientific judgment, whether a risk of one in a million (or one in 10 million) is "acceptable." The NAFTA parties are required to "take into account" the risk assessment techniques devised by international organizations, but that requirement still allows considerable scope for judgment.

29. By contrast, critics of the Uruguay Round draft text on S&P contend that it might establish international (primarily, Codex) standards as a "ceiling" on national S&P standards. In addition, the current Uruguay Round text has been criticized for its requirement that domestic S&P standards exceeding international norms must be supported by "scientific justification" and not be "maintained against available scientific evidence" (Mark Silbergeld, "NAFTA Food Safety Measures," Consumers Union internal memo, 15 September 1992).

30. It should be noted that the language "to the extent necessary" does not appear in the standards chapter; in that chapter the touchstones are scientifically based principles and nondiscrimination.

contexts by GATT panels to require, variously, a "least GATT-inconsistent" or "least trade-restrictive" environmental measure.

The GATT tests are designed to prevent environmental measures from becoming a new handmaiden of protection. However, in our opinion, the NAFTA could go part way toward recognizing Wirth's concerns without opening the door to trade protection masquerading as environmental protection. A suggestion offered by Justin Ward of the Natural Resources Defense Council points to a possible middle ground: a country's environmental measures should be sustained by a dispute panel, even if they are not in a theoretical sense the "least trade-restrictive," if no less trade-restrictive measure is both equally available and equally effective (Justin Ward, "NAFTA Assessment," memorandum to the authors, 4 November 1992).[31] In addition, the scope of potential controversy would be substantially narrowed if existing federal and subfederal regulations were exempt from the "least trade-restrictive" test.

Probably the biggest gap in the S&P and standards chapters is that they do not explicitly address process standards. In some cases, no traces of the production process show up in the exported product. Nevertheless, for example, an agricultural product may be grown in a way that destroys an underground aquifer or ruins a nearby wetland through the use of DDT. But nothing in the standards or S&P chapters would address that possibility.

In our view, some attention to process standards should properly be a major objective of the Environmental Protection Commission that Clinton called for in his campaign speech on NAFTA. But it is still an open question whether Clinton's proposed supplemental agreement on the environment should only address those processes that affect the global commons (such as taking dolphins from the sea) or spill effluents that cross international boundaries (such as pollution of the Rio Grande); processes that have irreversible effects but are contained within national borders (such as clearing a tropical forest); or processes that have strictly local and reversible effects (such as the emission of particulates into the atmosphere).[32] As discussed later, we think that the reach of NAFTA into process standards should reflect both the nature of the process and the extent of its economic impact.

The NAFTA dispute settlement procedures are environmentally friendly in various ways. First, to promote cooperation and harmonization, the agreement establishes a Committee on Sanitary and Phytosanitary Measures and a Committee on Standards-Related Measures. Both commit-

---

31. Consideration should also be given to cost: the hypothetical alternative should be preferred if it is less costly than the measure under dispute; if it is substantially more costly, it should not be regarded as a reasonable alternative.

32. This trichotomy was suggested by William Cline, Institute for International Economics, 24 November 1992.

tees are supposed to play a role in dispute resolution proceedings. Second, the S&P subchapter explicitly places the burden of proof on the party that challenges an environmental measure.[33] Third, the dispute settlement chapter gives the complaining party the right to have a dispute resolved either through the NAFTA dispute mechanism or through the GATT.[34] To the extent that NAFTA environmental standards are higher than the GATT standards, the complaining party will thereby have a better chance of achieving its objectives.[35]

The investment chapter permits each country to impose environmental requirements on inward foreign investment, so long as those requirements also apply to domestic investment. Critics of the NAFTA, particularly organized labor, have long claimed that the agreement will encourage US and Canadian companies to move south to take advantage of Mexico's weaker environmental standards.[36] Responding to this fear of "runaway plants," the investment chapter states: "The Parties recognize that it is inappropriate to encourage investment by relaxing domestic health, safety, or environmental measures" (Article 1114.2).

This language has a "green" character. Nevertheless, for a complaining NAFTA partner to prevail in a dispute, it would probably have to demonstrate that the other partner intends to encourage investment by its environmental measures. Intent is always hard to prove, and the offending country could almost always cite some other reason for altering its standards. Critics are therefore not satisfied with the language in the investment chapter. Further, they point out that if a country discovers one of its NAFTA partners relaxing its standards or enforcement measures, the concerned country can take no action to remedy the situation other than consultations. In this important respect, the agreement falls short of our recommendations.

Environmentalists argue that the NAFTA should explicitly state that lax environmental regulations or enforcement practices constitute unfair trade practices, which in turn should permit a partner country to apply trade remedies. Without such enforcement powers, environmentalists claim, the call in the NAFTA preamble to "strengthen the development and enforcement of environmental laws and regulations" will have little practical meaning. Ambassador Carla Hills, by contrast, has argued that

33. Under Article 723.6, "a Party asserting that a S&P measure of another Party is inconsistent with [the agreement] shall have the burden of establishing such inconsistency."

34. While parties are free to make the initial choice of forum—GATT or NAFTA—once dispute settlement procedures are initiated in one forum, they cannot be switched to another (NAFTA Article 2005).

35. However, since NAFTA does not cover process issues, cases in that realm would presumably go to the GATT (Charnovitz 1992a, 335–56; 1992b).

36. These criticisms were reiterated by Ross Perot, especially in the third presidential debate, held 19 October 1992.

there is no legitimate basis for concern that Canada or Mexico will lower standards to attract investment (Testimony before the US Senate Finance Committee, 8 September 1992). However, while NAFTA states that a party cannot relax its standards, the issue of better enforcement is not explicitly addressed.

In our view, the fear of runaway plants attracted by lax environmental standards or enforcement has been exaggerated. First, with rising per capita incomes, Mexican citizens will exhibit even stronger demands for a cleaner environment (The World Bank, *World Development Report 1992*, 36–41). Most Mexicans need no convincing that lax enforcement of environmental regulations is a bad idea. Second, as the Mexican political system becomes more open, these demands will be felt by Mexican leaders. Third, for the vast majority of US and Canadian companies, the cost of moving to Mexico could not be justified by the savings obtained from lax enforcement of environmental standards.[37]

Even though the runaway plant may be a problem of minor rather than major economic proportions, it plays a very large role in the US public's acceptance of free trade with a poorer country. Thus, it is a matter of concern that the agreement falls short of providing an explicit plan for the parties to raise their standards (including their enforcement efforts).

We recommend that the parties undertake negotiations to elevate, to the highest common denominator, those standards or enforcement practices that have a measurable effect on trade patterns. This should be a task for Clinton's Environmental Protection Commission (discussed below). If, after an appropriate period of consultation and negotiations, a country failed to enforce its own minimum standards, or if the countries could not agree on common NAFTA standards, the issue would be handed over to dispute settlement proceedings. As an ultimate sanction, after allowing a reasonable period for voluntary implementation of the recommendations, a second international panel could authorize a low-rate "green fee" on all the respondent nation's exports to the other NAFTA countries. The "green fee" (unlike countervailing duties) would not be imposed unilaterally and would not be specific to a particular product. Again (unlike countervailing duties), the fee would not be retained by the importing country. Instead, the funds generated would be either be paid to a binational institution (the NAFTA Fund in the

---

37. For most US industries, pollution abatement costs represent a small share of total production costs: 86 percent of US industries have abatement costs under 3 percent of total costs (World Bank, *World Development Report 1992*, 128). Companies for which the benefits of lax environmental standards substantially outweigh the costs of moving presumably were attracted to Mexico long before the NAFTA negotiations began. However, by eliminating tariffs on shipments to the United States, the NAFTA might attract additional companies seeking refuge from pollution standards.

case of US-Mexico trade) or to Canada (in the case of Canadian exports).[38] The green fee would thus discourage bad environmental practices and provide a funding source for better practices.[39] But the green fee would not become a mechanism for interrupting trade flows in particular products, and thus it should not become a lightning rod for protectionist initiatives.

The Border Plan

The Bush administration's second mechanism to address environmental concerns was the Integrated Environmental Plan for the Mexican-US Border Area (the "Border Plan"). The Border Plan, released in February 1992, commits the United States and Mexico to pursue specific objectives: strengthen the enforcement of existing environmental laws; reduce pollution through joint initiatives; expand planning, training, and education programs; and improve mutual understanding of environmental conditions along the border.

The Border Plan is an important first step in binational cooperation to address serious pollution along the 2,000-mile border. Critics of the Border Plan claim that it is vague, without formal links to the NAFTA. We do not think that formal links to the NAFTA are essential—after all, the United States and Mexico have negotiated many agreements that are not formally tied to the NAFTA text.[40] But we do think that the criticism of vagueness has merit. The Border Plan does not commit the parties to specific projects, and it lacks a long-term funding strategy.

Mexico promised $460 million for the Border Plan over the next three years. The Bush administration committed $379 million to the plan over the next two years, with $241 million allocated for 1993 (US Trade Representative 1992b, 14). However, the US funds have not been appropriated by Congress: in political terms, border environmental projects must compete with equally worthy projects elsewhere in the country, including a backlog of $80 billion of unfunded sewage treatment plants (*Journal of Commerce*, 24 August 1992, 8A).

Even assuming that Congress appropriates the full $379 million for the border, notwithstanding competing demands, our rough reckoning suggests that this amount falls far short of the resources required. We recommend that the United States budget at least $5 billion over the

---

38. The NAFTA Fund is explained in this chapter's subsequent section on financing the NAFTA.

39. To the extent that green fees, or other NAFTA Fund monies, are used to improve environmental practices, those uses should not be regarded as a countervailable subsidy under the laws of the NAFTA partners.

40. The recently signed (but not yet ratified) US-Mexico Income Tax Treaty is a case in point.

next five years to clean up and improve the sewage, water, and air basin condition in the border region.

In any event, opponents of the NAFTA believe that neither the Mexican nor the US governments will meet their environmental commitments once the agreement is ratified and political leverage is thus lost. The worsening problem of hazardous waste illustrates their concern. The Texas Water Commission (the state's primary environmental enforcement agency) has an annual budget of only $250,000 to cover an enforcement region of 8,800 square miles. Yet this commission must confront a large number of truckers that haul hazardous waste from the United States into Mexico for cheap and illegal disposal. A contributing factor is that many maquiladoras in Mexico do not follow prescribed rules for shipping hazardous waste back to the United States for legitimate disposal. The reason is cost: disposing of the hazardous waste legitimately can cost as much as $1,000 per barrel for some substances (*Wall Street Journal*, 10 November 1992, A1).[41]

In the case of hazardous waste, one possible solution is to set up a system of licensed and regulated hazardous waste disposal companies. In a given region, all factories would have to register with the licensed company. The licensed company would charge a lump-sum fee (set according to regulations) for each factory based on the projected amount and type of hazardous waste that it will generate (the fee would be periodically renegotiated to reflect actual waste generation). The disposal firm would then collect and dispose of the hazardous waste and in general serve the role of hazardous waste policeman in the region.[42]

The practical political question ahead is how to devise and implement such solutions, now that the NAFTA negotiations are completed. According to the Bush administration, the United States and Mexico "have developed one of the world's most comprehensive bilateral relationships in the area of environmental protection" (USTR 1992, 14). Despite myriad joint initiatives the two countries have undertaken to reduce border pollution and to address problems in the interior of Mexico, environmental groups are not convinced that these mechanisms will adequately deal with the environmental issues facing North America.

In response to this criticism, in September 1992 the three countries agreed to establish a North American Environmental Commission to promote long-term cooperation on improving the environment.[43] Ac-

---

41. One study found that only 33 out of 600 maquiladoras had registered to transport their hazardous waste back into the United States.

42. The regulatory body (for example, a committee of EPA and SEDESOL) would monitor the performance of the licensed company. The advantage of this approach over disposal by a government agency is that it minimizes bureaucratic cost and obstacles and provides funding outside the public budget process.

43. When the administration announced that it would establish the North American En-

cording to Ambassador Carla Hills, the commission will have three purposes: to provide a forum to discuss environmental issues of concern to
the three environmental ministers, to support cooperation on environmental matters and solutions to environmental problems, and to help
coordinate environmental expertise and information. In concept, the
mandate of the Environmental Commission was basically limited to common problems with a direct connection to NAFTA.

Clinton's Plan

In October 1992 Governor Clinton delivered a major speech in which
he endorsed the NAFTA and said he would not renegotiate the pact if
elected president (Clinton 1992). He would, however, negotiate three
supplementary agreements, one of which would create a trilateral Environmental Protection Commission, to be headed by Vice President
Gore.

In many ways, Clinton's Environmental Protection Commission is a
"bigger and better" version of the North American Environmental Commission proposed by President Bush in September 1992. Clinton's Environmental Protection Commission essentially gives more funding and
more enforcement power to the Bush administration's commission. According to Clinton, his commission would have "substantial powers and
resources to prevent and clean up water pollution" and would "encourage the enforcement of the country's own environmental laws through
education, training, and commitment of resources, and provide a forum
to hear complaints." Furthermore, the commission would have the "power
to provide remedies, including money damages, and the legal power to
stop pollution" (Clinton 1992, 14).

Details of the Clinton Environmental Protection Commission remain
to be drafted. Several bilateral commissions already deal with transboundary water-quality issues and other problems (for example, the
Canada-US International Joint Commission). Presumably, the Clinton
Environmental Protection Commission will coordinate these existing
bodies, as well as taking on new tasks. Beyond that obvious mandate,
Clinton, Salinas, and Mulroney must make a strategic decision of how
environmental convergence is to be sought:[44]

- through rhetorical complaints directed by each country against the
  other, with very little action (the situation with Canadian complaints
  about acid rain from US power stations until the late 1980s);

---

vironmental Commission, the National Wildlife Federation (the nation's largest conservation organization) endorsed the environmental provisions of the NAFTA, the first major
environmental group to do so.

44. This trichotomy was suggested by David Leyton-Brown in private remarks to the
authors, 17 December 1992.

- through enforcement actions against each other, by way of trade reprisals (as with US actions under the Marine Mammal Protection Act against imports of tuna from Mexico);

- through joint design of environmental product and process standards, initially with cooperation at the federal level and later with cooperation at the state and provincial levels.

While all three approaches are likely to be used, in our view, the sooner that emphasis is placed on joint design of product and process standards, the better. Toward this end, the new commission should sponsor broad assessments of environmental conditions in each country. The assessments would examine, for example, air basins, hazardous waste dumps, sewage treatment, forest practices, and similar problems. The assessments should be updated regularly to determine the extent to which the parties have achieved the environmental objectives of the NAFTA. Qualified experts should make these assessments on the basis of public hearings, available data, and field inspections. Where necessary, the commission would have the power to compel firms and municipalities to open their doors and books to provide evidence. The assessments should be published, on the theory that sunshine is the best disinfectant.

Second, the commission should perform a detailed and open evaluation of the means by which citizens and public interest groups can use legal and administrative processes to compel state and federal governments to enforce standards that have been legally established. This investigation should address both the problem of excessive litigation as well as the problem of inadequate legal remedies. It should examine the workings of judicial mechanisms, including the questions of standing, injunctive relief, and penalties for environmental abuse. For the foreseeable future, the commission should confine itself to suggesting, rather than prescribing, changes in national legal systems.

Third, the commission should establish a procedure to encourage the upward harmonization of environmental standards and enforcement, especially in the area of process standards (such as aquifer pollution).[45] Processes that abuse the global commons or the transboundary environment should be the subject of upward harmonization within the NAFTA, regardless of any trade effects.[46] In addition, process standards with a measurable trade effect should be subject to review, as discussed earlier, with the possibility of upward harmonization. At a later stage,

---

45. A timetable for upward harmonization of standards is suggested on page 152 of our 1992 book.

46. Processes that abuse the global commons will, of course, be discussed in multilateral forums as well as in the NAFTA. When progress is being made multilaterally, the NAFTA partners would normally recess their own talks.

say in 10 years, processes with an irreversible environmental impact, but an impact contained economically and physically within national borders, might also be the subject of upward harmonization within the NAFTA.

The fourth point deals with sanctions. In the vast majority of cases, commission review alone should lead to better process standards. In a few cases, additional sanctions may be required to redress trade distortions created by lax standards or enforcement. Our preferred sanction, mentioned earlier, is a system of "green fees" applied to all exports from any NAFTA country that, after a period of consultation, does not raise its environmental standards or enforcement rigor to the level recommended by an international panel. The green fees would be assessed by a second international panel only upon application by one of the NAFTA countries, and only upon clear and convincing evidence that the recommended higher standards are necessary to fulfill the objectives of the NAFTA.[47] Once assessed, the green fees would be remitted to the NAFTA Fund in the case of fees levied against US or Mexican exports, or to Canada in the case of Canadian exports.

Finally, the commission should seek wider implementation of the "polluter pays" principle. This principle was long ago endorsed by OECD nations, but it remains to be implemented in a wide range of activities, from industrial air emissions to household sewer connections (Rich 1992, 45). Implementation of the "polluter pays" principle should be the main way in which NAFTA countries correct industrial and municipal processes that have local and reversible pollution effects.

---

47. Petitioning nongovernmental organizations, such as the National Wildlife Federation, would present initial complaints to their home governments rather than to the commission. The home government would then decide which issues to bring to the commission.

4. Dispute Settlement

The NAFTA augments the highly successful dispute settlement provisions in chapters 18 and 19 of the Canada-US FTA. As we recommended, the NAFTA extends the FTA dispute settlement system to Mexico in return for trade law revisions that will align Mexican administrative practices more closely to US-Canadian norms.

Dispute Settlement Under NAFTA

The general NAFTA dispute settlement mechanism in chapter 20 parallels that of chapter 18 of the Canada-US FTA, with minor revisions in the procedures for selecting panelists to judge disputes (Article 2011).[48] Following the precedent of the Canada-US FTA, the NAFTA establishes a trilateral Trade Commission, comprising cabinet-level representatives from each of the three countries, to administer the agreement and to adjudicate disputes over the interpretation or application of NAFTA rules (Article 2001).

More importantly, the NAFTA extends to Mexico the innovative procedures of FTA chapter 19 for resolving disputes involving final determinations in antidumping and countervailing duty cases. As in the FTA, panel decisions effectively substitute for judicial review and are binding on the respective governments (Article 1904). This mechanism will continue to be an important check on the improper application of antidumping and countervailing laws but will not impede their use against unfairly traded goods.

Like their FTA predecessors, the NAFTA negotiators were unable to traverse the mine-field of trade law reform. In most respects, the negotiators deferred to efforts in the Uruguay Round that to date have achieved worthwhile improvements in the existing GATT code on subsidies but only modest changes in the antidumping code.

However, the three countries did commit to consider reform of subsidy and antidumping practices in future work of the NAFTA Trade Commission. In particular, they agreed to consult on subsidy rules and to consider a potential alternative "system of rules for dealing with unfair transborder pricing practices and government subsidization" (Article 1907:2); they commissioned a working group to study the relationship of trade and competition policies and to recommend further work in this area (i.e., with a view toward merging the antidumping laws with the general competition laws; Article 1504); and they agreed to consult on third-country dumping issues (Article 317). Moreover, unlike the FTA, the NAFTA establishes chapter 19 as a permanent process rather than

---

48. The NAFTA also contains specific dispute settlement procedures for cases involving investment (see chapter 11, section B) and financial services.

as a temporary process pending the negotiation of new subsidy, countervail and antidumping rules. In addition, the NAFTA does not include specific provisions that allow a partner country to withdraw from the NAFTA if new trade rules are not negotiated within a fixed period of time.[49]

During the negotiations, questions were raised as to whether the Mexican legal system could accommodate the FTA procedures and provide sufficient basis for the review of final determinations by Mexican officials. We believe these concerns have been assuaged by Mexico's commitment in the NAFTA to overhaul its trade laws and procedures. In particular, Mexico has agreed to undertake significant legal and judicial reforms to provide due process guarantees and effective judicial review for disputing parties. These reforms should create greater transparency in the application and administration of Mexican trade laws and enable Mexico to follow the administrative practices and procedures that were already established for chapter 19 panels under the Canada-US FTA. Indeed, Mexico is now preparing a series of constitutional amendments that will codify the reforms required by the NAFTA accord (*Journal of Commerce*, 21 September 1992, 4A).

The NAFTA also includes new provisions to ensure that a country complies with panel procedures. Special committees will be established to review allegations that a country has impeded the establishment, operation, or implementation of panel decisions. These special committees will have the power to grant the complaining country the right to deny the other country's right to invoke chapter 19 panels, or to otherwise suspend equivalent trade benefits, if the offending party fails to follow binding panel decisions.

Special provisions have also been added to the NAFTA for disputes involving environmental and health and safety issues (Article 2005:3 and 2005:4). The new procedures place the burden of proof in these cases on the complainant and allow panels to draw on scientific and environmental experts.

In addition, the NAFTA clarifies the question of the forum in which a dispute can be brought. To address the concerns of environmental and other groups, the NAFTA affords the complaining party the option to bring the dispute before a panel under the GATT or the NAFTA. However, once a forum is chosen, the case cannot be switched to the other body (Article 2005:6).

Finally, the NAFTA strengthens the existing extraordinary-challenge procedures of the FTA and should thus assuage concerns that NAFTA procedures circumvent judicial review of such cases.[50] The provisions

---

49. However, the final provisions allow a country to withdraw for any reason six months after notification is given to the other countries.

50. The National Council for Industrial Defense and the American Engineering Association

in NAFTA expand the scope for disputants to challenge panel rulings, lengthen the period of review of disputed decisions, and require that panels be "comprised of judges or former judges of a federal court of the United States or a judicial court of superior jurisdiction of Canada, or a Federal Judicial Court of Mexico" (Annex 1904.13).

Evaluation

The dispute settlement provisions represent one of the most noteworthy accomplishments of the NAFTA negotiations. In return for significant reform of its judicial and administrative practices in the application of its trade laws, Mexico gains full rights under the innovative dispute mechanism for reviewing antidumping and countervailing duty cases. In addition, the NAFTA fine-tunes the FTA by adopting compliance provisions to insure that the panel procedures are not impeded, and by strengthening the extraordinary challenge process.

---

filed suit in August 1992 challenging the constitutionality of the arbitration process of the FTA. The suit charges that chapter 19, which provides that disputes be settled by a binding panel of five Canadian and US lawyers, is an unconstitutional surrender of the judicial authority of US courts (*Journal of Commerce*, 20 August 1992, 1A).

5. Financing the NAFTA

The debate over NAFTA exposed important shortcomings in national programs for labor adjustment, public investment in infrastructure, and environmental control. While many of the problems predate NAFTA and range far beyond its scope, the agreement provided a political target for addressing long-neglected issues.

As we noted in our analysis of labor, environmental, and transportation issues, new programs will require substantial resources over the next 5 to 10 years. We estimate total needs at about $8 billion. Financing such programs raises important policy issues: Should funding come from existing resources within the budget, or should new taxes be levied? Should funds be appropriated in advance for these programs (a rare procedure), or should NAFTA funding be subject to the hazards of the annual budget cycle?

House Majority Leader Richard Gephardt, in a July 1992 speech, proposed an earmarked transactions tax as a means of funding labor, environment, and other programs necessitated by the NAFTA (speech on NAFTA at the Institute for International Economics, 27 July 1992, 5). In his remarks, Gephardt noted that the European Community spends over $20 billion annually to address its own regional adjustment needs. He stressed that, unless funds are found to deal with the problems created in the wake of expanded North American commerce, the idea of freer trade would be discredited.

The issue of financing the NAFTA raises three interrelated sets of questions: the scope of needs, the ways and means of funding, and the institutional structure for allocating money.

Scope of Needs

Within Europe, structural adjustment funds are used both to upgrade infrastructure in the poorest EC member states (notably, Ireland, Portugal, and Greece) and to address the problems of numerous designated districts spread throughout Europe (including rich countries such as Germany and France) with particularly high rates of unemployment. The underlying concept is to spark the creation of jobs (and preferably high-paying jobs) in distressed areas.

Nothing like the European approach in terms of scale or purpose seems remotely plausible in the North American context. Indeed, the question of public finance for the NAFTA barely surfaced in either the Canadian or Mexican debates prior to the NAFTA's signing. Canada already has an extensive range of worker adjustment and environmental programs. Mexico did not want to overload the negotiations by raising issues that seemed to call for fiscal transfers in its direction. However, in December 1992 Salinas announced that he would ask the incoming

Clinton administration for a special economic support fund (*The Wall Street Journal*, 8 December 1992, A11). This suggestion may have been intended as a counterproposal to Clinton's call for a supplementary environmental agreement.

These considerations suggest that the scope of NAFTA financing voted by the US Congress should be confined to three purposes:[51]

- worker adjustment for US employees identifiably dislocated by larger imports from other NAFTA partners;

- environmental cleanup in the US-Mexican border area, especially municipal services affecting air and water quality;

- transportation infrastructure at the US-Mexico border—especially bridges, roads, and customs facilities.

In an important sense, the US presidential campaign debate substantially reduced the scope of NAFTA-specific financing requirements. Both Bush and Clinton advocated economywide retraining programs to address the needs of dislocated workers. A broad approach should fold the comparatively small labor dislocation caused by NAFTA (under 150,000 workers over five years) into the much larger retraining needs facing the US economy.[52] Our expectation and recommendation is that President Clinton will devise a retraining program that is widely available to American workers, whether the precise cause of dislocation is the Clean Air Act, defense conversion, the NAFTA, the Uruguay Round, new technology, or some other event. But it seems unlikely that the new retraining program will be in place by 1 January 1994, when the NAFTA is scheduled to go into effect.

Moreover, we must anticipate the possibility that budget realities foreclose an economywide training program, just as they did in the Carter and Ford administrations. Hence, we strongly recommend a targeted program for NAFTA adjustment, budgeted at $1.67 billion over five years (as in the Bush proposal). NAFTA Adjustment Assistance should be authorized annually by Congress and expended upon speedy certification by the US International Trade Commission that a particular group of workers is entitled to adjustment assistance. Once an economywide program is enacted, the NAFTA program should be folded into the broader approach.

---

51. The Mexican Congress would, of course, want to consider its own programs to deal with worker dislocation, and in our proposals (sketched out later), Mexico would contribute an equal amount to environmental cleanup and transportation infrastructure.

52. The 1990 Displaced Workers Survey (Podgursky 1992, 19) found that 8.9 million US workers had been displaced between 1985 and 1990 (they lost their jobs because of a plant closing, because the employer went out of business, or because they were laid off and not later recalled).

With this qualification, the scope of NAFTA financing should be limited to US-Mexico environmental and infrastructure needs within a zone extending roughly 100 kilometers on either side of the border, and, for a temporary period (until economywide retraining is in place) to US labor adjustment resulting from NAFTA dislocation.

Ways and Means

In his speech, Majority Leader Gephardt suggested that NAFTA financing should be provided by an earmarked transaction tax, but he gave no specifics as to its base or rate. We agree on the need for dedicated financing (more on that subject later), but we are opposed to a new transactions tax, for two reasons.

First, a new transactions tax would strike against the conceptual foundation of the NAFTA—namely, North American trade without barriers, so that trade between Texas and Chihuahua is just as free as trade between Texas and California. Second, it would erode the attractions of NAFTA for significant US industries, particularly autos and electronics. In 1989, out of total US imports from Mexico of $26.6 billion, imports under the Generalized System of Preferences (GSP) amounted to $2.5 billion (these imports were tariff-free), while imports under the Harmonized Tariff Schedule (HTS 9802.00.60 and 9802.00.80) reached $11.9 billion. (These HTS imports, closely linked to the maquiladora program, paid an effective tariff of only 1.8 percent.) A transactions tax that included GSP and HTS products would inevitably impose a higher tax on shipments that are now virtually tariff-free.

In our opinion, the place to start is not with an earmarked tax, nor with a predesignated list of projects.[53] The place to start is with a fixed sum of money, the NAFTA Fund, to be spent over five years on infrastructure and environmental projects within the border zone. We suggest a sum of $3.0 billion, half to be contributed by the United States and half by Mexico. Each country would pledge to commit annual installments of $300 million to the NAFTA Fund, starting in 1994. On this schedule, full payment would be completed by January 1999. Depending on the success of the NAFTA Fund in meeting its goals, it might then be replenished by future governments.

According to our rough-and-ready estimates, border environmental programs could cost $5 billion over five years while border infrastructure could cost $2 billion.[54] For reasons spelled out below, the size of the

---

53. An attempt to designate worthy projects in the implementing legislation would invite serious delay, since any list of legislatively approved projects would require complicated logrolling within and between the US Congress and the Mexican Congress. Moreover, the best projects might not get priority funding under this sort of process.

54. See the sections on environment and transportation in this assessment.

NAFTA Fund is deliberately designed to be less than our estimate of the total cost of worthy projects.

The amount of money we contemplate for the NAFTA Fund does not, by itself, require either Mexico or the United States to enact a new tax. However, we would be sympathetic to the idea of appropriating $300 million annually out of existing tariff revenues derived from US-Mexico trade to the NAFTA Fund.[55] Once the first US appropriation was made, others would follow more easily, since the expenditure would have entered the budget base. On the US side, an alternative would be to request an appropriation of the entire $1.5 billion, available until expanded. If successful, this would ensure that all funds are available, but it would engender substantially greater congressional opposition at the outset. Hence, we prefer the risks of an annual appropriation.[56]

In addition to its NAFTA Fund contribution, the United States would need to budget about $335 million annually for NAFTA Adjustment Assistance—the precise amount would depend on the extent of labor dislocation caused by NAFTA—until an economywide training program is enacted.

We recognize that annual appropriations, cosmetically linked to existing tariff revenues, do not answer the persistent US problem of finding ways to close the budget deficit. In our view, that problem must be answered squarely and on a much larger scale than the NAFTA Fund or NAFTA Adjustment Assistance. However, we acknowledge that the creation of the NAFTA Fund and the provision of NAFTA Adjustment Assistance may, for example, require an additional 0.2 percentage point increase in the corporate income tax.[57]

Institutional Structure

We suggest the creation of a joint US-Mexican Commission to administer the NAFTA Fund. The commission would have six members, three appointed by each country, with a rotating chairman. Four affirmative

---

55. As a rough estimate, in 1990 US-Mexico trade generated tariff revenues of about $4.0 billion, approximately $1.0 billion on US imports from Mexico, and $3.0 billion on Mexican imports from the United States. These magnitudes are large enough so that, even with the tariff phaseout schedule in the NAFTA, each country can safely earmark $300 million a year of its tariff revenue over the next five years to underwrite the NAFTA Fund.

56. Some observers note the tardy US record in paying United Nations dues, which are now far in arrears. We think the more timely (though far from perfect) US record in paying its contributions to the World Bank and the Inter-American Development Bank provides a better precedent. We would expect NAFTA Fund appropriations to receive even faster congressional approval than appropriations for the multilateral development banks.

57. To be clear, we are not suggesting the enactment of a special increment to the corporate income tax to finance the NAFTA Fund. We are simply acknowledging that, as part of a larger revenue package, money must be found.

votes would be required to approve any project financed by the Fund. The commission would be backed up by a small staff with financial, engineering, and environmental expertise. The commission's task would not be to originate proposals but to pass judgment on proposals submitted and sponsored by other bodies: municipalities, states, or federal agencies.

The projects submitted would need to be fully staffed out by the sponsoring agency, and cofinancing of at least 50 percent should be required. Preference should be given to environmental and infrastructure projects that promise to generate a future stream of revenues for the sponsoring agency by way of tolls or user fees. In this manner, the NAFTA Fund would leverage its resources and point the way to self-funding of services in the border zone.

We recognize that establishing a NAFTA Fund does not guarantee success. Much would depend on the quality of the commission and the projects submitted by public agencies and private firms. If the commission does not support exemplary projects, its resources should not be replenished in 1999. If the commission succeeds, it could set useful precedents for fiscal cooperation within North America.

5

Implications for Nonmember Countries

The final issue that deserves mention is how NAFTA fits into the international trade relations of the three member countries. A number of countries, particularly those in Latin America, the Caribbean, and East Asia, are concerned that the NAFTA marks a drift away from the GATT multilateral trading system and threatens to divert trade and investment away from their firms. Those concerns can be expressed more specifically in terms of four questions: Is the NAFTA consistent with GATT obligations? Will it on balance be trade creating or diverting? Will the NAFTA be open to new members? Will it foster regionalism at the expense of the multilateral trading system?

Overall, we hold to our earlier conclusions that the NAFTA complements the GATT process, and that the scope of potential trade diversion is quite limited (Hufbauer and Schott 1992a, chapter 2). However, the NAFTA accession clause falls short of our recommendations in terms of clarity of purpose and procedure, and it will need supplementary guidance from the NAFTA Free Trade Commission (established in Article 2001) if it is to be of use to aspiring new members.

NAFTA and GATT Obligations

In our view, the NAFTA is consistent with the letter of the GATT obligations of the member countries, even though certain provisions (e.g., sector-specific rules of origin) seemingly run counter to the spirit of the GATT. GATT requirements are not difficult to meet and are open to flexible interpretation. GATT Article XXIV authorizes derogations from the most-favored-nation (MFN) obligation of Article I for FTAs and customs unions that meet two vague requirements: the accord must cover "substantially all" the trade among the partner countries, and the accord should not raise barriers to the trade of third countries. No agreement has ever failed these tests![1] Further, it must be stressed that the GATT tests do not refer or correspond to Jacob Viner's famous dichotomy between trade creation and trade diversion.

The NAFTA arguably meets the explicit GATT tests better than almost any other trade pact that has been notified to the GATT under Article XXIV. Nonetheless, like almost every other trade pact notified under Article XXIV, certain provisions will be questioned: likely candidates are industry-specific rules of origin and the dispute settlement procedures. As a result, the NAFTA is unlikely to be deemed fully consistent with the GATT. Instead, the NAFTA will probably be consigned to GATT limbo, in which the pact is neither approved nor disapproved and in which other GATT members reserve their rights to contest the agreement at some future date if their GATT rights are impaired by NAFTA preferences (Schott 1989, chapter 1).[2]

Why have GATT appraisals of prior FTAs been so ambiguous? In essence, the conclusions of GATT working parties that review Article XXIV notifications reflect a recognition that the GATT standards ignore practices that can have adverse effects on third-country trade. For example, Article XXIV skirts around problems caused by gray-area measures such as voluntary export restraints, contingent protection measures (antidumping and countervailing duties), and rules of origin. These measures may significantly distort trade and investment flows between the region and third countries, and thus third countries are reluctant to give pacts that include such measures unqualified approval.

Efforts to bolster Article XXIV requirements in the Uruguay Round and make them more specific and operational have produced feeble results. The proliferation of preferential trading arrangements in Europe, North America, and Latin America underscores an urgent need to do better and makes it increasingly important that GATT obligations under Article XXIV and GATT reviews of FTAs and customs unions be strengthened.

The first step should be to institute rigorous and continuous multilateral monitoring of all preferential trading arrangements—not just in North America, but also in the European Economic Area, the FTA be-

---

1. At the same time, few accords have been deemed to be fully consistent with the GATT.

2. The Canada-US FTA was a stellar example of a pact that met the letter of GATT tests, yet was denied the GATT seal of approval due to concerns about the pact's dispute settlement mechanism and loopholes in the FTA coverage of agricultural trade barriers.

tween members of the Association of Southeast Asian Nations, and perhaps other evolving partnerships (e.g., Asia Pacific Economic Cooperation, or APEC) in East Asia as well. The means to do so already exist. The GATT's new Trade Policy Review Mechanism could be used both to analyze the schedule of trade liberalization and the trade rules of each prospective agreement, guarding against opaque protectionism hidden in the woodwork, and to monitor the implementation of the final agreement to ensure that it does not adversely affect the trading interests of third countries. Regional partners should welcome increased GATT surveillance of preferential trade pacts because such surveillance would provide external pressure for partners to keep faith with liberalization undertaken within the region. Other GATT members should demand it to ensure the consistency of these arrangements with the spirit as well as the letter of GATT obligations.

We believe that the NAFTA members should be model GATT citizens in this regard. To promote the strengthening of GATT disciplines under Article XXIV and to assuage foreign concerns about potential adverse trade effects resulting from the NAFTA preferences, each NAFTA country should volunteer to allow GATT panels to review biennially the trade effects generated by NAFTA provisions and, where net trade diversion has occurred in particular sectors, to recommend compensatory measures. To the extent that the NAFTA, through internal liberalization, on balance diverts trade in a given sector from the baseline that would otherwise have been reached, and by more than *de minimis* amounts, trade compensation should be paid. Such a commitment would provide concrete evidence that the NAFTA members regard the NAFTA as complementary to their GATT obligations.

Is the NAFTA Trade Diverting?

As is evident from the preceding sections of this assessment, we believe there are only a few areas where the accord is likely to make a significant difference in existing opportunities for nonmember countries to trade in the North American market. In many areas, the NAFTA merely codifies the preferences already accorded to Mexican firms in the US market. The NAFTA is likely to cause some trade diversion in particular sectors. However, the positive income effects of the NAFTA, particularly on the Mexican economy, should increase overall import demand in the NAFTA region. On balance, we believe, the trade created by growth in the NAFTA region should more than offset the trade diverted in particular sectors. Nevertheless, as we suggested above, where there is significant diversion in individual sectors, the NAFTA members should offer trade compensation under GATT auspices.

It is important to emphasize that the NAFTA is designed to make it harder for foreign firms to compete in the North American market—not because of higher barriers against third-country trade, but because of the heightened competitiveness of North American firms. Nonetheless, the scope for trade diversion is limited because of the relatively unfettered access that Mexico already enjoys in the US market. Thus, we would expect little change from what otherwise would have occurred in the absence of the NAFTA in terms of foreign access to the US market (which represents 85 percent of regional output).

A further constraint on trade diversion results from the internal pressures within the NAFTA region to reduce MFN tariff rates down to the level of the low-tariff country to avoid potential investment diversion within the region. This concern led, for example, to the commitment in the NAFTA to harmonize computer tariffs in the three countries at the low US level. Subsequently, Canadian apparel producers requested tariff cuts on imported fabrics in order to maintain competitiveness against Mexican and other suppliers to the NAFTA market (*Inside US Trade*, 14 August 1992, 4).

One final point: the sectors in which the potential for trade diversion is the greatest (e.g., textiles and apparel, autos and parts, and agriculture) are likely to be subject to extensive liberalization in the Uruguay Round. In the event the Uruguay Round fails, however, concerns about trade diversion as the agreement is implemented would become more prominent. Such a situation would reinforce the case for *ex post* monitoring and review of the trade effects of the NAFTA and other preferential trading pacts.

Accession Clause

To avoid the evolution of a patchwork quilt of bilateral FTAs between individual NAFTA members and third countries, we recommended that the NAFTA include an accession clause based on GATT procedures and (for pragmatic political reasons) limited to countries in the Western Hemisphere. The NAFTA does include a vague accession clause, similar in wording to GATT provisions but without the GATT's procedural underpinnings, that is open to all countries.[3]

As negotiated, the NAFTA provision suffers from several flaws. First, several of the industry-specific provisions of the pact (e.g., auto and

---

3. The NAFTA provision states that "[a]ny country or group of countries may accede to this Agreement subject to such terms and conditions as may be agreed between such country or countries and the Commission and following approval in accordance with the applicable approval procedures in each country." In addition, like GATT Article XXXV, the NAFTA contains a "nonapplication" provision that allows existing members to deny new members at the time of their accession the benefits of the NAFTA in their markets without blackballing the candidate country or countries entirely from the club.

textiles origin rules) were designed without reference to their possible extension to additional countries. Second, the three countries did not spell out either the application procedures or the criteria that new members would have to meet to join the club. In addition, each country remains free to form its own network of FTAs with other countries that do not wish to join NAFTA or are blackballed from NAFTA membership.

As crafted, the accession clause has several interesting features. It requires unanimous approval of prospective new members by all the existing members (i.e., a one-country veto). Moreover, the accession negotiations will be conducted by the NAFTA Free Trade Commission (comprising all existing members), which presumably will act by consensus. However, as noted above, the NAFTA Free Trade Commission will need to decide how to deal with requests to join the club.

Finally, and in contrast to our recommendation, the accession clause does not include geographic limitations, primarily to forestall accusations that NAFTA was seeking to build a hemispheric "fortress." In principle, accession is open to all countries; in practice, the need for President Clinton to obtain new *bilateral* fast-track authority from the Congress before negotiating new FTAs will likely delay consideration of new NAFTA members in the near future.[4]

How the NAFTA, once implemented, responds to potential requests from middle-level trading powers (e.g., Singapore, Australia–New Zealand) is unclear.[5] Much will depend on whether US fast-track authority is renewed for the negotiation of bilateral and regional FTAs, and on whether the candidate country prefers to negotiate separately with the United States or with the NAFTA members as a whole.[6]

We still believe that enlargement of the NAFTA should proceed in measured steps, starting with countries in the Western Hemisphere under the framework of the Enterprise for the Americas Initiative (EAI). The negotiation of FTAs between the United States and other countries would be an ambitious undertaking—both politically and in terms of additional adjustment in the US economy—and would distract attention from multilateral negotiations. However, if the GATT talks falter, the

---

4. The Congress may be amenable to limited fast-track authority for an FTA with Chile but will be reticent to provide the president authority to negotiate FTAs with powerful competitors, thus limiting the prospects for large East Asian nations to join the NAFTA for at least the next few years.

5. The ambitious campaign proposal by President Bush to negotiate FTAs with countries in Eastern Europe and the ASEAN garnered little political support and is unlikely to be revived by the Clinton administration.

6. These issues raise questions that go well beyond the scope of this monograph; we will address them in our forthcoming analysis, *Prospects for Western Hemisphere Economic Integration*.

NAFTA members would then need to broaden their horizons, looking both South and West—perhaps coupling the EAI with a Pacific Basin initiative.

Drifting Toward Regionalism?

The successful conclusion of the NAFTA stands in sharp contrast to the oft-postponed and still unresolved Uruguay Round of multilateral trade negotiations. The juxtaposition of these talks, coupled with the growth of regionalism in Europe, has raised red flags in many countries that are concerned about a drift away from multilateralism by the world's trading powers.[7]

We do not regard the NAFTA as a shift in US policy away from its central focus on multilateralism. Indeed, as the economies of North America restructure and grow in response to domestic economic reforms and NAFTA commitments, a successful outcome in the GATT talks will become even more important, for one simple reason: the NAFTA will make North American firms more competitive in world markets and thus better able to take advantage of the increased trade opportunities created by the prospective Uruguay Round reforms. The objectives of the NAFTA and the Uruguay Round are thus complementary and mutually reinforcing.

One should see the NAFTA (and other regional initiatives such as the Enterprise for the Americas Initiative) as an integral part of a national competitiveness strategy, one that complements domestic economic reforms designed to improve productivity and promote the ability of local industries to compete more effectively against foreign suppliers at home and in world markets. The competitiveness rationale is important both for the United States, whose trade with Pacific Basin countries is greater than with its NAFTA partners,[8] and for Canada and Mexico, whose trade is primarily with the United States, because of the importance of the efficiency gains cited in chapter 2.

With a successful Uruguay Round, the NAFTA should continue to be outward-oriented. But if the Uruguay Round breaks down, the complementary relationship of multilateral and regional initiatives could be at risk. Although the GATT rules and obligations would still apply, confidence in using the multilateral process to resolve trade problems would ebb and would be hard to reverse, particularly among the major trading

---

7. Reactions have ranged from the constructive approach of the Cairns Group and APEC countries to build global coalitions in support of the GATT talks, to the xenophobic response of Malaysia, which initially called for a closed East Asian Economic Group.

8. Canada and Mexico combined account for about 26 percent of total US trade, while the Pacific Basin and Western Europe represent 35 percent and 24 percent, respectively.

powers that have the clout to pursue unilateral and bilateral remedies. In the absence of strong multilateral trade discipline, the temptation to discriminate against third countries will be strong. The fear of just such a result has already spawned regional initiatives in East Asia, which fears that access to its main markets in North America and Europe could be eroded by regional preferences and a spate of new contingent protection measures.

While the failure of the Uruguay Round would be a serious blow to world trade, we do not take an apocalyptic view of the ensuing developments. Instead, we would foresee a renewed interest in building a Pacific Basin trading arrangement—drawing on the nascent efforts of the APEC initiative—that would seek to replicate and perhaps extend GATT disciplines for regional trade. Such an outcome makes sense, considering that the Pacific Basin region already accounts for more than one-third of US trade and a substantial share of the trade of East Asian countries.

Failure of the Uruguay Round could thus result in the movement toward two competing trading blocs, pitting an expanding European Community against a looser Pacific Basin group of North American and East Asian countries. Both regions would be worse off than under a scenario of a successful Uruguay Round; but nonmember developing countries would be the hardest hit since they benefit most from GATT efforts to open markets on a global basis.

Appendix
AN EVALUATION OF THE NAFTA

MARKET ACCESS: Energy

RECOMMENDATIONS:

Investment

1. Focus on investment issues with a view to higher Mexican production. Mexico requires $20 billion in investment just through 1995 to meet domestic demand (increasing at 5% a year) and to keep exports constant at 1.3 million barrels a day.

2. Liberalize foreign investment restrictions in Mexico. Take a results-oriented rather than a rules-oriented approach. Mexico's constitution should not be amended, but it should be interpreted in a pro–free enterprise manner.

3. Restructure Pemex into three separate companies that operate as semiprivate firms. Permit foreign participation in the exploration and development of hard-to-access energy resources.

4. Permit foreign companies to invest in the Mexican petrochemical industry.

Trade

1. Simplify the regulatory patchwork that constrains electricity and natural gas trade between the US and Mexico.

2. Apply the US-Canada FTA qualifying tests on energy trade restrictions to Mexico. The FTA limits energy trade restrictions to special circumstances: to protect national security, to conserve exhaustible natural resources, to deal with a short-supply situation, or to implement a price stabilization plan. The FTA also requires that the burden of restrictions be shared between domestic and foreign consumers (except to protect national security).

NAFTA RESULTS:

Investment

1. Mexico will maintain most of its historic restrictions on foreign investment and private participation in the primary petroleum industry. The NAFTA does not ensure foreign investment in oil exploration, production, or refining; it does not provide for risk-sharing contracts; and it does not permit US and Canadian firms to enter Mexico's retail gasoline market.

2. Mexico will substantially lift investment restrictions on 14 of the 19 basic petrochemicals and entirely on 66 secondary petrochemicals.

3. Foreign investors may acquire, establish, and operate electric-generating facilities in Mexico for self-generation, cogeneration, and independent power production.

4. Mexico will immediately permit US and Canadian firms to own 100% of new coal mines and facilities but will continue for three years to limit US and Canadian ownership of existing mines and facilities to 49%.

Tariff/Nontariff Barriers

1. About half of all tariffs on oil and gas field equipment will be immediately reduced to zero. The other half will be phased out over 5 to 10 years.

2. US suppliers of natural gas and electricity can negotiate directly with Mexican firms but must contract through Pemex or CFE (the State Electricity Commission)—giving Pemex and CFE blocking or delaying powers.

3. Mexico will eliminate its 10% tariff on coal immediately and will guarantee national treatment to coal imported from the US or Canada.

Procurement and Contracts

1. Mexico will open Pemex and CFE procurement contracts to 50% foreign participation immediately, to 70% by year eight, and to 100% foreign participation by year 10. The provisions are modeled after the GATT Procurement Code. Pemex contracts are worth $5.5 billion a year, and CFE contracts are worth $3.0 billion a year.

2. Mexico will allow "performance contracts" under which US and Canadian oil and gas field service companies operating in Mexico can be paid a bonus for exceeding contract targets.

Energy Trade Restrictions

1. Mexico's ability to restrict energy trade is not limited to the specific circumstances set out in the US-Canada FTA, and Mexico did not commit to supply energy to the US or Canada during an energy emergency. Mexico did agree to abide by GATT standards when intervening in international trade; it has been exempted from GATT disciplines on energy trade under its protocol of accession to the GATT.

SCORE: BEATS, MEETS, OR FALLS SHORT

Beats

1. Opens Pemex and CFE procurement contracts.

Meets

√ 1. Allows foreign investment in the production of petrochemicals.

2. Although not part of the NAFTA text, Pemex is organizing itself into four separate companies.

3. Liberalizes trade in natural gas and electricity.

4. Liberalizes investment in electricity.

Falls Short

√ 1. Does not adequately liberalize Mexico's restrictions on foreign investment. Pemex retains a monopoly on oil exploration and development, and on gasoline and fuel oil sales.

2. Foreign suppliers must contract their natural gas and electricity sales through Pemex or CFE.

√ 3. The US-Canada FTA limits on energy trade restrictions will not apply to Mexico.

Note: A check mark (√) in the "Beats, Meets, or Falls Short" sections denotes points of particular economic significance that weighed most heavily in the authors' assignment of grades for the results of the NAFTA in specific areas.

MARKET ACCESS: Automotive Goods

RECOMMENDATIONS:

Tariff/Nontariff Barriers

1. Eliminate immediately all tariffs on auto and auto parts trade. Do not use a two-tier tariff or NTB system to discriminate between established and new firms.
2. Negotiate a common external tariff within 10 years.
3. Phase out Canadian and Mexican domestic-content requirements on a straight-line schedule over 10 years (the Mexican content requirement is 36%; the Canadian content requirement has not been binding for a decade). Phase out Mexico's trade balancing (or export performance) requirements over five years ($2 of exported autos and parts are now required for every $1 of new autos imported into Mexico). Phase out the Mexican quota on imports of new autos. Phase out the Mexican and Canadian bans on used-car imports.
4. Replace the foregoing Mexican NTBs and the Canadian content requirement with a single one-for-one production-to-sales ratio test (as in Canada) and then phase out the production-to-sales ratio tests in both Canada and Mexico over 10 years.

Rules of Origin

1. Keep the rule of origin at its current figure of 50% of North American factory cost to qualify for NAFTA benefits. Introduce a new overlay test to prevent "roll-up" abuses.
2. Apply the agreed rule of origin equally to all firms; do not use rules of origin to discriminate between established and new firms.

US CAFE Rules

1. Designate Mexican and Canadian production as either "domestic" or "foreign," at the option of the producer, for the purpose of meeting Corporate Average Fuel Efficiency rules.

Japanese transplants

1. Allow auto parts purchased by Japanese transplant firms in fulfillment of the "best-efforts" commitments made to the US in January 1992 to be sourced anywhere in North America.

NAFTA RESULTS:

Tariff/Nontariff Barriers

1. **Vehicle Tariffs:** All duties on North American vehicles are phased out over 10 years. Mexico will reduce its tariff on autos from 20% to 10% immediately, and then to zero over 10 years. Mexico will immediately cut its tariff on light trucks in half, and then phase out the remaining tariff over five years. Until 1999, Mexico will allow manufacturers to import heavy trucks equal to 50% of what they produced in Mexico that year; thereafter, import restrictions on new trucks will be lifted. The US will immediately eliminate its tariff on autos imported from Mexico, reduce its tariff on light trucks from 25% to 10%, and phase out the remaining tariff over five years.
2. **Parts Tariffs:** Each country will immediately eliminate its tariffs on certain automotive parts and will phase out duties on most other parts over five years (Mexico will eliminate tariffs on 75% of US and Canadian parts in five years). A small number of tariff lines will be phased out over 10 years.
3. **Domestic-Content Requirement:** Mexico will slightly lower its domestic-content requirement to 34% over five years, to 29% over the next five years, and to zero after 10 years. However, established manufacturers may use as their required percentage level the percentage of domestic content they achieved in model year 1992. For all manufacturers except one, this level is less than 34%. In addition, Mexican national parts suppliers are guaranteed a declining percentage of any growth in the Mexican auto market during the transition period (starting at 65% and declining to 50%). To be defined as a "Mexican national supplier," firms must source at least 20% of raw materials from Mexico, which should include independent maquiladoras.
4. **Trade Balancing Requirement:** Mexico will immediately reduce its trade balancing requirement from $2 of auto and parts exports for every dollar's worth of imported cars to

80 cents, gradually down to 55 cents in 2003, and then eliminate the requirement in January 2004. Established manufacturers can access trade balance "credits" earned prior to model year 1991 to import up to $150 million worth of automotive goods annually until the surplus has been exhausted. In 10 years, Mexico will eliminate the requirement that manufacturers produce in Mexico in order to sell in Mexico.

5. **Import Quotas:** Mexico will immediately lift its quota (15% of the market) on new auto imports. A transitional system of quotas for trucks and buses will apply for five years.

6. **Used-Car Imports:** Beginning 15 years after the NAFTA goes into effect, Mexico will phase out its ban on imports of North American used vehicles over the succeeding 10 years. Canada will phase out its prohibition on imports of Mexican vehicles over the same period.

Rules of Origin

1. To qualify for duty-free treatment, automotive goods must contain a specified percentage of North American content based on a net-cost formula (certain sales-related expenses are excluded in the net-cost calculation). For vehicles, engines, and transmissions, the percentage is 50% for the first four years of the agreement, 56% for the second four years, and 62.5% after eight years. New plants that produce a model not yet made in North America can operate for five years under the 50% rule but must meet the 62.5% rule in the sixth year. For other auto parts, the flat percentage is 60%. Cars produced by the General Motors–Suzuki joint venture in Canada (the CAMI plant) may use Japanese engines and still qualify for NAFTA benefits.

2. The new method for calculating regional content "traces" the value of foreign components, replacing the US-Canada FTA "roll-up" method (which counts a part as 100% regional if its domestic value exceeds 50%).

US CAFE Rules

1. Vehicle manufacturers may choose to have Mexican-produced parts and vehicles they export to the US classified as domestic. After 10 years, Mexican exports to the US will receive the same treatment as US or Canadian production for CAFE purposes.

SCORE: BEATS, MEETS, OR FALLS SHORT

Beats

√ 1. Mexico will eliminate immediately its quota on imports of new vehicles.

Meets

√ 1. Tariff reduction and rules of origin generally will not be applied on a discriminatory two-tier basis.

√ 2. Mexico will phase out its domestic-content requirement over 10 years.

3. "Roll up" abuse is addressed by the new tracing test.

4. The US will modify its CAFE rules so that for the first 10 years vehicle manufacturers can choose to have Mexican-produced parts and vehicles classified as domestic.

Falls Short

1. Does not immediately eliminate all tariffs on the automotive sector.

√ 2. Does not include plans to negotiate a common external tariff.

3. Retains for 10 years Mexico's requirement that manufacturers produce in Mexico in order to sell in Mexico.

4. Allows Mexican and Canadian prohibitions on used-vehicle imports to remain for 25 years after the agreement takes effect.

5. Does not consolidate the various Mexican (and Canadian) NTBs into a single test (our suggestion: a production-to-sales ratio test) and then phase out that test.

√ 6. Embraces a restrictive rule of origin: the ultimate figure will be 62.5%, compared with the current FTA figure of 50%.

MARKET ACCESS: Textiles and Apparel

RECOMMENDATIONS:

Tariff/Nontariff Barriers

1. Phase out tariffs over 10 years. Apply a special quota regime to Mexico based on a guaranteed access level (GAL) concept (distinct from the levels set by MFA quotas). Barring a finding of "market disruption," the GAL quotas should be adjusted upward upon request.

Rules of Origin

1. Rules of origin should not be stricter than those in the US-Canada FTA. Basically, the US-Canada rules call for a double transformation (e.g., from fabric to cut and sewn garment parts) in order for the imported component (in this case, fabric) to qualify for North American tariff and quota benefits.

Safeguards

1. Special safeguard measures should be available during the transition period. At the end of the transition period, all quotas and tariffs should be eliminated, and GATT safeguards procedures should apply.

Caribbean Basin Initiative (CBI)

1. NAFTA benefits should not be extended to CBI countries until they join NAFTA.

NAFTA RESULTS

Tariff/Nontariff Barriers

1. The partners will eliminate tariffs immediately, or phase them out over a maximum of 10 years, on textiles and apparel that meet the strict NAFTA rules of origin.

2. For trade between the US and Mexico, tariffs covering about $250 million of US exports to Mexico will be eliminated immediately. Tariffs covering about $700 million of US exports to Mexico will be phased out over six years (these tariffs will be cut immediately by their face level, e.g. a 20% tariff will be cut immediately to 16%, and the remaining tariff will be phased out in equal amounts over six years).

3. The US will immediately lift import quotas on goods produced in Mexico that qualify under the rules of origin and will phase out import quotas on Mexican textiles and apparel that do not qualify. The NAFTA countries may not impose new quotas, except under the safeguard provisions.

4. For US-Canada trade, tariffs will be phased out by 1999 at the pace established under the US-Canada FTA. Canada apparel exporters will receive a slightly larger quota in the US market that will allow duty-free entry for goods that do not meet the NAFTA content requirements.

Rules of Origin

1. To qualify for NAFTA preferential treatment, textiles and apparel must be produced from yarn spun in North America or from fabric made from North American fibers (the "yarn forward" and "fiber forward" rules). Apparel made from certain imported fabrics that are in short supply in North America, such as silks and linens, can also qualify for preferential treatment.

2. Yarns, fabrics, and apparel that are made in North America but do not meet the rules of origin still can qualify for preferential treatment up to specified import levels ("tariff preference levels," or TPLs). The three countries have established a process to permit annual adjustments in TPLs.

3. The TPLs for Canada set out in the Canada-US FTA have been increased and will grow annually for at least the next five years.

4. The partners will review the textile and apparel rules of origin prior to January 1, 1998. Meanwhile, they will consult on whether different rules of origin should apply to specific goods.

MARKET ACCESS: Textiles and Apparel *(continued)*

Safeguards
1. During the transition period a partner that faces "serious damage" as a result of increased imports from another NAFTA country may increase tariffs or, with the exception of Canada-US trade, impose quotas to provide temporary relief to that industry. However, for goods that meet NAFTA's rules of origin, safeguard measures can only take the form of tariff increases. Safeguard actions may not last longer than three years and may not be imposed on a particular product more than once during the transition period. Once a safeguard action is lifted, the product will be subject to the tariff that would have been in effect one year after the action was imposed.

SCORE: BEATS, MEETS, OR FALLS SHORT

Beats
√ 1. Immediately eliminates import quotas on Mexican textiles and apparel that meet the strict NAFTA rules of origin.

Meets
√ 1. All tariffs on textile and apparel trade will be eliminated within 10 years. Most US-Mexico textile trade will be tariff-free in six years, and the rest in 10 years.
√ 2. Quotas on Mexican goods that do not qualify for preferential treatment will be phased out within 10 years.
3. Special safeguard measures will apply, but only during the transition period.
4. The NAFTA benefits will not be extended automatically to the CBI countries.

Falls Short
√ 1. The "yarn forward" and "fiber forward" rules of origin (a triple transformation test) are much stricter than those in the US-Canada FTA. However, certain goods that do not meet the rules of origin will still receive preferential duty treatment through TPLs.

Third-Country Concerns
1. The NAFTA textile and apparel trade chapter is far more liberal than US rules on imports under the CBI. This could prompt a significant diversion of investment and trade from the Caribbean Basin to Mexico.
2. Free regional trade in textiles and apparel could cause the NAFTA countries (especially the US) to adopt a go-slow approach to reform of the MFA in the Uruguay Round.

MARKET ACCESS: Agriculture

RECOMMENDATIONS:

Tariff/Nontariff Barriers

1. Link Mexican liberalization of field crops to US and Canadian liberalization of horticulture; allow a 15-year transition period to implement free trade.
2. Following the Uruguay Round reforms, remove all remaining tariff and nontariff barriers to wheat trade over five years.
3. Cut Mexican tariffs on meat products to zero in five years. Exempt Mexico from US Meat Import Law quotas; eliminate the Mexican tax on beef exports. Update Mexican health and safety procedures so that they do not act as nontariff barriers. Create better facilities for inland and border inspections.
4. Remove Mexico's licensing requirements for poultry imports in exchange for US approval of Mexican poultry exports from disease-free zones.
5. Withdraw US and Mexican participation in the International Coffee Organization (ICO). Eliminate Mexico's domestic price-support program for coffee and allow coffee imports.
6. Defer liberalization of sugar quotas within NAFTA until a liberal global sugar bargain has been struck in the Uruguay Round.
7. Further liberalize US-Canada farm trade and resolve the dispute over Canadian grain export subsidies.

NAFTA RESULTS:

The NAFTA has separate bilateral agreements for agricultural products: one for Mexico and the US and one for Mexico and Canada. The rules of the US-Canada FTA will apply to US-Canada trade.

Mexico-US Trade

1. Both countries will immediately eliminate all nontariff barriers by converting them into regular tariffs or tariff-rate quotas (TRQs). Mexico will lift all farm import licenses (which covered 25% of US agricultural exports in 1991). The US will exempt Mexico from its Section 22 rules, which impose quotas on peanut, cotton, dairy, and sugar imports in times of import surges.
2. Tariffs will be eliminated immediately on 57% of the value of US-Mexico agricultural trade ($3.1 billion). Tariffs on 94% of bilateral farm trade will be eliminated within 10 years, and the remaining 6% (highly sensitive products) will be eliminated after 15 years (these totals include goods subject to TRQs).
3. The TRQ quantities eligible for duty-free treatment will be based on recent average trade levels and will grow at 3% or 5% per year. The over-quota duty, which will equal the tariff equivalent of existing nontariff barriers, will be phased out over a period of 10 to 15 years. For example, Mexico will import, duty-free, a quota of 2.5 million metric tons of corn in the first year, growing by 3% a year over the next 15 years. Tariffs on corn imports above the quota will start at 215% and will be phased out over the next 15 years.
4. Restrictions on sugar trade will be largely eliminated in 15 years. Over the first six years, the US over-quota tariff will be reduced by 15 percent of its base level; starting in year 7, the remaining tariff surcharge will be phased out linearly through year 15. If Mexico becomes a net sugar exporter on a global basis, the quota will increase to the amount by which Mexico is a net exporter up to 25,000 metric tons during the first six years, and 150,000 MT starting in year 7 (and then increased annually by 10 percent through year 15).
5. The partners will take into account the interests of other NAFTA parties and consult with them prior to providing export subsidies for agricultural goods. The parties will establish a Working Group on Agricultural Subsidies that will work toward eliminating all agricultural export subsidies among the partners.

6. The NAFTA provides for national treatment regarding classification, grading, and marketing. Mexico and the US will establish a bilateral working group to address quality standards issues.

Mexico-Canada Trade

1. Mexico and Canada will phase out all tariffs over 10 years (over 85% of Canada's agricultural imports from Mexico already enter duty-free). Mexico will continue to apply its MFN tariffs on sugar from Canada (Canada may apply an equal duty on Mexican sugar).
2. Most nontariff barriers on sensitive products remain intact: Canada will maintain its import quotas and Mexico its import licenses on bilateral trade in dairy, poultry, and eggs.

Safeguards

1. Special safeguards in the form of TRQs are allowed during a 10-year phase-out period for a specific group of products for each country. For Mexico, this group includes pork, apples, potatoes, barley, and malt. For the US, the group includes in-season eggplant, watermelons, onions, tomatoes, and squash.
2. The US will apply TRQs over a 15-year phase-out period to orange juice, peanuts, and sugar. Mexico will apply TRQs over a 15-year phase-out period to corn, dried beans, and nonfat dried milk.
3. In the case of serious injury or threat of serious injury, a country may suspend further tariff reduction or snap back to the pre-NAFTA level (for three to four years depending on the product).

SCORE: BEATS, MEETS, OR FALLS SHORT

Beats

√ 1. Tariffs on over half of US-Mexico agricultural trade will be eliminated immediately; the remaining tariffs will be phased out within 15 years.

Meets

√ 1. Loosely links Mexican liberalization of field crops (corn, dry beans, potatoes) to US horticulture liberalization.
√ 2. All nontariff barriers between the US and Mexico are eliminated or converted into regular tariffs or TRQs.
3. Exempts Mexico from the US Meat Import Law.
4. Provides safeguard measures for sensitive products.

Falls Short

1. Mexico and the US did not agree to withdraw their participation from the ICO. Mexico has not agreed to end its price support program for coffee and allow coffee imports.
2. The US and Canada failed to further liberalize bilateral farm trade.
3. Rather than tackling farm export subsidies, the NAFTA created a trilateral working group to address the problem.

Third-Country Concerns

1. Sugar liberalization could hurt non-NAFTA countries. The outcome will depend on the extent of sugar liberalization negotiated in the Uruguay Round.

MARKET ACCESS: Financial Services

RECOMMENDATIONS:

Banking Industry

1. Allow foreign banks to acquire immediately voting minority shares of up to 49% in Mexican institutions and to offer wholesale banking services; after five years, allow foreign banks to acquire controlling stakes.

2. Allow foreign banks to establish branch offices in Mexico within five years and allow Mexican banks similar access to the US. Benefits of Mexican banking reforms should be extended to all foreigners. If and when major US banking reforms are carried out, the US should allow Canadian and Mexican banks to operate anywhere in the US.

Insurance Industry

1. Open the Mexican insurance market immediately to majority foreign ownership of existing Mexican companies and allow free competition via newly minted subsidiaries within five years.

Brokerage Industry

1. Gradually open the Mexican securities industry to match US and Canadian practice. Foreign competition should be phased in in three steps. First, trading in shares of foreign firms should be permitted on the Mexican stock exchange. Second, foreign firms should be permitted to underwrite securities and become members of the Bolsa. Finally, within five years, foreign firms should be allowed to offer their full range of financial services to the Mexican public.

NAFTA RESULTS:

Banking Industry

1. Foreign banks will be allowed a gradual expansion of their share of the Mexican banking market, starting at 8% when the NAFTA enters into force and increasing in equal amounts to 15% as of January 1999. All restrictions will be eliminated by January 2000.

2. Between 2000 and 2004, if US and Canadian banks obtain more than 25% of the market, Mexico can impose a one-time three-year freeze on further acquisitions by US or Canadian firms. No market share caps will be permitted after 2007.

3. An individual cap of 1.5% of the market will apply until January 2000. Once this cap expires, individual foreign banks will not be able to obtain more than 4% of the overall market through acquisition of Mexican banks—which would effectively protect four of the largest Mexican banks from a foreign takeover.

4. The NAFTA allows but does not require a country to permit the establishment of branches. Canada requires establishment in the form of a subsidiary; Mexico has indicated it will do so as well. Glass-Steagall restrictions and interstate branching requirements are maintained for Mexican and Canadian banks in the United States. However, the US is effectively giving Mexico a five-year exemption from the Glass-Steagall divestiture requirement.

5. The three countries will consult on further liberalization of cross-border financial services no later than January 2000.

Insurance Industry

1. US and Canadian insurance companies may not sell cargo, life, health, accident, or travel insurance on a cross-border basis (they can sell these policies only to Mexicans who come to the US or Canada). Only reinsurance providers can solicit business in Mexico.

2. US and Canadian insurance firms with existing joint ventures in Mexico may increase their ownership to 100% by January 1996. No market share cap is applied.

3. New US and Canadian entrants that wish to form a joint venture with an existing Mexican insurance firm will be restricted to 30% ownership initially, rising to 51% by 1998 and

100% by 2000. New entrants will not be subject to aggregate or individual market share limits.

4. New entrants may start their own wholly owned subsidiaries on the date the NAFTA enters into force but will initially be subject to an aggregate market share limit of 6%, increasing to 12% by the beginning of 1999. A 1.5% individual market share cap will apply throughout this period but will be eliminated in January 2000. The largest eight Mexican insurance firms are thus protected from takeover during the transition.

5. Intermediary and auxiliary insurance services companies can establish subsidiaries with no ownership or market share limits when the NAFTA goes into effect.

Brokerage Industry

1. Foreign ownership initially will be limited to 10% of the total market, which will rise to 20% six years after the agreement enters into force, and to 30% over the next four years.

2. An individual market share cap of 4% will apply during the transition period. This cap will be lifted in January 2000 and cannot be reimposed. Thus, Mexican brokerage firms are not protected from foreign takeover.

SCORE: BEATS, MEETS, OR FALLS SHORT

Meets

√ 1. Mexico will phase out restrictions on foreign ownership of and participation in its financial services market.

Falls Short

1. Although Mexico has agreed to phase out restrictions on foreign ownership of financial services, the transition periods are longer than recommended.

2. Majority foreign ownership of existing Mexican insurance firms will not be allowed until 1996, rather than immediately; moreover, the 1996 date only applies to joint-venture firms as of July 1992.

3. The partners are not required to allow branching. Canada and Mexico have indicated they will not permit branching of North American firms into their countries.

4. For insurance and security firms, individual or market caps will apply throughout the transition period, thereby limiting prospective competition. For banks, an individual cap on growth through acquisition will still apply even after the transition period.

MARKET ACCESS: Transportation

Note: The NAFTA book discusses transportation issues but does not make specific recommendations.

NAFTA RESULTS:

Cross-Border Access for Bus and Trucking Services

1. Current laws prevent US truckers from carrying cargo across the border, even though 90% of US-Mexican trade moves by land (Mexican truckers currently are allowed limited access to the US). NAFTA permits US, Mexican, and Canadian trucking companies to carry international cargo to and from the contiguous US and Mexican states by the end of 1995 and to have cross-border access to all the US and Mexico by the end of 1999. Mexican carriers will enjoy sole service to maquiladora operations along the border for the first few years (until access provisions take effect).

2. US and Canadian charter and tour bus operators will have full and immediate access to the Mexican market, and the US will grant equivalent rights to Mexican charter and tour bus operators (Canada already has rights to the US market).

3. Three years after the NAFTA goes into effect, US and Canadian bus firms may begin scheduled cross-border bus service to and from any part of Mexico. The US will provide the same treatment to bus firms from Mexico. Seven years after implementation, the US will allow Mexican bus firms to apply for domestic operating authority.

Investment in Bus and Trucking Services

1. US and Canadian companies may set up international cargo subsidiaries in Mexico three years after implementation. US and Canadian firms may acquire minority ownership of Mexican bus companies and truck companies providing international cargo services by the end of 1995, 51% ownership by 2001, and 100% ownership by 2004. However, Mexican carriers that only carry domestic cargo will be protected from foreign ownership.

Technical and Safety Standards

1. Over a period of six years, the NAFTA partners will seek to harmonize their technical and safety standards with respect to motor carrier and rail operations. A Land Transportation Services Standards Subcommittee will be established to make standards compatible.

2. Nonmedical standards will be compatible 1.5 years after the agreement enters into force, and medical standards will be compatible 2.5 years after entry into force. The NAFTA calls for the study of differing vehicle size and weight standards of US and Mexico truck fleets.

3. Under a memorandum of understanding signed in 1991, the US and Mexico agreed to accept the other's commercial driving licenses beginning in April 1992.

Maritime Services

1. No change in the restrictive cabotage requirements of the US Jones Act and parallel restrictions by Canada and Mexico.

2. The NAFTA liberalizes land-side aspects of port activities. Mexico will immediately allow 100% US and Canadian investment in, and operation of, port facilities such as cranes, piers, terminals and stevedoring companies for enterprises that handle their own cargo. For enterprises handling other companies' cargo, 100% US and Canadian ownership will be allowed after screening by the Mexican Foreign Investment Commission.

Rail Services

1. US and Canadian railroads can continue to market their services directly to Mexican customers; use their own locomotives; construct and own terminals in Mexico; and provide infrastructure financing. Mexico will have full access to the Canadian and US railroad systems.

2. Mexico will retain its constitutional restriction on foreign investment in the state-owned railroad system.

Ocean and Air Transport are exempt from the NAFTA and are addressed under existing bilateral agreements.

SCORE: BEATS, MEETS, OR FALLS SHORT

Note: While the NAFTA book did not make specific recommendations, this scoring follows our general standards.

Beats
√ 1. Permits cross-border access for trucking companies carrying international cargo.

Meets
√ 1. Allows foreign investment in bus and trucking services.
2. Harmonizes some technical and safety standards.

Falls Short
1. Maritime is still a sacred cow.
2. Only a vague promise is made to address the differing vehicle size and weight standards of US and Mexico truck fleets.
3. Lacks adequate provisions to improve infrastructure and border inspection facilities.

MARKET ACCESS: Telecommunications

Note: The NAFTA book does not make specific recommendations for the telecommunications industry.

NAFTA RESULTS:

Tariff/Nontariff Barriers

1. The majority of Mexico's tariff and nontariff barriers on telecommunications equipment will be eliminated immediately, including private branch exchanges, cellular systems, satellite transmission and earth station equipment, and fiber-optic transmission systems. Tariffs on central office switches and certain mobile equipment will be phased out over five years. Mexico's telecommunications equipment market is projected to exceed $1 billion in 1992.

2. The parties agreed to work to the greatest extent practicable to making their respective standards-related measures compatible. The Telecommunications Standards Subcommittee will develop by mid-1994 a work plan for making compatible the standards-related measures for authorized equipment. By 1995, each party shall adopt the necessary provisions to accept the test results from the other NAFTA members.

Access to and Use of Public Networks

1. North American firms will have access to and use of public telecom networks and services on a reasonable, nondiscriminatory, cost-oriented basis to conduct their business. The three countries will allow North American firms to lease private lines; attach terminal or other equipment to public networks; interconnect private circuits to public networks; perform switching, signalling, and processing functions; and use operating protocols of the user's choice. The operation and provision of public networks and services are not covered by the NAFTA.

2. US and Canadian firms may operate private intracorporate communications systems in Mexico and between Mexico and Canada and the United States.

3. The three countries may prohibit noncitizens from holding radio licenses (consistent with the US Communications Act) and may prohibit the use of private lines for the provision of switched services.

Investment

1. Mexico will immediately lift restrictions (currently 49%) on foreign investment in voice-mail and other value-added and information services (except restrictions for videotext and enhanced packet switched data services, which will be lifted by July 1995).

2. Current ownership restrictions for radio and television will be maintained by all three countries.

3. Mexico will not lift its restrictions on investment in the provision of telecommunications transport networks (e.g., basic local and long-distance telephone services).

SCORE: BEATS, MEETS, OR FALLS SHORT:

Note: While the NAFTA book did not make specific recommendations, this scoring follows our general standards.

Meets

√ 1. Eliminates all tariffs on telecommunications equipment within five years.

√ 2. Removes most controls on trade and investment in enhanced or value-added services.

TRADE RULES: Rules of Origin

RECOMMENDATIONS:

Rules

1. Incorporate the existing US-Canada rules of origin into the NAFTA; do not negotiate on a product-by-product basis.
2. Transform existing value-added tests into change-in-tariff-heading tests.
3. Do not use rules of origin to discriminate between new entrants and established firms.
4. Introduce a new overlay test for autos to prevent "roll-up" abuses.

Administration

1. Establish a trinational commission to determine necessary rule changes; for example, when a rule is overly burdensome or invites abuse, or when new tariff headings are required. The commission's recommendations should take effect within 120 days, unless overruled by the Canadian Parliament, the Mexican Congress, or the US Congress.

Maquiladoras

1. Maquiladoras now benefit from the US Harmonized Tariff Schedule (HTS) provisions, which exclude the US portion of the imported good from US tariffs. Continue these HTS benefits until January 1996 (whether or not the final product meets the NAFTA rules of origin). After that, deny HTS benefits to goods that do not meet the NAFTA rules of origin.

Duty Drawback

1. Eliminate duty drawback on all US-Mexico and Canada-Mexico trade by 1996 (duty drawback will be eliminated on all US-Canada trade under the FTA by 1994).

NAFTA RESULTS:

Rules

1. Under the NAFTA, goods qualify for preferential treatment according to the following rules:

■ The goods are wholly obtained or produced in North America;

■ The goods contain nonoriginating materials but are sufficiently transformed in North America so as to undergo a specified change in tariff classification under the HTS;

■ For sensitive sectors, goods must include a specified percentage of North American content, or specified components, in addition to meeting the requirement of a change in tariff classification (e.g., autos, computers, and textiles and apparel);

■ If a good meets the required regional value content test but does not change its tariff classification, it can still receive preferential treatment;

■ Goods that fail to meet a specific rule of origin will be considered North American if the value of non-NAFTA materials constitutes no more than 7% of the price or total cost of the good (the *de minimis* rule).

Calculation Method

1. Producers generally have the option of using either the "transaction-value" or the "net-cost" method to calculate regional content. The transaction-value method is based on the price paid or payable for a good; the net-cost method limits allowable interest and is based on the total cost of the good less the costs of royalties, sales promotion, and packing and shipping. The net-cost method must be used for certain products, such as automotive goods, and where the transaction value is not acceptable under the GATT Customs Valuation Code.

Administration

1. The three countries will establish uniform regulations; a uniform certificate of origin and certification requirements; common recordkeeping requirements; rules for traders and customs authorities to verify the origin of goods; and the right of traders and producers to obtain advance rulings on the origin of goods from the customs authorities.

TRADE RULES: Rules of Origin *(continued)*

Duty drawback

1. Duty drawback programs will end by January 2001 for Mexico-US trade and Canada-Mexico trade. The deadline established in the Canada-US FTA for the elimination of drawback will be extended for two years to 1996. When all duty drawback programs are eliminated, each NAFTA country will adopt a procedure for goods still subject to duties in the free trade area (e.g., because they do not meet the NAFTA rules of origin) to avoid double tariffs.

SCORE: BEATS, MEETS, OR FALLS SHORT

Beats

√ 1. Embraces a more liberal rule of origin for computers. The three countries will harmonize their external tariff within 10 years.

Meets

1. Does not use rules of origin to discriminate between new and established firms.
2. "Roll-up" abuse is addressed by the new tracing test, although this test might make the effective rule of origin for autos greater than 62.5% in some instances.

Falls Short

√ 1. Embraces stricter rules than the US-Canada FTA rules for autos (62.5% rather than 50%) and for textiles and apparel.
2. Does not eliminate value-added tests.
3. Does not eliminate duty drawback on Mexican trade until 2001, five years later than recommended. Extends the US-Canada FTA deadline for two years to 1996.
4. Does not establish a formal council for regular review and revision of rules of origin.

TRADE RULES: Safeguards

RECOMMENDATIONS:

Conditions for Relief

1. Allow customary GATT safeguards and special "snapback" provisions, as in the US-Canada FTA, during the transition period.

2. Create new sectoral safeguard actions for sensitive sectors, e.g., autos, steel, agriculture, and textiles. Grounds for relief under the sectoral safeguards would exist when a partner experiences a "substantial adverse surge" over base-year levels in its North American trade balance in a sensitive sector.

Relief Actions

1. Allow only the affected country's authorities to initiate a sectoral relief action, not individual firms.

2. Designate the preferred remedy as accelerated liberalization in the relevant product sector by the partner experiencing an export surge.

3. If trade barriers need to be raised temporarily, allow only a snapback to prior tariffs (or to the tariff equivalent of prior restraints).

NAFTA RESULTS:

Rules

1. Partners can impose a safeguard action during the transition period of a product if, as a result of the NAFTA, increased imports of that product constitute a "substantial cause or threat" of "serious injury" to a domestic industry. This follows GATT practice.

2. A safeguard action may be taken only once, and for a maximum period of three years (four years for goods in the C + category, if the industry undertakes adjustment). Bilateral safeguard actions may be taken after the transition period only with the consent of the exporting country. These limits narrow the scope of safeguards available under the GATT.

Relief Actions

1. The affected country may suspend further reduction of the good's tariff or reestablish the prior tariff on the good (the tariff may not exceed the pre-NAFTA levels). Once the safeguard action is lifted, the product will be subject to the tariff level that would have prevailed one year after the safeguard was imposed.

2. The partner taking the action must compensate the other country in the form of trade concessions equal to the value of lost trade. If the countries cannot agree on the appropriate compensation, the exporting country may take trade measures of equivalent effect to compensate for the trade effect of the safeguard.

3. When a country takes a safeguard action on a global or multilateral basis, each NAFTA partner must be excluded unless its exports account for a "substantial share of total imports" of the good in question and "contribute importantly" to the serious injury or threat of injury. To account for a "substantial share" of imports, the country must be among the top five suppliers of the good in question.

Additional Safeguards

1. To a large extent, NAFTA safeguards are built into the long transition periods applied to sensitive products.

2. Special safeguards in the form of tariff rate quotas (TRQs) are provided for sensitive agricultural products.

3. A different causation (serious damage or actual threat of serious damage) test will apply to textile and apparel products.

TRADE RULES: Safeguards *(continued)*

SCORE: BEATS, MEETS, OR FALLS SHORT

Beats

1. Limits relief available under safeguard actions more narrowly than relief allowable under the GATT.

Meets

1. Allows customary safeguard actions during the transition period.

Falls Short

√ 1. Does not create special sectoral safeguards, with a preferred remedy of accelerated liberalization.

TRADE RULES: Dumping and Subsidies

RECOMMENDATIONS:

Dispute Resolution Procedure

1. Over the long term, aim to replace antidumping actions on intraregional trade with harmonized competition policies.

2. Extend to Mexico the special dispute resolution rules and binding panel procedures of chapter 19 of the US-Canada FTA (where FTA panels substitute for judicial review of final antidumping and countervailing duty decisions).

Mexico

1. Require Mexico to align its administrative procedures (in terms of open proceedings and written opinions) with US and Canadian norms. Mexico should adhere to the GATT Code on Subsidies and Countervailing Measures.

NAFTA RESULTS:

Dispute Resolution Procedures

1. The NAFTA extends to Mexico the US-Canada FTA chapter 19 procedures by providing for independent binational panels to review final antidumping (AD) and countervailing duty (CVD) determinations made in each country. Panel decisions will be binding.

2. Following a panel decision, either of the countries involved may request a three-person "extraordinary challenge" committee, comprising judges or former judges from those countries. If the committee determines that one of the grounds for the extraordinary challenge has been met, it will establish a new panel to hear the case.

3. A country may request a "special committee" to determine if another country's domestic law has undermined proper functioning of the panel system. If the special committee makes an affirmative ruling and the countries cannot resolve the matter, the complaining country may suspend the chapter 19 panel system with respect to the other country, or suspend equivalent trade benefits.

4. The NAFTA explicitly preserves each country's right to retain its AD/CVD laws. Once the NAFTA takes effect, any amendment a country makes to these laws may be subject to panel review for inconsistency with the object and purpose of the NAFTA, the GATT, or the relevant GATT codes.

5. The parties agreed to consider reform of subsidy and antidumping practices in future work of the NAFTA Trade Commission, and to consider a potential alternative "system of rules for dealing with unfair transborder pricing practices and government subsidization."

Mexico

1. In an annex to the NAFTA, Mexico agreed to undertake legal and judicial reforms to provide full due-process guarantees and effective judicial review of AD/CVD cases to US exporters.

SCORE: BEATS, MEETS, OR FALLS SHORT

Meets

√ 1. Extends the AD/CVD rules and panel procedures of the US-Canada FTA (chapter 19) to Mexico.

2. Commits Mexico to undertake legal and judicial reforms.

Falls Short

1. Does not make the replacement of antidumping actions with harmonized competition policy a specific long-term goal of the NAFTA. Instead, reform of subsidy and antidumping rules is put on a future work agenda with unspecified goals and time limits.

TRADE RULES: Government Procurement

RECOMMENDATIONS:

1. Abolish preferential state, provincial, and parastatal procurement methods.
2. Require Mexico to adhere to the GATT Procurement Code.

NAFTA RESULTS:

1. Modeled after the GATT Procurement Code. Covers procurement by specified federal government departments and agencies and federal government enterprises in each country.

2. For federal departments and agencies, the NAFTA applies to procurement of over $50,000 for goods and services, and over $6.5 million for construction services. For federal enterprises, such as Mexico's oil and electricity monopolies, the NAFTA applies to procurement of over $250,000 for goods and services, and over $8 million for construction services.

3. Each country must give sufficient notice of procurement opportunities to ensure equal competitive conditions for foreign and domestic firms and must set up a bid system to allow suppliers to challenge procedures and awards.

4. Mexico will phase out its procurement restrictions over 10 years. For Pemex, CFE, and construction contracts, 50% of total annual dollar procurement above the NAFTA thresholds will be open to US and Canadian bidders immediately. This percentage will grow to 70% by year 8, and to 100% by year 10. For pharmaceuticals, Mexico will open procurement of patented drugs immediately and nonpatented drugs in eight years.

5. The three countries agreed to hold further talks on opening their respective government procurement markets no later than five years after implementation. The countries also agree to encourage their subnational governments to enter into the obligations of the agreement.

Exceptions

1. This chapter does not apply to the procurement of arms, ammunition, weapons, and other national security procurement.
2. Each country may favor national suppliers for procurements specified in the agreement.
3. All three countries excluded transport services, public utilities, research and development, and basic communications.

SCORE: BEATS, MEETS, OR FALLS SHORT

Meets

√ 1. Mexico will open Pemex and CFE procurement contracts to foreign participation.

Falls Short

1. Does not abolish preferential subnational government procurement methods. Each country reserves the right to favor national suppliers in specific circumstances.
2. Mexico does not commit to adhere to the GATT Code on Procurement.

TRADE RULES: Dispute Settlement

RECOMMENDATIONS:

Dispute Resolution Procedures

1. Model the dispute resolution provisions of the NAFTA after those of the US-Canada FTA (extend the FTA dispute settlement system to Mexico).

2. Require Mexico to align its administrative procedures with US and Canadian norms in terms of open proceedings and written opinions.

Panel Procedure

1. Continue to draw panelists from the disputing parties. If all three countries are involved in a dispute, each should be represented, and the three should then select a fourth as chair.

NAFTA RESULTS:

Dispute Resolution Procedures

1. Extends the dispute settlement provisions of chapters 18 and 19 of the US-Canada FTA to Mexico. Establishes a trilateral North American Free Trade Commission, composed of cabinet-level representatives from each country, to administer the agreement and adjudicate disputes over the interpretation or application of NAFTA rules.

2. The first step in the dispute settlement process is consultation with the other party or parties. If the consultations fail to resolve the matter within 30 to 45 days, any country may call a meeting of the commission, which is to use "good offices, mediation, conciliation, or other means" to resolve the dispute. In the absence of a mutually satisfactory solution, any country may institute panel proceedings. The complaining party may choose to bring the dispute under the GATT or the NAFTA.

Panel Procedure

1. If the case is to be heard through NAFTA procedures, the commission will create a panel of private-sector experts. Panels will be composed of five members, chosen from a trilaterally agreed-upon roster of trade and legal experts, including panelists from countries outside the NAFTA. Each party to the dispute will choose two members from the roster supplied by the other country. The chair of the panel will be chosen by mutual agreement or by drawing lots.

2. The panel will issue its initial report within 90 days of panel selection and its final report 30 days later.

Compliance and Challenge Procedures

1. After receiving the report, the disputing parties are directed to "comply in a timely fashion" with the determination of the panel. Failure by the defending party to comply with a binding panel ruling allows the complaining country to suspend equivalent trade benefits until the dispute is resolved.

2. Once a panel decision has been made, either country may request a three-person extraordinary-challenge committee, composed of judges or former judges from the two countries. If any of the grounds of the extraordinary challenge are met, the panel decision will be overturned, and a new panel will be set up.

Other

1. NAFTA also establishes processes for resolving disputes between investors and host governments and facilitates commercial arbitration of private disputes.

2. Special provisions for disputes involving environmental and health and safety issues place the burden of proof on the complainant and allow panels to draw on scientific and environmental experts.

TRADE RULES: Dispute Settlement *(continued)*

SCORE: BEATS, MEETS, OR FALLS SHORT

Beats

√ 1. Includes new provisions to ensure that a country complies with panel procedures and rulings.

√ 2. Strengthens existing extraordinary-challenge procedures of the US-Canada FTA.

Meets

1. Extends the US-Canada FTA dispute settlement system to Mexico.

√ 2. Requires Mexico to undertake legal and judicial reforms to provide full due-process guarantees and effective judicial review for disputing parties.

3. Panelists will be drawn from the disputing parties and from countries outside NAFTA.

NEW ISSUES: Investment

RECOMMENDATIONS:

Foreign Investment
1. Achieve in Mexico the degree of liberalization achieved in the US-Canada FTA. Specifically, Mexico should give national treatment to foreign investors, phase out export and production-based performance requirements, implement a new tax treaty that limits Mexican tax rates on interest and royalties, and liberalize foreign participation in the energy sector.

NAFTA RESULTS:

Foreign Investment
1. NAFTA investors will receive the more favorable of national or MFN treatment in setting up operations or acquiring firms. Unless they have requested specific exceptions, states, provinces, and local governments must accord national treatment to investors from any NAFTA country.
2. A NAFTA country may not impose new performance requirements, including specified export levels, minimum domestic content, preferences for domestic sourcing, trade balancing, technology transfer, or product mandating. Most existing requirements of this type are phased out over periods up to 10 years. Government procurement, export promotion, and foreign aid activities are exempt from these restrictions.
3. A NAFTA country may not expropriate investments of NAFTA investors except for a public purpose, in which case compensation must be paid to the investor at the fair market value of the investment.
4. Investors have the right to obtain hard currency, which may be freely transferred for profit and capital repatriation.
5. The NAFTA permits each country to require that investors adopt pollution abatement and other environmental technologies.

Exceptions
1. The investment provisions do not apply to Mexico's energy and rail sectors, the United States' airlines and radio communications, or Canada's cultural industries. Also exempt are state or provincial measures notified within two years of entry into force of the pact, government procurement, export promotion, and foreign aid activities.
2. Canada may require technology transfer on an intracorporate basis.
3. Mexico may screen acquisitions with an initial threshold of $25 million, increasing to $150 million after 10 years. Canada will maintain the $150 million threshold as provided in the Canada-US FTA. The US will retain the right to review all foreign takeovers of US companies and block those judged to threaten national security.
4. Mexico retains individual caps for foreign banks beyond the transition period.

US-Mexico Tax Treaty
1. In September 1992 Mexico and the US signed a tax treaty that significantly reduces the withholding rates charged on interest, dividends, and royalties flowing in both directions.

Dispute Settlement
1. A NAFTA investor may seek binding arbitral rulings in an international forum. Remedies for NAFTA violations include monetary damages or return of property. The investor can go to a court in any of the three NAFTA countries for enforcement of arbitral awards.

SCORE: BEATS, MEETS, OR FALLS SHORT

Beats
√ 1. The dispute settlement process allows private investors to seek relief for NAFTA violations in an international forum, rather than relying on their own domestic courts or those of the host country.

NEW ISSUES: Investment *(continued)*

Meets

1. With important exceptions, the NAFTA commits all three countries to provide national treatment to all foreign investors.

√ 2. Mexico will phase out export and production-based performance requirements.

√ 3. The US and Mexico signed a tax treaty that significantly reduces tax rates on interest and royalties.

4. Mexico further opens foreign investment in the production of petrochemicals.

Falls Short

√ 1. Does not adequately liberalize foreign investment and participation in Mexico's energy and rail sectors.

2. Individual caps will apply to US and Canadian banks and brokerage firms investing in Mexico after the transition period.

NEW ISSUES: Intellectual Property

RECOMMENDATIONS:

Intellectual Property Protection

1. Eliminate Canada's compulsory pharmaceutical licensing practices. Future intellectual property disputes should be handled within the NAFTA framework, thus preempting recourse by US firms to section 337 and Special 301 remedies.

2. Lock in recent intellectual property reforms in Mexico. Commit the NAFTA partners to adhere to the prospective GATT accord on intellectual property or undertake equivalent obligations if the GATT talks fail.

3. Mexico should give patent protection to biotechnology and computer program inventions; improve the protection accorded to semiconductor mask works; clarify the protection of trade secrets; and ensure comprehensive protection of all classes of literary works, particularly computer software.

Enforcement Procedures .

1. Include a surveillance mechanism to monitor the patent licensing practices and the enforcement of intellectual property laws, and to ensure compliance with NAFTA obligations.

NAFTA RESULTS:

Copyrights

1. Calls for adherence to the Berne Convention. Provides copyright protection for North American producers in two new areas: computer programs and compilation of individually unprotected material.

2. Gives copyright owners of computer programs and sound recordings the right to prohibit the rental of their products.

3. Establishes a minimum 50-year term for the protection of sound recordings and motion pictures. Because of differences between US and Mexican approaches, the NAFTA does not require national treatment for the performer's right in secondary uses of sound recordings.

4. Canada will retain an exemption for its motion picture, sound recording, and other "cultural" industries. The exemption has been expanded to include copyrights.

5. Does not protect against the parallel importation of copyrighted or patented works.

6. Includes a provision to protect satellite transmissions.

Trademarks, Industrial Designs, and Geographical Indicators

1. Requires companies to register both service marks and trademarks.

2. Initial registration of a trademark is for 10 years, renewable for successive terms of not less than 10 years.

3. Prohibits compulsory licensing or mandatory linking of trademarks.

4. Provides protection for independently created industrial designs that are new or original.

5. Non-NAFTA countries can establish separate bilateral agreements with Mexico and Canada in which geographical appellations preclude or supersede the use of conflicting trademarks.

Patents and Trade Secrets

1. Limits the ability of NAFTA countries to impose compulsory licensing on patent holders. Canada will eliminate its system of compulsory licensing for pharmaceuticals and will abolish retroactively all compulsory licenses issued since December 20, 1991.

2. NAFTA will protect foreign patents for a minimum of 20 years and will provide protection for patents in the approval pipeline.

3. NAFTA countries must provide product and process patents for most types of inventions, including pharmaceuticals and agricultural chemicals. Inventions to protect human, animal,

or plant life are exempt, which means biotechnical inventions and diagnostic, therapeutic, and surgical methods will be excluded from patentability.

4. Provides protection of trade secrets and proprietary information.

5. Provides for at least five years of exclusive use for the owners of proprietary data required by governments for the marketing approval of pharmaceutical and agrichemical products that contain new chemical entities.

SCORE: BEATS, MEETS, OR FALLS SHORT

Meets

√ 1. Canada will eliminate its compulsory licensing practices.

√ 2. Mexico will adhere to the GATT accord on intellectual property. Strengthens Mexico's protection for patents, copyrights, trademarks, and trade secrets.

3. Establishes enforcement procedures.

NEW ISSUES: Environment

RECOMMENDATIONS:

Environmental Standards

1. Maintain and enforce existing standards. Provide a dispute settlement procedure to resolve complaints that internationally recognized standards are being applied in a discriminatory fashion.

2. Allow parties to challenge federal and subfederal standards that come into place after the NAFTA is approved if they act as disguised protection against NAFTA commerce. A NAFTA dispute panel would rule if the standard is discriminatory in its design or application.

3. Provide for the NAFTA countries to harmonize their process standards upward in a staged fashion. For example, in the first three years the parties would commit themselves to strict enforcement of their own standards and would issue an annual trinational report on enforcement practices in each country. Three years after implementation of the agreement, the countries would negotiate to raise to the highest common denominator those standards that are found to cause trade diversion (or attract "runaway plants"). After the three-year transition period, a country that fails to enforce its own standards or the agreed NAFTA standards would be subject to dispute settlement and trade compensation.

The Border Region

1. The US should budget at least $5 billion over the next five years to clean up and improve sewage, water, and air basin conditions in the border region. Such environmental improvement should be funded from general budget resources. Private responsibilities should be addressed by progressive implementation of the polluter-pays principle.

NAFTA RESULTS:

Environmental Standards

1. Maintains existing federal and subfederal health, safety, and environmental standards. Allows a country to prohibit entry of goods that do not meet its standards. Does not explicitly address process standards.

2. Explicitly states that parties, including their subfederal entities, may enact tougher standards. Encourages the NAFTA parties to harmonize their process standards upward.

3. Allows a government to challenge any environmental measure but places the burden of proof on the challenging party. The complaining party may choose to bring the dispute through the NAFTA dispute mechanism rather than through the GATT. However, the NAFTA dispute mechanism can be invoked only where standards covered by the agreement are violated. Each country is responsible for enforcing its own environmental laws.

4. Requires that technical standards have a scientific basis and are applied in a nondiscriminatory manner. The NAFTA closely follows, but improves upon, the proposed standards for industrial and agricultural products negotiated in the Uruguay Round.

5. Permits each country to impose environmental requirements on inward foreign investment, as long as those requirements also apply to domestic investment. States that it is "inappropriate" for countries to relax standards to attract foreign investment but does not provide a mechanism to remedy such a situation if it occurs.

6. Preserves a country's right to enforce international treaty obligations, including limits on trade in products such as endangered species and ozone-depleting substances.

The Border Region

1. The US and Mexico released a Border Plan that commits the two countries to strengthen enforcement of existing environmental laws; reduce pollution through joint initiatives; expand planning, training, and education programs; and improve mutual understanding of environmental problems along the border.

2. The Bush administration proposed spending $379 million on the Border Plan over the next two years. The administration opposed a transaction tax to fund environmental cleanup along the border.

3. Mexico has committed $460 million over three years for border environmental programs. President Salinas has increased Mexico's environmental budget 700% in the last four years; the number of inspectors in the border area has increased from 50 to 203. Mexico will spend 1% of its GDP on the environment this year.

The North American Environmental Commission

1. In September 1992 the three countries agreed to establish a North American Environmental Commission to promote long-term cooperation on improving the environment.

SCORE: BEATS, MEETS, OR FALLS SHORT

Meets

√ 1. Allows each country to maintain and enforce existing federal and subfederal standards.

√ 2. Seeks to prevent a country from using technical standards to restrict trade.

3. Does not implement a "transaction tax" to fund environmental initiatives.

Falls Short

√ 1. Encourages countries to harmonize their process standards upward but does not provide an explicit plan for the countries to achieve this goal.

2. Does not provide a mechanism to prevent countries from relaxing standards or enforcement measures to attract foreign investment.

√ 3. The Border Plan, while an important first step, does not commit the parties to specific projects and lacks a long-term funding strategy. The US has proposed only $379 million for border environmental programs, which falls far short of the $5 billion we recommended for the next five years.

NEW ISSUES: Labor Adjustment

RECOMMENDATIONS:

1. The NAFTA will create about 316,000 gross new jobs in the US by 1995, but it also will displace about 145,000 workers; the US should budget $1.2 billion over five years for adjustment assistance.

2. Encourage Mexico to enforce its labor laws, allow trade union representation among maquiladora workers, and upgrade its labor standards. Issue biennial trilateral reports on labor conditions and adjustment in each country.

3. Ease US restrictions on Canadian and Mexican performers/entertainers working in the US on a temporary basis.

NAFTA RESULTS:

US Worker Adjustment Program

1. In August 1992, President Bush proposed the Advanced Skills through Education and Training (ASETS) worker adjustment program, which would spend $10 billion over five years on skills training and adjustment help for displaced workers. Current spending on programs for all displaced workers is $740 million per year; therefore, Bush's plan would require about $6.3 billion in new funding over five years.

2. ASETS would spend at least $335 million annually for five years ($1.67 billion total) specifically to educate and retrain workers displaced by the NAFTA. If the $335 million a year is inadequate, the secretary of Labor can draw up to double that amount from a discretionary fund.

3. Under the plan, displaced workers will receive vouchers of up to $3,000 a year for two years for job training.

4. ASETS was designed to replace two existing adjustment programs under the Economic Dislocation and Worker Adjustment Assistance Act and the Trade Adjustment Assistance Act with a single new program. Bush's previous 1993 budget called for the elimination of the Trade Adjustment Assistance program.

Binational Cooperation

1. In May 1991 the US and Mexico signed a five-year memorandum of understanding, which has produced several comparative studies of labor conditions and laws in each country. These studies are designed to provide the substantive basis for new bilateral programs.

2. In September 1992 the US and Mexico established a new "Consultative Commission on Labor Matters." This permanent body will be charged with implementing a bilateral work program and consulting on the enforcement of national labor laws and regulations.

SCORE: BEATS, MEETS, OR FALLS SHORT

Beats

√ 1. Clinton is likely to augment Bush's proposed $1.67 billion over five years to assist workers displaced by the NAFTA, which is more generous than our recommended $1.2 billion.

Meets

√ 1. Most money is scheduled for education and retraining rather than income maintenance, with vouchers issued for training at qualified private institutions in addition to federally run programs.

2. The memorandum of understanding and the Commission on Labor Matters will encourage Mexico to upgrade its labor standards and enforce its labor laws.

NEW ISSUES: Maquiladora Program

RECOMMENDATIONS:

1. Eliminate by 1996 all duty drawbacks on third-country components included in maquiladora exports to the US and Canada.
2. Apply the NAFTA rules of origin to maquiladora shipments after a short transition period (by 1996).
3. Eliminate within three years all linked domestic content and export requirements outside the automotive sector. Allow maquiladoras to sell freely within Mexico, upon payment of duties at the appropriate rate on imported components.

NAFTA RESULTS:

1. All duty drawbacks on third-country components will be eliminated by January 1, 2001.
2. Mexico will eliminate over seven years the 50% limitation on sales by maquiladoras into the local market. These sales will be subject to duties.
3. The domestic-content requirement and foreign exchange balancing requirements will be eliminated immediately.

SCORE: BEATS, MEETS, OR FALLS SHORT

Meets
1. The NAFTA rules of origin will apply to maquiladora shipments.
2. Linked domestic content and export requirements are eliminated (except autos).

Falls Short
1. Duty drawback on third-country components will be eliminated for maquiladora exports but not until January 1, 2001.
2. Eliminates the 50% limitation on maquiladora sales into Mexico, but over a seven-year transition period (we recommended a three-year transition).

NEW ISSUES: Accession Clause

RECOMMENDATIONS:

1. Membership in the NAFTA should be open to all countries in the Western Hemisphere that agree to all its obligations.
2. The NAFTA should include an accession clause, modeled on GATT procedures, that enables candidate countries to negotiate the terms of their accession protocols with the existing NAFTA members but also allows current members to invoke a nonapplication provision and deny extension of the pact to any country at the time of its accession.

NAFTA RESULTS:

1. Provides that any country or group of countries may be admitted into the NAFTA, subject to the agreement of existing members and the completion of members' domestic approval procedures. The criteria and procedures for accession are not spelled out in the NAFTA.

SCORE: BEATS, MEETS, OR FALLS SHORT

Beats
1. In principle, NAFTA membership is open to any country.

Meets
1. Includes an accession clause and nonapplication provision.

Falls Short
1. Criteria and procedures for enlargement remain to be spelled out by the NAFTA Trade Commission.

Addendum

Addendum

NAFTA'S Side Agreements and a Postscript on Jobs

In August 1993, exactly one year after the conclusion of the NAFTA negotiations, the United States, Canada, and Mexico reached agreement on three NAFTA side accords dealing with environmental issues, labor issues, and import surges. The side accords supplement the rights and obligations contained in the NAFTA; they do not amend the provisions previously negotiated.

The NAFTA side accords establish new North American institutions to monitor environmental and labor market conditions in the region, promote compliance with national laws and regulations in each of the three countries, and administer new dispute settlement procedures. In addition, the side agreement on import surges creates an early-warning monitoring system to scan sectors where explosive growth in regional trade is emerging.[1]

By focusing public attention on both inadequate enforcement measures and on environmental and labor standards that do not meet international norms, the new commissions should ferret out problems that can then be redressed before they fester into trade disputes. The new procedures encourage transparency and voluntary compliance; as a last resort, they levy fines and trade sanctions in select instances. The primary objective is not to punish, but to promote compliance with national laws and regulations. To that extent, the side accords have "teeth."

The new agreements accomplish the basic objectives set by President Clinton. They represent modest enhancements of the rights and obligations undertaken by the three countries in the NAFTA, especially with regard to environmental and labor matters. However, the new agreements take only the smallest step toward creating supranational institutions: neither Mexico, nor Canada, nor the United States is prepared to surrender significant sovereignty to regional institutions. While the agreements establish a foundation for further cooperation, they do not magically change a sow's ear into a silk purse. The NAFTA as originally

---

1. This assessment is largely based on the summaries of the supplemental agreements provided by the US Trade Representative and drafts of legal texts that were leaked to publications specializing in trade issues. The final legal text of the agreements was made available just as this book went to press.

negotiated was not a sow's ear, and the side agreements are the work of technicians, not magicians.

In addition to the side agreements, over the past year both Mexico and the United States have independently addressed concerns about the NAFTA raised by environmental and labor groups. For example, Mexico has initiated improvements in its environment and infrastructure by committing $245 million for wastewater and solid waste treatment and $168 million for transportation infrastructure for 1992–94.[2] President Salinas will soon announce details of a plan to link average productivity gains to periodic increases in Mexico's minimum wage (*Wall Street Journal*, 19 August 1993, A6). Mexico will also station international inspectors on its fishing boats to deter excessive dolphin kills.[3] Cooperative efforts are also being made. The Mexican environmental ministry, the US Environmental Protection Agency, and the US State Department plan to create an Air Pollution Control Zone for the El Paso–Cuidad Juarez residents. At first, joint pollution monitoring and voluntary control programs will be established. Eventually, the joint authority will have the power to establish and enforce emission standards (*Wall Street Journal*, 10 September 1993).

In hopes of alleviating environmental concerns, the Clinton administration is preparing a "white paper" on NAFTA sanitary and phytosanitary provisions. The white paper will clarify the US understanding of the NAFTA text concerning the regulation of agricultural products grown with pesticides or containing food additives. It will probably deal with such issues as who should bear the burden of proof required to upset existing state and federal environmental laws,[4] and the oft-repeated but erroneous assertion that, with NAFTA, lower Codex Alimentarius

---

2. US Council of the Mexico-US Business Committee, "Analysis of Environmental Infrastructure Requirements and Financing Gaps on the U.S./Mexico Border," July 1993, p. 21; and *Investors Business Daily*, 24 August 1993.

3. *The Economist*, 21 August 1993, 2. While Mexican boats kill less than one dolphin for every shoal of tuna they net, this figure still exceeds the average for the US fishing fleet, mainly because the US fleet operates in different waters with few or no dolphins swimming among the tuna. Because Mexico's tuna boats kill more dolphins than the US boats, Mexico remains in violation of the US Marine Mammal Protection Act.

4. *Inside U.S. Trade*, 27 August 1993, 2. Lori Wallach from Citizens Trade Committee (a coalition of 70 organizations opposing the NAFTA) argues that the NAFTA "sets up a whole system of rules and a court system that is basically placed on top of U.S. law." According to Wallach, under NAFTA, Mexicans could theoretically bring a case to the commission, and if a dispute panel declares that the current US DDT ban is an illegal trade barrier, then the United States would either have to repeal the law or be subject to trade sanctions (transcript, "MacNeil/Lehrer Newshour," 13 August 1993, 6.) However, it is highly improbable that Mexico could prevail in such litigation, inasmuch as present US standards would almost certainly pass the scientific evidence and risk assessment tests laid out in the NAFTA.

standards will undercut higher US federal and state standards (Perot and Choate 1993, 82–83).

The administration is also seeking to overturn Judge Charles Richey's decision of 30 June 1993, ruling that NAFTA should be accompanied by an environmental impact statement (EIS). The administration's main arguments are that the Administrative Procedures Act (APA) does not permit judicial review where, as with NAFTA, only the president may take final action; that the National Environmental Policy Act (NEPA) does not apply to presidential actions; and that insistence on an EIS would inevitably insert the judiciary into the complex negotiation of trade agreements.[5] The Court of Appeals for the District of Columbia Circuit was expected to rule on this case in fall 1993, though it had not done so before this book went to press.

Funding provisions for environmental and labor projects remain to be designed in order to complete the NAFTA package and to gain congressional acceptance. Secure revenues are needed for environmental projects in the US-Mexico border region and for addressing the needs of dislocated US workers.

Side Agreements on Environment and Labor

The side agreements broadly conform with our recommendations in terms of structure of the commissions and the processes for consultation and dispute settlement. The environmental agreement, however, falls short of our recommendations in two important areas: review of existing legal systems and establishment of a procedure to encourage the upward harmonization of environmental standards and enforcement.[6]

While the labor agreement also broadly carries out our recommendations, it falls short in two respects.[7] First, only three labor areas (occupational health and safety, minimum wages, and child labor) can be subject to fines and trade sanctions. Second, any trade sanction will apparently apply to total trade and not necessarily be directed against the specific firm or industry that is engaged in a pattern of labor abuse.

---

5. For a description of the litigation see *Wall Street Journal*, 1 July 1993, A1 and *Inside U.S. Trade*, 2 July 1993, 1; 9 July 1993, 1; 16 July 1993, 6; 6 August 1993, 4; and 27 August 1993, 4.

6. See pages 100 and 101 of this book for more details on our recommendations.

7. While we give the labor side agreement a passing grade, the AFL-CIO gives it an "F". According to AFL-CIO President Lane Kirkland, the labor side agreement is "bad joke. . .a Rube Goldberg structure of committees all leading nowhere" (*The Washington Post*, 1 September 1993, F13).

Structure of the Commissions

The Commission on Environmental Cooperation and the Commission on Labor Cooperation are structured according to traditional models: a council of the top three officials in each country is formed; in turn, a trinational secretariat provides technical and administrative support to the council [Article 8 of the North American Agreement on Environmental Cooperation (NAAEC) and Article 8 of the North American Agreement on Labor Cooperation (NAALC)]. In addition, the Commission for Environmental Cooperation will have a Joint Public Advisory Committee with five nongovernmental members from each country to advise the council (Article 11:2e of the NAAEC). While the Commission on Labor Cooperation does not have a citizen advisory committee, it will be served by three National Administrative Offices (NAOs)[8] (Article 15 of the NAALC). The NAOs are charged with providing information to the secretariat, other NAOs, and an Evaluation Committee of Experts (ECE) on domestic labor laws and their enforcement (Article 16 of the NAALC). Each commission also has its own roster of experts that can be convened to examine a particular issue if consultations fail (Article 25 of the NAAEC).

First Step: Consultations and Action Plans

Under Article 14 of the NAAEC, any organization or individual can make a complaint, known as a "submission," to the secretariat alleging a party's failure to effectively enforce its national environmental or labor laws. However, submissions concerning labor issues must first go to the National Administrative Office, which will attempt to resolve the dispute through consultations with its counterpart NAOs (Article 21 of the NAALC). If the issue cannot be resolved at the NAO level, ministerial consultations and analyses by an ECE will follow (Articles 22 and 23 of the NAALC).

For the environment, submissions may be raised on a wide variety of issues, including process standards, a subject not addressed in the NAFTA provisions.[9] For labor, 11 areas are covered, divided into three groups with procedures for each group. The first group includes the three areas that can ultimately become the subject of fines and trade

---

8. The NAOs will be units within labor ministries; the US NAO, for example, will be a unit reporting to the Undersecretary for International Affairs in the Department of Labor.

9. However, as the Sierra Club and Greenpeace have pointed out, natural resource conservation, promoting clean energy alternatives, and the export of hazardous waste are not included among the topics that may be the subject of a submission (*Orlando Sentinel*, 23 August 1993).

sanctions (occupational health and safety, child labor, and minimum wages) (Annex 41B:2 of the NAALC). The second includes five areas that can only be the subject of official consultations and review by independent experts (migrant workers, forced labor, employment discrimination, equal pay for men and women, compensation in cases of work accidents or occupational diseases). The third group includes three areas that can only be the subject of consultations at the ministerial level (the right to strike, the right to bargain collectively, and the right to freely associate and organize).[10] (See Articles 22, 23:2, and 49 of the NAALC.)

Based on the complainant's submission, the respective secretariat will develop a factual record. It can seek information from a variety of sources (including information developed by independent experts). The factual record will be made public if two of the three parties concur. If, after 60 days of consultation, the matter is not resolved, the complaining party may request a meeting of the council, which must convene within 20 days of the request (Articles 15 and 23 of the NAAEC, and Article 28 of the NAALC).

If, after 60 days, the council cannot resolve a dispute, an arbitration panel may be established from a previously agreed roster of experts. However, the creation of a panel requires an affirmative vote of two of the three council members. Within 180 days after the last panelist is selected, the panel will present its initial report. The final report must be presented within the following 60 days (Articles 24, 31, and 32 of the NAAEC; Articles 29, 30, 36, and 37 of the NAALC).

If the panel rules that a party is responsible for a pattern of failing to effectively enforce its environmental or labor law, the parties may agree on a mutually satisfactory remedy (Article 33 of the NAAEC; Article 38 of the NAALC). The action plan will be made public.

If the parties cannot agree on an action plan, then the panel is reconvened 60 to 120 days after the final panel report to evaluate the plan proposed by the party accused of wrongdoing (Article 39 of the NAALC). The panel will either accept that plan or devise its own (Article 34 of the NAAEC).

Next Step: Fines

If the action plan is not fully implemented, the arbitration panel will determine a fine (Article 34:5 of the NAAEC). The maximum amount in the first year is $20 million per infraction. The cap increases in subsequent

---

10. *Inside U.S. Trade*, 20 August 1993, 6. The placement of labor organization issues in the third group partly reflects the fact that the most important labor confederation in Mexico, the Confederación de Trabajadores Mexicanos (CTM) and its leader, Fidel Velázquez (leader of the CTM for over 50 years) have strong ties to the PRI, which in turn has controlled the government for 60 years.

years as the total level of NAFTA trade increases, but it cannot exceed 0.007 percent of total merchandise trade between the parties during the preceding year (Annex 34, Article 1 of the NAAEC; Annex 39 and Article 39:4b of the NAALC).[11] In the case of Canada, a domestic court will enforce the action plan and if necessary assess the fine against the government (Annex 36A of the NAAEC; Annex 41A of the NAALC).

Fines assessed in connection with environmental abuses are in accord with our recommended "green fee" (see p. 96). The fines (unlike countervailing duties) will not be specific to a particular product. Moreover, the money collected will be paid to a binational institution (the NAFTA Fund in the case of US-Mexico trade) or the Canadian Finance Ministry (in the case of Canadian exports) and is specifically earmarked for environmental purposes (Annex 34, Article 3 of the NAAEC).

Final Step: Trade Sanctions

In the case of environmental disputes, trade sanctions will be applied only in exceptional circumstances: when the party found not in compliance continues to inadequately enforce its environmental law (or otherwise violate its NAFTA obligations) and does not pay the fine assessed by the dispute panel. Trade sanctions are limited to the withdrawal of unspecified NAFTA benefits in an amount that does not exceed the original fine (Article 36 of the NAAEC; Article 41 of the NAALC).

Moreover, the possibility of trade sanctions only applies to the United States and Mexico. Canada has a special exemption from the imposition of trade sanctions because, in theory, Canadian courts will supposedly ensure that the action plan is carried out or that the fine is paid. In practice, Canada was excepted from trade sanctions because this remedy would have created an explosive political problem for the Canadian government (Annex 36A of the NAAEC).[12] Recall that a key Canadian objective in the Canada-US FTA was to constrain the use of US trade sanctions under US trade laws; the ability to impose trade sanctions would have been labeled a surrender by Canadian opposition parties (Schott and Smith 1988, 1–64).

In any event, the consultation and fine procedures specified in the environmental side agreement provide ample opportunity to settle the vast majority of environmental cases that arise. Trade sanctions will probably be used rarely, if at all.

---

11. *Inside U.S. Trade*, 20 August 1993, 16. In 1992, total three-way commerce between the United States, Canada, and Mexico was $271 billion (0.007 percent of this amount is $19 million).

12. Ambassador Mickey Kantor in Public Broadcasting Service transcript, "MacNeil/Lehrer Newshour," 13 August 1993, 4. Another consideration is that US environmental and labor groups have focused their worries on Mexico, not Canada.

In the case of labor disputes, the same process and criteria apply for the application of trade sanctions. However, as mentioned earlier, only occupational health and safety, child labor, and minimum wages can be the subject of fines and trade sanctions.

Along the lines of our recommendation to limit trade remedies to those specific firms and industries that show a persistent pattern of labor abuse, Annex 41B of the NAALC provides for trade sanctions in the same sector where the persistent failure has occurred. If this is not practicable or effective, other sectors can be targeted.

Side Agreement on Import Surges

The focus of the agreement on import surges is to establish a new mechanism for monitoring trade so that the parties can anticipate rapid and harmful import growth and not necessarily wait until a particular industry complains (Article 3 of the Understanding Between the Parties to the North American Free Trade Agreement Concerning Chapter Eight—Emergency Action). This is an ambitious task; the success of the monitoring process will in part depend on the data available. Much better and more timely data should be collected on US trade and investment with Mexico and on the jobs affected in both countries. Data are required not only to anticipate surges, but also to examine the longer term connection between investment, employment, productivity, and wages (box 1).

The US sugar, citrus, and vegetable producers were the strongest proponents of this supplementary agreement. These industries worry about the potential for rapid increases in the volume of Mexican exports and the possible depressing effect on US prices.[13] The surge agreement does not satisfy citrus and vegetable growers, mainly because the snapback mechanism in the NAFTA—namely, a raising of tariffs to pre-NAFTA levels—will only be triggered if there are large import volume increases, not if there are sudden price declines in the US market (Article 3:3a of the Understanding Between the Parties . . . ; *Inside U.S. Trade*, 6 August 1993, 1; and *Orlando Sentinel*, 23 August 1993, A1). In response to these concerns, Ambassador Kantor said in early August that he was seeking to tighten the sugar provisions and include a special price-based safeguard for fruits and vegetables in a "letter of clarification" (*Inside U.S. Trade*, 6 August 1993, 1).

---

13. Specifically, US sugar producers are concerned that corn sweeteners will be substituted for cane sugar in domestic Mexican consumption (as has occurred to some extent in the US market), thus freeing up cane sugar for export to the United States. Sugar producers have thus insisted that corn sweeteners be included in the "net exportable surplus" definition (*Christian Science Monitor*, 26 August 1993; and *Inside U.S. Trade*, 3 September 1993, 5). Orange juice producers are likewise concerned that Brazilian juice will be shipped to Mexico, consumed there, and that Mexican juice will be sold in the US market.

Box 1 Better and more timely data

Reconcile trade data. Mexico and the United States report different figures for bilateral merchandise imports and exports. Mexico does not report bilateral trade in business services. Following the precedent set by the United States and Canada, the statistical authorities of both countries should be directed to reconcile their figures.

Reconcile investment data. Mexico and the United States report different figures for US direct investment in Mexico. The Mexican figures, which are reported on a global basis (but which largely reflect US direct investment) are substantially higher than the US figures. Again, a reconciliation exercise is required.

Econometric assessment of job dislocation by imports. The US Commerce Department has carefully evaluated the connection between US exports and US jobs using input-output techniques. It should apply the same techniques to evaluate the connection between US imports and US jobs dislocated. In particular, it should examine the fine-grained impact of two-way trade in two major sectors: automotive goods, and textiles and apparel.

Case-by-case assessment of job dislocation. An important concern of American workers is that the NAFTA will cause plant closures and job layoffs. Mexican and Canadian workers have the same fears. These concerns should be addressed by setting up a statistical task force to identify and tabulate case-by-case instances of job losses linked to changes in North American trade and investment patterns by comparison with a base year, say 1990. The task force will have to do most of its work in the field. To start, it should issue reports every six months. The task force should attempt to distinguish between job losses resulting from liberalization under the NAFTA and job losses that might have occurred under pre-NAFTA trade rules.

Case-by-case assessment of job creation. The same task force should likewise identify case-by-case instances of job gains associated with trade and investment changes, again distinguishing between pre-NAFTA and post-NAFTA rules.

Wage suppression. An equally important concern of American workers is that NAFTA will lead to wage suppression. Here there are three concerns: first, that US workers will find themselves in head-to-head competition with Mexican workers who achieve, say, 50 percent of US productivity but who are paid only 15 percent of the US wage rate; second, that US firms will use the threat of relocation to Mexico as a bargaining chip in wage negotiations with US unions; and third, that the migration of Mexican workers to the United States will hold down wages for the lowest paid US workers. These concerns point to three separate statistical initiatives:

- A sector-by-sector comparison of wage and productivity levels between the United States, Canada, and Mexico at the three-digit SIC level.
- A longitudinal study to evaluate whether a "Mexico effect" can be detected in the wage settlements negotiated by large and medium-sized US firms.
- A greater effort should be made to estimate the annual two-way flow of immigrants, their geographic/industry sources and destinations, and the number of Mexican workers who permanently settle in the United States.

Moreover, the side agreement provides that a working group can make recommendations for revisions in the NAFTA text, based on the success of NAFTA provisions in alleviating harmful import surges (Article 3:6 of the Understanding Between the Parties . . .). If the worst fears of the citrus and sugar industries are realized, this provision might eventually be used to modify the snapback mechanism.

Unfinished Business

As of early September 1993, the administration had not made final decisions on funding environmental or transportation infrastructure projects or on paying for US labor adjustment due to NAFTA. Negotiations for funding environmental projects in the US-Mexico border region have made some progress. The EPA and other federal agencies are currently developing a program that will propose projects on border clean-up, related infrastructure, and enforcement ("The NAFTA: Expanding U.S. Exports, Jobs, and Growth," President's Briefing Synopsis to Congress, August 1993, Section K, p. 8).

Some progress has also been made in determining the funding needs for other border infrastructure, such as customs facilities, roads, and bridges. At the end of September 1993, a study will be released by the Federal Highway Administration (FHWA), as required by the Intermodal Surface Transportation Efficiency Act of 1991; the study will contain broad policy recommendations relating to current and future border infrastructure conditions ("The NAFTA: Expanding U.S. Exports, Jobs, and Growth," President's Briefing Synopsis to Congress, August 1993, Section K, p. 36).

Funding Environmental Projects

The negotiating results so far appear to be in line with our recommendations. A new institution, a border authority, will be responsible for approving projects and assembling the appropriate financing sources for each project. The border authority will have an executive board (presidentially appointed), an advisory committee (with representatives from the 10 border states and with backgrounds in environmental, engineering, and other related fields),[14] and a financing mechanism, the Border Environmental Finance Bank (BEFB).[15] The mandate of the border

---

14. The 10 border states are California, Arizona, New Mexico, Texas, Baja California, Sonora, Chihuahua, Coahuila, Nuevo Leon, and Tamaulipas.

15. The provisions relating to the establishment of the BEFB are along the lines of the proposal for a North American Development Bank first made by Raúl Hinojosa-Ojeda and Albert Fishlow, both with the University of California, in April 1993. The possibility of housing the BEFB within the Inter-American Development Bank is still being studied.

authority will include water and sewage systems, air pollution, municipal solid waste disposal, hazardous waste, and related infrastructure within the border region (including the region's watershed ecosystems).

The border authority will assess the technical feasibility of projects and assemble financing from three possible sources: BEFB resources, government support (federal, state, or local), and private capital. Financing for each project will be different. For example, projects with good prospects for collecting fees or tolls will finance up to 70 percent of their cost through self-liquidating debt. The emphasis on payment of fees by those firms and individuals who cause environmental pollution and those who benefit from a cleaner environment embraces our recommendation of the "polluter pays" principle. The US financial responsibility for capitalizing the BEFB will be 85 percent, and the Mexican responsibility will be 15 percent. The initial capitalization will be $5 billion,[16] of which the paid-in portion will be $500 million. In addition, $25 million will be provided for administrative expenses over five years. The remaining $4.5 billion of BEFB capitalization will take the form of callable capital. Based on a loan-to-capital ratio of 1 to 1, the BEFB will be able to make loans of $5 billion over five years. According to the administration's initial thinking, US appropriations for the BEFB (85 percent of $105 million, or $89 million per year for 5 years) will come either from the budget of the Environmental Protection Agency or from shifting funds out of other unnamed domestic expenditure categories into the international affairs account (the so-called 150 account). In addition to the $89 million per year for the BEFB, the US will also contribute $61 million per year in direct grants, for a total yearly contribution of $150 million.

Will the BEFB and associated financing meet the border environmental needs? Estimates of financing needs are imprecise and prone to political massage. Given the scope of existing environmental problems in the border region and the prospect of increased economic activity, environmental programs will require substantial resources over the next 5 to 10 years. According to our rough estimates, environmental programs to clean up and improve the sewage, water, and air basin conditions in the border region would cost about $5 billion over a five-year period. Other estimates of funding needs over a 5- to 10-year period generally fall in the range of $4 billion to $12 billion (table A1).

Some money has already been appropriated for environmental improvement both by the United States and Mexico. The US Congress in fiscal 1992 and fiscal 1993 appropriated $137 million for EPA and for the International Boundary Water Commission to help fund environmental projects in Nuevo Laredo, Nogales, and San Diego. The Mexican government has committed $245 million in public funds for wastewater and

---

16. This amount can later be raised if the mandate of the BEFB is expanded to other areas.

Table A1 Estimated environment-related funding needs[a]
(billions of dollars, except where noted)

	Treasury Department	Sierra Club	US Council of the Mexico–US Business Committee	Funds already committed
Period covered	5 to 10 years	10 years	10 years	
Wastewater treatment	3.3[b]	6.0	4.3	3.7
Water supply	0.5	2.0	1.0	0.7
Municipal solid waste		0.7	0.4	0.2
Hazardous waste disposal		2.0	0.8	
Air quality infrastructure		1.3	n.e.	
Conservation		0.1	n.e.	
Total	3.8	12.1	6.5	4.6

n.e. = not estimated
a. These figures refer to the US-Mexico border region. Estimates for regulations, maintenance, and operation are generally not included.
b. Includes maintenance and operation costs.

Sources: Inside U.S. Trade, 25 June 1993, p. 21; *Inside U.S. Trade*, 9 July 1993, p. 14; US Council of the Mexico-US Business Committee, "Analysis of Environmental Infrastructure Requirements and Financing Gaps on the U.S./Mexico Border," July 1993; and Sierra Club, "Funding Environmental Needs Associated with the North American Free Trade Agreement," 7 July 1993.

solid waste treatment during the 1992–94 period. In addition, the World Bank and the Inter-American Development Bank have committed about $500 million for water programs in Mexico.[17]

While the total BEFB capitalization of $5 billion is much the same as our back-of-the-envelope calculation of required border environmental projects, the means of funding are different than we envisaged. To minimize demands on the US budget, the plan relies to a much larger extent on callable capital than we recommended. Accordingly, the implied emphasis on state and local funding, and on revenue-yielding projects, will be greater.

A final point deserves mention. We suggested that project selection should be distanced from the establishment of financial resources. It remains to be seen how much independence the border authority will

---

17. For more details, see US Council of the Mexico-US Business Committee, "Analysis of Environmental Infrastructure Requirements and Financing Gaps on the U.S./Mexico Border," July 1993, 21–26.

have from the day-to-day politics of the two congresses and the border states.

A Labor Adjustment Program

Our estimates of NAFTA-related job losses, some 145,000 jobs over five years, have been challenged as too low by some NAFTA critics. One estimate, made by responsible economists, claims that the number of US jobs dislocated might be as high as 490,000 (Koechlin and Larudee 1992, 19). We think this figure is far too pessimistic. But neither our figure nor the higher Koechlin-Larudee figure represents a significant share of the nearly 9 million jobs dislocated in the US economy for a variety of reasons (layoffs, bankruptcies, plant closings, etc.) over a typical five-year period. Nonetheless, a decisive issue in the current debate is whether NAFTA on balance gains or loses US jobs, and what employment alternatives are available to dislocated US workers. In the postscript that follows, we examine the job impact numbers in greater detail. Here we focus on labor adjustment policies.

Details on the design of a training and adjustment program for workers dislocated by NAFTA, and its funding, are still unknown. However, it seems that the administration may have opted for an economywide training program instead of a program specifically aimed at workers displaced by NAFTA ("The NAFTA: Expanding U.S. Exports, Jobs, and Growth," President's Briefing Synopsis to Congress, August 1993, Section K, p. 5). In broad public policy terms, there is much to say for an economywide program. After all, why should adjustment benefits differ for workers displaced by NAFTA, workers displaced by the Clean Air Act, or workers laid off by Eastman Kodak as it responds to new technology and fresh competition?

The administration's comprehensive worker adjustment program will provide a new mix of unemployment insurance benefits, training programs, and other adjustment services. It will also have a "national reserve account" to answer the needs of industries, firms, and communities affected by specific structural changes such as NAFTA. Implementation of the new program is planned for October 1994 ("The NAFTA: Expanding U.S. Exports, Jobs, and Growth," President's Briefing Synopsis to Congress, August 1993, Section K, p. 5). In the meantime, workers displaced by NAFTA will have to use the present adjustment programs (the Trade Adjustment Assistance program and the Economic Dislocation and Worker Adjustment Assistance funds available under the Job Training Partnership Act).

Labor Secretary Robert Reich in his outline of President Clinton's economywide work force strategy pointed out that the new program will identify potential displaced workers early on—before they are actually laid off. It will shift the emphasis from unemployment insurance to retraining. Further, the program will identify the higher-wage skills that are in short supply and provide the necessary training for US workers "regardless of the reason they lost their job" (Remarks of Labor Secretary Robert B. Reich to the Center for National Policy's News Luncheon, "Beyond the Politics of Preservation: the Clinton Administration's Workforce Strategy," 1 September 1993).

These are all laudable goals, but President Clinton's immediate need is to secure congressional approval of NAFTA. An adjustment program targeted on NAFTA might gain a few congressional votes, both because it could be more immediate and because it would likely be far more generous on a per-worker basis than an economywide program. Thus, the politics of NAFTA ratification may well require a specific NAFTA adjustment program in 1993. In four or five years, after the effects of NAFTA can be better assessed, the NAFTA program could then be folded into an economywide training and adjustment program.

Postscript on the Job Impact of NAFTA

Central to the congressional debate is the prospective impact of NAFTA on US jobs and US wages. Our own forecasts of the job impact are set forth in table 2.1 of this book.[18] Briefly, we project that 316,000 US jobs will be gained because of larger US merchandise exports to Mexico as a result of NAFTA and ongoing Mexican reforms; that 145,000 US jobs will be lost on account of larger US merchandise imports from Mexico; and that, on balance, 171,000 net US jobs will be gained. These job gains and losses are calculated against the base of 1990 bilateral merchandise trade between the United States and Mexico.

Our projections, first made early in 1992, may be contrasted with actual trade developments since 1990, as summarized in table A2. This table covers bilateral trade both in merchandise and business services. Trade in business services will have a jobs impact just like that of merchandise trade. Available data do not permit a close estimate of the number of jobs associated with the export or import of $1.0 billion of business services, nor a breakdown of the occupational composition of jobs affected. However, the overall number of jobs resulting from a change in business services trade is probably somewhat higher than the 1990 figure of 19,600 US jobs per $1.0 billion of US manufactured exports to Mexico.[19]

---

18. The estimating methodology is explained in detail in our *North American Free Trade: Issues and Recommendations*, 1992, chapter 3.

19. Business services include travel, tourism, transportation, insurance, telecommunications, legal and accounting services, and royalties and license fees. On average, these services probably require less physical capital per employee than manufacturing activity; hence, the job impact per $1.0 billion of receipts or expenditures is likely to be greater.

Table A2 US-Mexico bilateral trade in merchandise and business services (billions of dollars, except where noted)

	1990	1991	1992	1993	1994
US statistics					
Merchandise exports	28.1	33.1	40.5	42.1[a]	47.3[b]
Business services exports	7.7	8.1	8.6[c]	9.1[c]	9.6[c]
Total	35.8	41.3	49.1	51.2	56.9
Merchandise imports	30.5	31.5	35.6	38.8[a]	43.5[b]
Business services imports	7.4	7.8	8.2[c]	8.6[c]	9.0[c]
Total	37.9	39.3	43.9	47.4	52.6
Bilateral trade balance	−2.1	2.0	5.3	3.8	4.4
Calculated net change in US jobs (thousands)[d]				115,600	126,900
Mexican statistics					
Merchandise exports[e]	32.3	33.9	37.4[f]	40.6[b]	45.6[b]
Business services exports[g]	8.0	8.7	9.1[f]	9.9[b]	11.1[b]
Total	40.3	42.6	46.5	50.5	56.7
Merchandise imports[e]	30.8	36.8	44.2[f]	47.6[b]	53.5[b]
Business services imports[g]	9.9	10.5	11.5[f]	12.3[b]	13.5[b]
Total	40.8	47.4	55.7	59.9	66.9
Bilateral trade balance	−0.5	−4.7	−9.2	−9.4	−10.2

a. Estimated on the basis of January-June 1993 trade data.
b. Estimated on the basis of CIEMEX-WEFA forecasts.
c. US business service reports to Mexico are assumed to increase $0.5 billion annually, while US business service imports are assumed to increase by $0.4 billion annually.
d. Calculated as 19,600 jobs per $1.0 billion change in bilateral US trade balance since 1990 (when the bilateral trade deficit was $2.1 billion).
e. Includes maquiladora trade.
f. Preliminary.
g. Mexican receipts and expenditures for business services represent trade on a global basis. Mexican statistics do not separately identify business service trade with the United States.

Sources: US Department of Commerce, *Survey of Current Business,* September 1992 and June 1993, p. 76 and 78; CIEMEX-WEFA, July 1993; US Department of Commerce, *Commerce News,* "US Merchandise Trade: June 1993"; Banco de Mexico, "The Mexican Economy—1993," p. 200.

For purposes of an interim review of US job effects, we rely on US statistics concerning bilateral merchandise and services trade. As table A2 shows, Mexican statistics are comparable to US data, but the Mexican figures show a larger swing in the trade balance since 1990 in the United States' favor.[20] Hence, if Mexican trade statistics were used, the favorable impact to date on US jobs would be larger than the picture that follows.

---

20. As table A2 indicates, US and Mexican statistics on bilateral trade differ somewhat. While the levels and overall direction are much the same, the individual components and year-to-year changes differ. US statistics show a $7.4 billion swing in the United States's favor between 1990 and 1992, while Mexican statistics show an $8.7 billion swing in the US's favor.

By comparison with 1990, the promise of NAFTA, coupled with unilateral Mexican reforms, has attracted large sums of foreign capital to the Mexican economy; the resulting bilateral Mexican trade deficit will add about 116,000 jobs to the US economy in 1993. Based on CIEMEX-WEFA trade projections, this figure could rise to a US job gain of nearly 127,000 in 1994. These figures seem to confirm our projection of net US gains of 171,000 jobs by the mid-1990s resulting from NAFTA and continuing Mexican reforms.

The Oligarchy Thesis

A key criticism of NAFTA, stridently advanced by Perot and Choate (1993, 45) and by the Economic Policy Institute (1992, 10), is that, with new capital investment and on-the-job training, Mexican labor productivity will fast approach US levels. These critics further claim that Mexican wages will be held down by an oligarchy of Mexican and US business firms working together with the Mexican government. Hence there will be a "giant sucking sound" as firms close their US plants and move to Mexico. In support of their argument, the critics point to the rapid growth of maquiladora operations, from 67,000 Mexican workers in 1975 to 505,000 in 1992. This line of criticism is preposterous for several reasons:

- First, as shown in table A3, the ratio between value added per US manufacturing worker and value added per Mexican worker in the maquiladora plants actually increased between 1980 and 1991, from a ratio of 5.8 times to 8.2 times.[21] In other words, in the battle for better productivity, US workers have gained ground relative to their Mexican counterparts in maquiladora establishments, not vice versa.[22]

- Second, while maquiladora operations in Mexico show a progressive increase in value added per worker, they do not exhibit Korean-style double-digit productivity growth. Over the entire 12 years between 1980 and 1992, Mexican productivity in the maquiladoras, measured in current dollars, increased by 47 percent. Allowing for inflation (as measured by the US producers price index) real Mexican productivity in maquiladora operations increased only 17 percent, or by less than 2 percent per year.

- Third, after a sharp fall coinciding with economic chaos in the early 1980s, wage rates in Mexico have advanced far more rapidly since 1987

---

21. Robert Z. Lawrence was the first scholar to use maquiladora value-added data to refute the oligarchy story ("The Real Wage/Productivity Story" *The International Economy*, July/August 1993).

22. In portraying the Mexican "threat," critics of NAFTA usually point to maquiladora operations as the harbinger of job competition with US manufacturing operations.

Table A3 Mexico and United States: value added per worker and hourly compensation, 1975–92

	Mexico (based on maquiladora experience)					United States (based on all manufactures)	
Year	Number of maquiladora plants	Total maquiladora employment	Maquiladora net exports (millions of dollars)	Annual value added per maquiladora employee (dollars)[b]	Average hourly compensation per Mexican production worker (dollars)[c]	Annual value added per US manufacturing employee (dollars)	Average hourly compensation per US production worker (dollars)
1975	454	67,213	332	4,940	1.44	24,177	6.36
1980	578	119,546	772	6,458	2.18	37,480	9.87
1981	605	130,973	976	7,452	2.73	41,330	10.87
1982	585	127,048	851	6,698	1.90	43,161	11.68
1983	600	150,867	818	5,422	1.42	47,143	12.14
1984	722	199,684	1,155	5,784	1.54	51,415	12.55
1985	789	211,968	1,268	5,982	1.58	53,209	13.01
1986	844	249,833	1,295	5,183	1.10	56,366	13.25
1987	1,432	305,253	1,598	5,235	1.01	61,516	13.52
1988	1,441	369,489	2,337	6,323	1.25	65,928	13.91
1989	1,699	429,725	3,047	7,091	1.48	68,693	14.32
1990	1,938	460,293	3,611	7,845	1.64	70,400	14.91
1991	1,925	467,454	4,122	8,818	1.95	72,740	15.60
1992	2,075	505,053	4,808	9,520	2.35	n.a.	16.17

a. All money figures are in current dollars not adjusted for inflation.

b. Calculated as net exports divided by the number of employees. Note that value added by maquiladoras is nearly the same as net exports (i.e., maquiladora exports of finished goods minus imports of raw materials and components). However, the net export figure also includes both the cost of energy and the cost of inputs purchased from the Mexican economy, and neither of these is part of value added.

c. This series refers to all Mexican production workers employed in manufacturing. The average compensation for Mexican production workers is probably higher than the average compensation for maquiladora workers. See tables 6.7, 6.8 and 6.9 in Gary C. Hufbauer and Jeffrey J. Schott, 1992, *North American Free Trade: Issues and Recommendations*, Washington: Institute for International Economics.

Sources: CIEMEX-WEFA, *Maquiladora Industry Analysis*, 1993; Banco de Mexico, *The Mexican Economy*, 1993; US Census Bureau, *1991 Annual Survey of Manufacturers*, 1992; US Bureau of Labor Statistics, *International Comparisons of Hourly Compensation Costs for Production Workers in Manufacturing—1992*, April 1993.

than the oligarchy story would suggest. Perot and Choate erroneously claim (p. 44) that "since 1987, Mexico has fixed wages through a complex government-business-labor arrangement." In fact, as table A3 shows, average Mexican hourly compensation per production worker advanced from $1.01 in 1987 to $2.35 in 1992.

- Fourth, in 1991, the ratio between US production worker hourly compensation and Mexican production worker hourly compensation was 8.0 ($15.60 vs. $1.95). This compensation ratio is consistent with the manufacturing productivity ratio between the two countries, shown by the 8.2 ratio between value added per employee in all US manufacturing ($72,740) and value added per employee in Mexican maquiladora operations ($8,818). Set side by side, the two ratios (8.0 and 8.2) hardly suggest that Mexican manufacturing workers are dramatically underpaid relative to their productivity.

- Fifth and finally, the "sucking sound" proposition completely ignores the stimulating effect that larger Mexican payrolls and greater capital spending would exert on US exports. About 80 percent of all Mexican imports come from the United States—in this sense, Mexico is one of the world's best markets for US goods and services.

Perot and Choate vs. the Economic Models

A number of scholars have used economic techniques to forecast the effect of NAFTA on key economic variables. The leading models are summarized in table A4. It is worth contrasting these models with the "analysis" offered by Perot and Choate.

In terms of trade balance effects, most of the modelers believe that any effect on the US or Mexican trade balance will be quickly offset by forces elsewhere in the respective economies. The Almon model and our own calculations, however, suggest significant positive effects on the US trade balance and a negative effect on the Mexican trade balance. In stark contrast, the assertions made by Perot and Choate about prospective US job losses ("millions") imply a US trade deficit with Mexico of at least $100 billion annually as a consequence of NAFTA.[23]

Practically all the models project that NAFTA will exert no effect, or a very small positive effect, on average US wages. Many of the models see moderate gains (up to 8 percent) in Mexican wages. Again, Perot and Choate are at striking odds with serious economic research. They claim that significant wage losses will result both in the United States and Mexico as a consequence of NAFTA.

---

23. This figure is calculated on the basis of 19,600 US jobs per $1.0 billion change in the US trade balance with Mexico and assumes a US job loss of 2.0 million workers.

Table A4 Comparison of NAFTA forecasts[a]

Model	Type[b]	Change in annual trade balance (billions of dollars)		Effect on average wages (percentage change)		Effect on US employment (thousands of jobs)			Cumulative investment in Mexico (billions of dollars)[a]
		US	Mexico	US	Mexico	Jobs gained	Jobs lost	Net effect	
Adams, Alanis, Del Rio	(1)		+1.7						none
	(2)		−7.2						27
Almon[d]	(2)	+6.6	−3.0	none		+60	−15	+45[e]	2
Bachrach and Mizrahi	(1)	none	+0.9	none	none			none	none
	(2)	+0.1	+4.7	none	none			none	25
Boyd, Krutilla, McKinney[f]	(1)	+1.8	−1.8	none					none
Brown, Deardorf, Stern	(1)	none	none	+0.1	+0.4			none	none
	(2)	none	none	+0.1	+7.2			none	33
Hinojosa-Ojeda and Robinson	(1)	none	none	+0.4[g]	+2.3[g]			−234	none
	(2)	none	none	+0.2[g]	+8.4[g]			none	26[h]
Koechlin and Larudee[i]	(2)		+4.0	−2.0	none			−490[j]	53
KPMG	(2)	−1.1		none				none	25
McCleery	(1)	none	none	+0.3[k]	−0.1[k]			none	none
	(2)	none	none	+0.7[k]	−0.1[k]			none	46
Robinson et al.	(1)	none	none	−0.1[g]	+0.8[g]			none	none
	(2)	none	none	none[g]	+3.6[g]			none	33
Roland-Holst et al.	(1)	none	none	none	none			+95[l]	
Hufbauer and Schott[m]	(2)	+9.0	−12.0	none	+8.7	+316	−145	+171	60
Perot and Choate[n]	(2)	−102.0	+102.0	"standards of living sacrificed"	"workers are exploited"	"loss of millions of jobs"			"The flow of US companies moving factories to Mexico . . . threatens to become a flood"

a. Different models envisage different periods for the estimated effects to occur. Generally the period between 1995 and 2000 is referenced. A blank means the model was not used to estimate the magnitude in question; "none" means, in the case of trade balance, a change of less than $0.05 billion; in the case of average wages and the effect on US employment, a change of less than 0.05 percent; in the case of investment in Mexico, a cumulative change in the capital stock of less than $1 billion.

b. Model type refers to whether investment effects in Mexico are, or are not, built into the model: (1) model with no investment effects; (2) model with investment effects and a consequent change in the Mexican capital stock.

c. Generally, estimates for cumulative investment in Mexico refer to a period of about 10 years, unless noted otherwise.

d. The trade figures in the Almon report are based on 1977 price levels. They were adjusted to 1992 price levels by applying a multiple of 1.9 (based on the US producer price index for industrial commodities). The employment figures in the almon model are for 1995.

e. This figure represents the net job effect five years after the elimination of tariffs and nontariff barriers.

f. The percentage change figures in the Boyd et al., study are applied to 1989 trade flows to produce these estimates.

g. The percentage change in US and Mexican average wages are weighted averages of the estimates for rural, unskilled urban workers, skilled urban workers, and white-collar workers.

h. This estimate is for five years.

i. These figures are the upper-bound estimates made by Koechlin and Larudee.

j. This job-loss estimate is based on the average amount of capital used by each worker in US manufacturing, and the assumption that additional investment in Mexico means less investment in the United States.

k. These figures are unweighted averages of low-wage service workers, high-wage service workers, and high-wage manufacturing workers.

l. The value for the Roland-Holst et al. study covers the effects of eliminating tariff barriers to US-Canadian trade as well as US-Mexico trade. The baseline for US employment is the 1989 figure.

m. The Hufbauer-Schott trade figures refer to changes induced by NAFTA and continuing Mexican economic reforms by the mid-1990s.

n. The trade balance figure is calculated on the basis of 19,600 US jobs per $1.0 billion change in the US trade balance and assumes that NAFTA results in a net US job loss of 1.0 million workers (Perot and Choate assert that US job losses will be "millions"). The quotes are from pages 52 and 55 of Ross Perot and Pat Choate, 1993, Save Your Job, Save Your Country, New York: Hyperion.

Sources: Gary Clyde Hufbauer and Jeffrey J. Schott, 1992, North American Free Trade: Issues and Recommendations, Washington: Institute for International Economics, table 3.4; and 1993, NAFTA: An Assessment, Washington: Institute for International Economics, table 2.1; Ross Perot and Pat Choate, 1993, Save Your Job, Save Our Country, New York: Hyperion, p. 52 and 55; Timothy Koechlin and Mehrene Larudee, 1992, "The High Cost of NAFTA," Challenge, (September-October); KPMG Peat Marwick, 1991, The Effects of a Free Trade Agreement Between the U.S. and Mexico, Washington: KPMG Peat Marwick, (May). All other models are summarized in Congressional Budget Office, 1993, "Estimating the Effects of NAFTA: An Assessment of the Economic Models and Other Empirical Studies," CBO Papers, Washington: CBO, (June).

Box 2 Critique of the Perot-Choate claim that "millions" of US jobs will be lost

Perot and Choate start with the AmeriMex Maquiladora Fund prospectus, which identified companies that might move all or part of their manufacturing operations to Mexico (Perot and Choate 1993, 52). The Fund emphasized two criteria for its marketing efforts: firms with a labor cost component of 20 to 30 percent of goods sold that also employ workers with low to medium skills with average compensation in the $7 to $10 per hour range. The Fund prospectus did not specify what percentage of the target population of firms might seriously consider a move to Mexico.

However, Perot and Choate count the jobs of all US manufacturing firms with labor costs of 20 percent or more as "jobs at risk."[1] They omit the $7 to $10 per hour criterion as a filter in identifying at-risk jobs. Thus, a very large fraction of their 6 million US production jobs claimed to be "at risk" do not even meet the stated AmeriMex criteria. Instead, high-wage, high-skill sectors such as SIC 376 ("guided missiles, space vehicles, and parts") and SIC 384 ("medical instruments and supplies") are included in the "at risk" listing. In California, the state with the most "jobs at risk" (747,600), more than half of the supposed at-risk jobs (386,300) pay wages over $11 per hour. In their book (p. 55), Perot and Choate drop the "at-risk" qualifier altogether when they write of "the loss of millions of jobs that the United States sorely needs."

Perot and Choate do not consider how Mexican workers or firms would spend the money earned from their new jobs and their much larger export sales. The positive effects of higher Mexican income on US exports and US jobs are thus simply ignored.

Nor do Perot and Choate consider the macroeconomic consistency of their estimates. In order to displace 2 million US manufacturing workers, Mexico would have to run a huge bilateral trade surplus (about $100 billion) with the United States, employ at least 10 million more workers (the current Mexican labor force is about 30 million), and increase exports by more than one-third of total Mexican GNP (1992 level, about $300 billion). These magnitudes are the economic equivalent of catapulting Noah's Ark to Mars.

---

1. The same procedure was followed in a preliminary study by Choate: *The Manufacturing Policy Project*, Jobs at Risk: Vulnerable US Industries and Jobs under NAFTA, Washington, DC, April 1993.

Next, there is the question of cumulative new investment in Mexico as a result of NAFTA. Where estimated, figures generally range between $25 billion and $60 billion, a very small fraction of the total US stock of plant and equipment (about $10,000 billion in 1992) or the annual level of US plant and equipment investment, or about $550 billion (*Statistical Abstract of the United States*, 1992, table 735; *Economic Report of the President* 1993, table B1). In contrast, Choate and Perot claim that NAFTA will prompt a "flood" of US companies to move to Mexico.

The hallmark of the Perot and Choate criticism is their claim of potential US job losses. In the 1992 presidential campaign, "the great sucking sound" became Perot's most memorable sound bite; it has now become his rallying cry against NAFTA. Prior to publication of *Save Your Job, Save Our Country*,[24] the largest negative projection for US jobs was the figure of 490,000 by Koechlin and Larudee.[25] Perot and Choate, however, claim that millions of US jobs will be lost as a consequence of NAFTA. To arrive at this figure, they use analytic methods that bear a closer kinship to astrology than economics (box 2).

---

24. *Save Your Job, Save Our Country* was preceded by an April 1993 study financed by Perot—*The Manufacturing Policy Project, Jobs at Risk: Vulnerable US Industries and Jobs under NAFTA*, Washington, DC, April 1993.

25. This estimate is critiqued in this book on pages 15–19.

Evaluation of Side Agreements

SIDE AGREEMENT: Environmental Cooperation

RECOMMENDATIONS:

Environmental Assessments

1. To determine the extent to which the parties have achieved the environmental objectives of the NAFTA, we recommend that a new commission be established to sponsor assessments on a broad variety of environmental conditions in each country and to periodically update the findings.

2. The assessments should be made by qualified experts on the basis of public hearings, available data, and field inspections. The commission should have the power to compel firms and municipalities to open their doors and books to provide evidence, as necessary.

3. The assessments should be published, on the theory that sunshine is the best disinfectant.

Legal Systems

1. The commission should perform a detailed and open evaluation of the means by which citizens and public interest groups can use legal and administrative processes to compel state and federal governments to enforce standards that have been legally established.

2. This investigation should examine the workings of judicial mechanisms, including the questions of standing, injunctive relief, and penalties for environmental abuse. It should address both the problem of excessive litigation as well as the problem of inadequate legal remedies.

3. For the foreseeable future, the commission should confine itself to suggesting, rather than prescribing, changes in national legal systems.

Process Standards with a Trade Effect

1. We recommend that the parties undertake negotiations to elevate, to the highest common denominator, those process standards or enforcement practices that have a measurable effect on trade patterns. Petitioning organizations, such as the National Wildlife Federation, would present initial complaints to their home governments. The home government would then decide which issues to bring to the commission.

2. In the vast majority of cases, commission review alone should lead to better process standards. If, after an appropriate period of consultation and negotiations, a country failed to enforce its own minimum standards, or if the countries could not agree on common NAFTA standards, the issue would be handed over to dispute settlement proceedings.

Green Fees

1. As an ultimate sanction, after allowing a reasonable period for voluntary implementation of the recommendations, an international panel could authorize a low-rate "green fee" on *all* the respondent nation's exports to the other NAFTA countries. The green fee (unlike countervailing duties) would not be imposed unilaterally and would not be specific to a particular product.

2. Again (unlike countervailing duties), the fee would not be retained by the importing country. Instead, the funds generated would either be paid to a binational environmental institution (the NAFTA Fund in the case of US-Mexico trade) or earmarked to a Canadian environmental fund (in the case of Canadian exports).

3. The green fee would thus discourage bad environmental practices and provide a funding source for better practices. But the green fee would not become a mecha-

nism for interrupting trade flows in particular products, and thus it should not become a lightning rod for protectionist initiatives.

Upward Harmonization (Especially of Process Standards)

1. The commission should establish a procedure to encourage the upward harmonization of environmental standards and enforcement, especially in the area of process standards (such as aquifer pollution), even where there is no measurable trade effect.[1]

2. In the first stage, processes that abuse the global commons or the transboundary environment should be the subject of upward harmonization within the NAFTA, regardless of any trade effects.

3. At a later stage, say in 10 years, processes with an irreversible environmental impact, but an impact contained economically and physically within national borders, might also be the subject of upward harmonization within the NAFTA.

Polluter Pays Principle

1. Finally, the commission should seek wider implementation of the "polluter pays" principle. This principle was long ago endorsed by OECD nations, but it remains to be implemented in a wide range of activities, from industrial air emissions to household sewer connections.[2] Implementation of the polluter pays principle should be the main way by which NAFTA countries correct industrial and municipal processes that have local and reversible pollution effects.

RESULTS:

Commission for Environmental Cooperation

1. The North American Agreement on Environmental Cooperation establishes a Commission for Environmental Cooperation, comprising a governing council of the environmental ministers of each country, a central secretariat staffed proportionally to population by independent nationals of each country, and a Joint Public Advisory Committee consisting of five public members from each country.

2. The Joint Public Advisory Committee will meet at least once a year, concurrent with the regular session of the council, and will provide the secretariat with technical, scientific, and other information to help inform reports issued by the commission.

3. Assessments by the commission will be based on information submitted by interested parties and developed by independent experts. The agreement does not grant the commission power to compel firms and municipalities to open their doors and books to provide information.

4. The council will administer the agreement, including the dispute settlement procedures. The council will meet at least once a year, with all regular sessions open to the public. Findings and reports of dispute settlement panels will normally be made public.

5. The council will consider and develop recommendations regarding the environmental implications of process and production methods with significant transboundary effects. It will also consider (and may develop recommendations on) public access to information, appropriate limits for specific pollutants, and reciprocal access to rights and remedies for damage or injury resulting from transboundary pollution.

---

1. A timetable for upward harmonization of standards was suggested on page 152.

2. Jan Gilbreath Rich, "Planning the Border's Future: The Mexican-US Integrated Border Environmental Plan," US-Mexican Occasional Paper No. 1, LBJ School of Public Affairs, University of Texas at Austin, March 1992, 45.

6. Each country can call for an arbitral panel if consultations by the council do not result in resolution of a dispute relating to a persistent pattern of failure to effectively enforce its environmental laws with respect to traded goods. If the party complained against does not implement the action plan recommended by the panel, the panel can impose a fine of up to $20 million in the first year, which is to be paid into an environmental fund. If the party complained against (except Canada) still refuses to act on the complaint or to pay the fine, it will be liable to trade sanctions.

Legal Systems

1. Parties guarantee that all people with a legally recognized interest in a particular matter have access to national courts. Parties will ensure open and equitable judicial and administrative proceedings.

Upward Harmonization (Process Standards)

1. Parties commit to effectively enforce their domestic environmental laws to ensure high levels of environmental protection and to continue to work cooperatively in enhancing environmental protection. All domestic environmental laws are covered by this pledge with the exception of natural resource management programs (at Canada's request).

2. In addition, the commission will encourage the three countries to examine the need to harmonize NAFTA standards at levels that are not lower than the highest minimum standards within the NAFTA region. However, the agreement does not provide a specific timetable or plan for the harmonization of standards.

3. The rights of local authorities under the NAFTA to maintain standards at levels higher than the federal governments are not affected.

Other Matters

1. As a unilateral matter, each country will periodically issue reports on the state of its environment. In addition, the parties will limit trade in toxic substances that are banned domestically.

SIDE AGREEMENT: Labor Cooperation

RECOMMENDATIONS:

1. Establish a trinational commission to review the enforcement practices of national authorities, to send out field investigators, to hold public hearings, to publish reports, and to make recommendations.

2. Labor unions and industry associations should be able to file reports with their home government on the labor practices in any member country. However, petitions to the commission should only be made by member governments. In the event of a petition, NAFTA panels should rule on whether national authorities have faithfully pursued their own labor laws and regulations. Commission reports should encourage enforcement of national laws by exposing offenders to public scrutiny. In most cases, the glare of publicity should be sufficient to promote compliance.

3. However, if this spotlight and subsequent government measures prove inadequate, the commission should be empowered to authorize trade remedies against firms or industries that show a persistent pattern of labor abuse. The commission should not have the power to levy fines or award damages against particular firms or industries. Such remedies should remain the responsibility of national agencies and courts.

RESULTS:

Commission on Labor Cooperation

1. The agreement creates a new Commission on Labor Cooperation, with each country represented on the council by its ministerial-level labor official. The council has a broad mandate to work cooperatively on labor issues. Individuals or groups will have access to legal and administrative proceedings.

2. Countries will also appoint a National Administrative Office to serve as a point of contact for public input, a clearinghouse for information on labor matters, and a first-stage dispute settlement forum.

3. An independent coordinating Secretariat will provide technical support to the council and will itself report periodically to the council on a wide range of labor issues.

4. The agreement encourages voluntary compliance by exposing problems in commission reports. Fines and trade sanctions are a last resort, and applicable only in cases involving workplace health and safety, minimum wage, and child labor. These areas are subject to a full array of dispute procedures, including consultations, evaluation by expert panels, and ultimately fines and sanctions if a persistent pattern of failure to enforce labor laws is demonstrated.

5. Disputes involving other labor laws as defined by the agreement (except labor organization) may be discussed among ministers, who can decide to establish expert groups to prepare reports. However, such disputes cannot be the subject of fines or trade sanctions.

6. Disputes relating to labor organizations' right to strike, to bargain collectively, and to freely associate and organize can only be discussed in ministerial-level consultations. They cannot be the subject of expert reports, fines, or trade sanctions.

National Measures

1. Each country agrees to publish its labor-related laws, regulations, and procedures and to promote public awareness of labor rights. Each country will encourage compliance with domestic laws through appointment and training of inspectors, monitoring and on-site inspections, mandatory reporting, and strict enforcement actions.

SIDE AGREEMENT: Import Surges

RECOMMENDATIONS:

1. The NAFTA contains adequate provisions to safeguard US industry from sudden and overwhelming import surges of Mexican goods. Hence, we recommend no additional substantive provisions in the side agreement on import surges.

RESULTS:

1. The supplemental Agreement on Import Surges establishes an early warning system through constant monitoring of trade flows and domestic market conditions; however, no new safeguard mechanisms are created.

2. The agreement establishes a working group to evaluate how well NAFTA's safeguard provisions alleviate harmful import surges and to recommend revisions as appropriate.

FUNDING: Border Environmental Projects

RECOMMENDATIONS:

In order to provide secure financing for projects that address environmental problems along the US-Mexico border, we recommend the following steps:

Institutional Structure

1. The establishment of a joint US-Mexican Commission to administer a NAFTA Fund. The commission should be backed up by a small staff with financial, engineering, and environmental expertise. Concerns about establishing a new bureaucracy could be mitigated by nesting the commission within the Inter-American Development Bank.
2. The commission's task should not be to originate proposals, but to pass judgment on proposals submitted and sponsored by other bodies: municipalities, states, federal agencies, or private corporations. The projects submitted would have to be fully staffed by the sponsoring agency.
3. Project selection should be distanced from the provision of financial resources, lest politicians condition overall funding on support for their pet projects. (Demands that the NAFTA Fund include projects in the United States beyond the border regions indicate that these pressures already exist.) Politicians should create the fund and leave it to technicians to evaluate project proposals.

Financing

1. We recommend endowing the NAFTA Fund with $3 billion ($1.5 billion contributed each by the United States and Mexico) to be spent over five years on environmental and infrastructure projects within the border zone. Each country would pledge annual installments of $300 million to the NAFTA Fund, starting in 1994. On this schedule, full payment would be completed by January 1999.
2. Funding provided by the two federal governments can be used to leverage much larger resources through cofinancing both with state and local governments and with private firms. Cofinancing of at least 50 percent of project cost should be required. Preference should be given to environmental and infrastructure projects that promise to generate a future stream of revenues for the sponsoring agency by way of tolls or user fees. In this manner, the NAFTA Fund would leverage its resources and point the way to self-funding of services in the border zone.
3. According to our rough-and-ready estimates, border environmental programs could cost $5 billion over five years, while border infrastructure projects could cost an additional $2 billion. Other estimates of the costs of border environmental programs for the next 10 years include the US Council of the Mexico-US Business Committee, $6.5 billion; Sierra Club, $12.1 billion; US Treasury Department, $3.8 billion.
4. We strongly oppose institution of a transaction tax to finance border projects. A transaction tax would simply reimpose a large share of the trade barriers that are scheduled to be eliminated by the NAFTA: for example, a 1 percent tax would clawback more than 50 percent of the prospective reductions in US tariffs imposed on Mexican imports.[3]

---

3. The Congressional Budget Office estimates that US tariff revenues from imports from Mexico in 1991 totaled less than $600 million, or only 1.9 percent of the total value of US imports from Mexico (CBO, "A Budgetary and Economic Analysis of the North American Free Trade Agreement," July 1993, 32).

5. Our strong preference is that US contributions to the NAFTA Fund come out of general Treasury revenues: the cost is relatively small and extends over a five-year period.[4]

RESULTS:

Institutional Structure

1. A new, binational border authority will coordinate environmental infrastructure projects in the border area. Its tasks include approving projects that are initiated by local jurisdictions on both sides of the border and assembling a financing package for each project.

2. The new institution will be governed by an executive board consisting of presidentially appointed representatives of the United States and Mexico. The board will select a managing director, who supervises an integrated financial and engineering staff of US and Mexican professionals and reports to the board.

3. The US-Mexican executive board will be advised by a committee representing the 10 border states and consisting of representatives with backgrounds in environmental planning, engineering, or related fields.

4. The Border Environmental Finance Bank (BEFB) will serve the border authority as an official financing mechanism for environmental infrastructure projects. A possible link with the Inter-American Development Bank remains to be explored.

Financing

1. The binational border authority will assemble its financing packages from three sources: the BEFB; direct support from federal, state, and local governments; and the private sector.

2. The initial capital of the BEFB is $5 billion plus $25 million to cover administrative expenses, to be capitalized over five years. Ten percent of BEFB's capital ($500 million) plus the administrative costs ($25 million) will be paid in by the two governments, in five annual installments of $105 million. Eighty-five percent of this sum ($89 million) will be paid by the United States and 15 percent ($16 million) by Mexico. The remaining exposure ($900 million per year) will be callable capital, committed in like percentages by the two governments.

3. In addition, the United States will provide $304 million in federal grants, credits, and partial guarantees over five years. In total, the United States will thus have to appropriate $150 million per year for five years: $89 million for its paid-in share of BEFB capital and $61 million for direct grants, etc.

4. The BEFB's initial capital will be used as the basis to leverage federal, state, local, and private funds for environmental infrastructure. Proposed burden sharing of the portion of the project costs financed through direct government support (federal, state, or local) is 50 percent for each country.

5. Where possible, projects will be financed through revenue bonds issued by the project sponsors. User fees will be levied to pay the debt service on these bonds.

6. The funding agreement does not deal with nonenvironmental infrastructure such as roads and bridges, even though the deferral of such projects could contribute to existing pollution problems. Also, the inclusion of nonborder environmental projects remains to be decided.

---

4. However, we could also support the transfer of funds allocated to other capital programs to cover part of the US commitment. For example, part of the funds could come from temporarily halting the fill of the Strategic Petroleum Reserve (SPR). Alternatively, an SPR drawdown and sale of 100 million barrels (about 17 percent of the total SPR reserve) over five years could yield about $1.5 billion (at $15 per barrel).

FUNDING: Labor Adjustment

RECOMMENDATIONS:

1. We recommend worker adjustment assistance for US employees that are identifiably dislocated by larger imports from other NAFTA partners. For a temporary period, i.e., until an economywide training program is enacted, a targeted program for NAFTA adjustment should be created, to be budgeted at approximately $1.67 billion over five years. The precise amount would depend on the extent of labor dislocation caused by NAFTA. Once an economywide program is enacted, the NAFTA program should be folded into the broader approach.

RESULTS:

1. A NAFTA Adjustment Assistance program still remains under consideration by the Clinton administration.

References

Advisory Committee for Trade Policy and Negotiations. 1992. "Report of the Advisory Committee for Trade Policy and Negotiations (ACTPN) on the North American Free Trade Agreement" (September).

Agricultural Policy Advisory Committee for Trade. 1992. "Report of the Agricultural Policy Advisory Committee for Trade (APAC) on the North American Free Trade Agreement" (September).

Bergsten, C. Fred, Thomas Horst, and Theodore H. Moran. 1978. *American Multinationals and American Interests*. Washington: Brookings Institution.

Berry, Steven, Vittorio Grilli, and Florencio López-de-Silanes. 1992. "The Automobile Industry and the Mexico-US Free Trade Agreement." NBER Working Paper 4152 (October).

Charnovitz, Steve. 1992a. "Environmental and Labour Standards in Trade." *The World Economy* (May).

Charnovitz, Steve. 1992b. "GATT and the Environment: Examining the Issues." *International Environmental Affairs*, vol. 4, no. 3 (Summer).

CIEMEX-WEFA. 1992. *Perspectivas Económicas de México*. Bala Cynwyd, PA: CIEMEX-WEFA (December).

Clinton, Bill. 1992. "Expanding Trade and Creating American Jobs." Remarks by Governor Bill Clinton, North Carolina State University, Raleigh, NC (4 October).

Competitiveness Policy Council. 1992. "First Annual Report to the President and the Congress: Building a Competitive America." Washington: CPC (1 March).

Competitiveness Policy Council. 1993. "Annual Report to the President and the Congress: Building a Competitive America." Washington: CPC. Forthcoming (March).

The Cuomo Commission on Competitiveness. 1992. *America's Agenda: Building Economic Strength*. New York: M. E. Sharpe.

Dorsey, Tom. 1992. "Estimating the Restrictive Effect of FTA Rules of Origin." Washington: Office of Management and Budget. Unpublished memorandum (November).

Economic Strategy Institute. 1992. *NAFTA: Making It Better*. (December). Washington: ESI.

Faux, Jeff, and William Spriggs. 1991. *U.S. Jobs and the Mexico Trade Proposal*. Washington: Economic Policy Institute.

Faux, Jeff, and Thea Lee. N.d. "The Effect of George Bush's NAFTA on American Workers: Ladder Up or Ladder Down?" Washington: Economic Policy Institute.

Gephardt, Richard. 1992. Remarks of Congressman Richard A. Gephardt, "Address on the Status of the North American Free Trade Agreement before the Institute for International Economics." (27 July).

Haberler, Gottfried. 1936. *The Theory of International Trade*. London: William Hodge.

Hinojosa-Ojeda, Raúl, and Sherman Robinson. 1991. "Alternative Scenarios of U.S.-Mexico Integration: a Computable General Equilibrium Approach." Berkeley, CA: Department of Agriculture and Resource Economics, Division of Agriculture and Natural Resources, University of California at Berkeley. Working Paper No. 609 (April).

Hufbauer, Gary Clyde. 1992. *US Taxation of International Income: Blueprint for Reform*, Washington DC: Institute for International Economics.

Hufbauer, Gary Clyde, Diane T. Berliner, and Kimberly Ann Elliott. 1986. *Trade Protection in the United States: 31 Case Studies*. Washington: Institute for International Economics.

Hufbauer, Gary Clyde, and Jeffrey J. Schott. 1992a. *North American Free Trade Issues and Recommendations*. Washington: Institute for International Economics.

Hufbauer, Gary Clyde, and Jeffrey J. Schott. 1992b. "Western Hemisphere Economic Integration: Starting Point, Long Term Goals, Readiness Indicators, Paths to Integration." Washington: Institute for International Economics. Mimeo (September).

Hufbauer, Gary Clyde, and Jeffrey J. Schott. 1993. *Prospects for Western Hemisphere Economic Integration*. Washington: Institute for International Economics. Forthcoming.

Industry Functional Advisory Committee for Trade in Intellectual Property Rights. 1992. "Report of the Industry Functional Advisory Committee for Trade in Intellectual Property Rights (IFAC-3) on the North American Free Trade Agreement." (September).

Industry Policy Advisory Committee for Trade (IPAC) on the North American Free Trade Agreement. 1992. "Report of the Industry Policy Advisory Committee for Trade (IPAC) on the North American Free Trade Agreement." (September).

Industry Sector Advisory Committee on Services. 1992. "Report of the Industry Sector Advisory Committee on Services (ISAC 13) on the North American Free Trade Agreement." (14 September).

Industry Sector Advisory Committee for Trade in Textiles. 1992. "Report of the Industry Sector Advisory Committee for Trade in Textiles (ISAC-15) on the North American Free Trade Agreement." (14 September).

Industry Sector Advisory Committee for Trade in Transportation Equipment, Construction Equipment, and Agricultural Equipment. 1992. "Report of the Industry Sector Advisory Committee for Trade in Transportation Equipment, Construction Equipment, and Agricultural Equipment (ISAC-16) on the North American Free Trade Agreement." (14 September).

Industry Sector Advisory Committee for Trade in Energy. 1992. "Report of the Industry Sector Advisory Committee for Trade in Energy (ISAC-6) on the North American Free Trade Agreement." (14 September).

Intergovernmental Policy Advisory Committee for Trade. 1992. "Report of the Intergovernmental Policy Advisory Committee for Trade (IGPAC) on the North American Free Trade Agreement." (September).

Koechlin, Timothy, and Mehrene Larudee. 1992. "The High Cost of NAFTA." *Challenge* (September/October).

Marshall, Ray. 1992. "The North American Trade Agreement: Implications for Workers." (Mimeo).

Martin, Lynn. 1992. Testimony of Secretary of Labor Lynn Martin before the Senate Finance Committee (10 September).

Martin, Philip L. 1992. *Trade and Migration: The Case of NAFTA*. Washington: Institute for International Economics. Draft of forthcoming monograph.

McKenna & Cuneo. 1992. *The NAFTA Papers,* no. 2 (October). Washington: McKenna & Cuneo.

McKinsey & Company. 1992. *Service Sector Productivity.* Washington: McKinsey & Company (October).

Morrison, Philip D. 1992. "US-Mexico Income Tax Treaty Breaks New Ground—Implications for the New US Model for Latin America." *Tax Notes International* (19 October).

National Commission for Employment Policy. 1992. *The Employment Effects of the North American Free Trade Agreement: Recommendations and Background Studies.* Special Report (October). Washington: National Commission for Employment Policy.

North American Free Trade Agreement. 1992. Vols. 1 and 2. Washington: Government Printing Office.

Organization for Economic Cooperation and Development. 1991. *Financing and External Debt of Developing Countries, 1990 Survey.* Paris: OECD.

Organization for Economic Cooperation and Development. 1992. *OECD Economic Surveys: Mexico.* Paris: OECD.

Perot, Ross, with Pat Choate. 1993. *Save Your Job, Save Our Country: Why NAFTA Must Be Stopped—Now!* New York: Hyperion.

Podgursky, Michael. "The Industrial Structure of Job Displacement, 1979–1989." *Monthly Labor Review* (September).

Reifman, Alfred. 1992. "NAFTA and Jobs: An Overview." Washington: Congressional Research Service (December 21).

Rich, Jan Gilbreath. 1992. "Planning the Border's Future: The Mexican-US Integrated Border Environmental Plan," US-Mexican Occasional Paper No.1. Austin, Texas: LBJ School of Public Affairs, University of Texas at Austin (March).

Richardson, J. David. 1989. "Empirical Research on Trade Liberalization With Imperfect Competition: A Survey." *OECD Economic Studies* (Spring) no.12. Paris: Organization for Economic Cooperation and Development.

Robinson, Sherman, Mary Burfisher, Raúl Hinojosa-Ojeda, and Karen Thierfelder. 1992. "Agricultural Policies and Migration in a U.S.-Mexico Free Trade Area: A Computable General Equilibrium Analysis." Berkeley, CA: Department of Agriculture and Resource Economics, Division of Agriculture and Natural Resources, University of California at Berkeley. Working Paper No. 617 (October).

SaKong, Il. 1993. *Korea in the World Economy.* Washington: Institute for International Economics.

Schott, Jeffrey J., ed. 1989. *Free Trade Areas and US Trade Policy.* Washington: Institute for International Economics.

Schott, Jeffrey J., and Murray G. Smith, eds. 1988. *The Canada–United States Free Trade Agreement: The Global Impact.* Washington: Institute for International Economics.

Shiells, Clinton, and Robert C. Shelburne. 1992. "A Summary of 'Industrial Effects of a Free Trade Agreement Between Mexico and the USA' by the Interindustry Economic Research Fund, Inc. " In US International Trade Commission, *Economy-wide Modeling of the Economic Implications of a FTA with Mexico and a NAFTA with Canada and Mexico.* USITC Publication 2508 (May).

Sierra Club. 1993. "Funding Environmental Needs Associated with the North American Free Trade Agreement." Washington: Sierra Club (7 July).

Uimonen, Peter, and John Whalley. 1992. "Trade and Environment: Setting the Rules." Washington: Institute for International Economics. Mimeo (draft of forthcoming monograph).

US Chamber of Commerce. 1992. *A Guide to the North American Free Trade Agreement: What it Means for US Business.* Washington: US Chamber of Commerce.

US Council of the Mexico-US Business Committee. 1992. *Investment, Trade, and U.S. Gains in the NAFTA.* Washington: Council of the Americas.

US Council of the Mexico–US Business Committee. 1993. "Analysis of Environmental Infrastructure Requirements and Financing Gaps on the U.S./Mexico Border." Washington: US Council of the Mexico–US Business Committee (July).

US Department of Commerce. 1992a. "U.S. Jobs Supported by U.S. Merchandise Exports." (April).

US Department of Commerce. 1992b. "US Jobs Supported by US Merchandise Exports to Mexico." Supplement to "US Jobs Supported by Merchandise Exports" (May).

US Department of Labor, Bureau of Labor Statistics. 1992. "International Comparisons of Hourly Compensation Costs for Production Workers in Manufacturing, 1991." Report 825 (June).

US Department of Labor and Mexican Secretariat of Labor and Social Welfare. 1992a. *A Comparison of Labor Law in the United States and Mexico: An Overview.*

US Department of Labor and Mexican Secretariat of Labor and Social Welfare. 1992b. *A Comparison of Occupational Safety and Health Programs in the United States and Mexico: An Overview.* Washington: Government Printing Office.

US Department of Transportation. 1992. "Fact Sheet on Mexican Trucking" (March).

US General Accounting Office. 1991. "US-Mexico Trade: Survey of US Border Infrastructure Needs" (November).

US International Trade Commission. 1991. *The Economic Effects of Significant US Import Restraints, Phase III: Services.* USITC Publication 2422 (September).

US International Trade Commission. 1973. "Implications of Multinational Firms for World Trade and Investment and for US Trade and Labor." Report to the Senate Committee on Finance. Washington: USITC.

US Trade Representative. 1992. "Overview: The North American Free Trade Agreement." Washington: USTR (August).

US Trade Representative. 1992. "Report of the Administration on the North American Free Trade Agreement and Actions Taken in Fulfillment of the May 1, 1991, Commitments," (18 September).

Walters, David. 1992a. "Comparison of Export Sector Wages to Overall Sector Wages." Washington: Office of the US Trade Representative (June).

Walters, David. 1992b. "Comparison of Mexican Export Sector Wages to Overall Sector Wages." Washington: Office of the US Trade Representative. Unpublished.

Ward, Justin. 1992. Testimony before the Subcommittee on International Trade, Committee on Finance, US Senate, (16 September).

Whalen, John. 1992. "The North American Free Trade Agreement, the Liberalization of the Mexican Trucking Industry, and the Removal of Obstacles to the Free Flow of Goods Via Truck Between the United States and Mexico." Unpublished paper, Georgetown University Graduate School of Foreign Service (30 April).

Index

Other Publications from the
Institute for International Economics

POLICY ANALYSES IN INTERNATIONAL ECONOMICS Series

1 **The Lending Policies of the International Monetary Fund**
John Williamson/*August 1982*
ISBN paper 0-88132-000-5   72 pp.

2 **"Reciprocity": A New Approach to World Trade Policy?**
William R. Cline/*September 1982*
ISBN paper 0-88132-001-3   41 pp.

3 **Trade Policy in the 1980s**
C. Fred Bergsten and William R. Cline/*November 1982*
(out of print)   ISBN paper 0-88132-002-1   84 pp.
Partially reproduced in the book *Trade Policy in the 1980s.*

4 **International Debt and the Stability of the World Economy**
William R. Cline/*September 1983*
ISBN paper 0-88132-010-2   134 pp.

5 **The Exchange Rate System, Second Edition**
John Williamson/*September 1983, rev. June 1985*
(out of print)   ISBN paper 0-88132-034-X   61 pp.

6 **Economic Sanctions in Support of Foreign Policy Goals**
Gary Clyde Hufbauer and Jeffrey J. Schott/*October 1983*
ISBN paper 0-88132-014-5   109 pp.

7 **A New SDR Allocation?**
John Williamson/*March 1984*
ISBN paper 0-88132-028-5   61 pp.

8 **An International Standard for Monetary Stabilization**
Ronald I. McKinnon/*March 1984*
ISBN paper 0-88132-018-8   108 pp.

9 **The Yen/Dollar Agreement: Liberalizing Japanese Capital Markets**
Jeffrey A. Frankel/*December 1984*
ISBN paper 0-88132-035-8   86 pp.

10 **Bank Lending to Developing Countries: The Policy Alternatives**
C. Fred Bergsten, William R. Cline, and John Williamson/*April 1985*
ISBN paper 0-88132-032-3   221 pp.

11 **Trading for Growth: The Next Round of Trade Negotiations**
Gary Clyde Hufbauer and Jeffrey J. Schott/*September 1985*
ISBN paper 0-88132-033-1   109 pp.

12 **Financial Intermediation Beyond the Debt Crisis**
Donald R. Lessard and John Williamson/*September 1985*
ISBN paper 0-88132-021-8   130 pp.

13 **The United States-Japan Economic Problem**
C. Fred Bergsten and William R. Cline/*October 1985, 2d ed. January 1987*
(out of print)   ISBN paper 0-88132-060-9   180 pp.

Korea in the World Economy
Il SaKong/*January 1993*

ISBN cloth 0-88132-184-2   328 pp.

ISBN paper 0-88132-106-0   328 pp.

Pacific Dynamism and the International Economic System
C. Fred Bergsten and Marcus Noland, editors/*May 1993*

ISBN paper 0-88132-196-6   424 pp.

Economic Consequences of Soviet Disintegration
John Williamson, editor/*May 1993*

ISBN paper 0-88132-190-7   664 pp.

Reconcilable Differences? United States-Japan Economic Conflict
C. Fred Bergsten and Marcus Noland/*June 1993*

ISBN paper 0-88132-129-X   296 pp.

Does Foreign Exchange Intervention Work?
Kathryn M. Dominguez and Jeffrey A. Frankel/*September 1993*

ISBN paper 0-88132-104-4   192 pp.

Sizing Up U.S. Export Disincentives
J. David Richardson/*September 1993*

ISBN paper 0-88132-107-9   192 pp.

NAFTA: An Assessment
Gary Clyde Hufbauer and Jeffrey J. Schott/*rev. ed. October 1993*

ISBN paper 0-88132-199-0   216 pp.

Adjusting to Volatile Energy Prices
Philip K. Verleger, Jr./*November 1993*

ISBN paper 0-88132-069-2   288 pp.

The Political Economy of Policy Reform
John Williamson, editor/*January 1994*

ISBN paper 0-88132-195-8   624 pp.

Measuring the Costs of Protection in the United States
Gary Clyde Hufbauer and Kimberly Ann Elliott/*January 1994*

ISBN paper 0-88132-108-7   144 pp.

The Dynamics of Korean Economic Development
Cho Soon/*March 1994*

ISBN paper 0-88132-162-1   272 pp.

Reviving the European Union
C. Randall Henning, Eduard Hochreiter and Gary Clyde Hufbauer/*April 1994*

ISBN paper 0-88132-208-3   192 pp.

China in the World Economy
Nicholas R. Lardy/*April 1994*

ISBN paper 0-88132-200-8   192 pp.

SPECIAL REPORTS

1   **Promoting World Recovery: A Statement on Global Economic Strategy**
by Twenty-six Economists from Fourteen Countries/*December 1982*

(out of print)   ISBN paper 0-88132-013-7   45 pp.

FORTHCOMING

For orders outside the US and Canada please contact:

Longman Group UK Ltd.
PO Box 88
Harlow, Essex CM 19 5SR
UK

Telephone Orders: 0279 623925
Fax: 0279 453450
Telex: 817484